MARTIN ROBINSON
JASON ZAHORCHAK

SEOUL
CITY GUIDE

INTRODUCING SEOUL

Late-night shoppers roaming Hongdae (p88)

Seoul is the grinning devil on your shoulder that whispers 'play'. Its teeming night markets, 24-hour barbecues and surging clubs all beg the question, 'Why sleep?'

But turn onto a side street, away from the shimmer of skyscraper against buzzing neon, and you're met with the hushed, gentle tones of the past. Seoul was once a city of philosophers and kings. Monks still serenade the morning with guttural chants and a bell's clear tone, and majestic palaces skirt the base of craggy mountains. Stroll the centuries-old passageways along the palace walls and you can almost hear court intrigue whispered into the ancient stones.

What was once a small village cradled in a river valley is now a rambunctious metropolis of 11 million people. And what a smorgasbord for the senses. Marvel at the breathtaking Joseon-era royal architecture, perfectly melded with its natural backdrop. Tuck in to Seoul's sumptuous spreads, from delicate court fineries to pungent, bubbling stews. Take in the latest Korean blockbuster in a tiny private DVD theatre. Bear witness to the scars of the 20th century at the disquieting DMZ that separates South from North.

As your taxi whisks you through a blur of light and humanity, you may find yourself reflecting quietly upon the tiny wooden teahouse you just visited, or first the cherry blossoms of spring glowing in the moonlight along the Han River. Congratulations: you've begun to embrace the raucous alongside the genteel – just the first peel of the disarming, enticing layers of Seoul.

SEOUL LIFE

Seoul is a modern Asian dynamo – strong, resilient, surging with energy. Restless, as well: the wave of humanity that pours out of the subways and onto the streets seems determined to outrun time itself.

The flash and fervour can make it easy to forget a century marked by occupation, war, poverty and spirited recovery. After a fervent, successful end to the last century (which included riding out the Asian financial crisis), Seoulites now find themselves increasingly reflective. South Korea's spirited economy has hit a lull and the most recent housing bubble has sputtered. In the past two decades they have catapulted forward in every category: living standards, self-governance and consumerism, to name a few. Now they're pausing to contemplate what it is they have wrought. Like no other point in history, the direction of the nation sits squarely in the hands of the next generation.

The topics of the day are borne out of this introspection: the bottoming birth rate; an environmentally sustainable Seoul; the creeping disparity that accompanies new wealth. At first glance, there may not seem much in common between the young businessman sitting down to a solitary bowl of noodles in a marketplace tent and the group of stylistas in a chic, glass-sided café checking their mobile phones between sips. But the same question occupies them: what will life be like in Seoul's 21st-century megalopolis?

The answer is in its history – endlessly renewing and reinventing itself, Seoul will be whatever its myriad denizens make it. There's a constant, transformative energy here, one that takes into account what has been lost but also gained. It's in the team of early-bird hikers getting ready to meet the dawn from a Bukhan mountain shrine. It's in the merry Seoulites joining a foreign melange for beers in Itaewon. And it's in the elderly man warbling into a karaoke microphone at Jongmyo Park, swaying to the rhythm, his sweetheart in his arms.

Changing of the guards ceremony at Deoksugung (p42)

HIGHLIGHTS

ROYAL SEOUL

The Joseon dynasty (1392–1910) left its architectural imprint on Seoul. Six palaces, a World Heritage memorial shrine, a colossal fortress wall and clusters of royal tombs offer an insight into a unique kingdom based on Confucian principles, values and beliefs.

❶ Gyeongbokgung
Seoul's grandest palace is being restored to its former glory, cermonial guards and all (p38)

❷ Seolleung Park Royal Tombs
The final resting place of several Joseon-era kings and queens (p72)

❸ Deoksugung
A potpourri of East-meets-West architectural styles (p42)

① Seodaemun Prison
The prison is a monument to the cruelty of the colonial era (p74)

② War Memorial & Museum
Relive the Korean War at this huge in- and outdoor museum (p73)

③ National Museum of Korea
An impressive modern museum housing Korea's ancient treasures (p73)

MUSEUM DISCOVERIES

Alongside the major 'must sees', Seoul features a plethora of hobbit-sized museums; one (at least) for everything from jewellery, embroidery and straw craft to funeral carvings, owls and chickens.

❶ Namdaemun Market
Lose yourself bargain hunting in this massive, exciting market (p86)

❷ Free Market
Hongdae's small weekend craft market is Seoul's trendiest (p88)

❸ Dongdaemun Market
A major fashion hot spot where new trends begin – also a good spot for random knick-knacks (p83)

❹ Gyeongdong Market
All sorts of Eastern medicines, health foods and teas are piled high here (p91)

BUSTLING MARKETS

Seoul is awash with traditional markets. Jump in and rub shoulders with the locals, whether you're after anchovies or antiques, local teas or T-shirts, fashion brands or one-off craft items.

FOOD ADVENTURES

From raw fish to barbecued meat, from hot-as-hell dishes to mild royal cuisine, Seoul's best restaurants spread an array of gourmet delights before you. For budget travellers, few cities can match Seoul's street eats, with thousands of stalls all over the city.

❶ Royal Cuisine
Elaborate presentation is key for this specialised style of dining (p105)

❷ Noryangjin Fish Market
For Seoul's freshest fish and seafood, just follow your nose (p89)

❸ Menus
Photos help visitors choose their meals

❹ Sanchon
Sample some Buddhist temple food at this Insa-dong restaurant (p101)

mushroom stew

❶ Ttukseom Seoul Forest Park
Kids love the fountains at this large park just east of the city centre (p76)

❷ Cycling
Cycling along the Han River cycleway is always enjoyable (p141)

❸ Palace Gardens
Gardens once reserved for royalty are now open to all, such as those at Gyeongbokgung (p38)

❹ Cheonggye Stream
The restored stream flows again from downtown to beyond Dongdaemun (p32)

GREEN SEOUL

The rush to modernise after the Korean War left very little room for green spaces, but recently trees and flowers have been given more priority, and an old stream has been 'rediscovered'. Mayors now promise more parks rather than more bulldozers.

CONTENTS

THE AUTHORS

Martin Robinson

This is Martin's third edition of *Seoul*. Yet again he has tramped the city's streets and alleyways to check on old haunts and many new places. He toured every tourist sight, walked every walk and sampled many strange brews, including sweet potato latte. He chomped through more than his weight in Korean food, and inspected hundreds of hotel rooms from the grotty to the grandiose. He even ventured north across the border to Korea's dark side.

Born in London, Martin has travelled widely throughout Asia. He's written for magazines and newspapers, and authored a hiking guide to the province of Jeollabuk-do. He worked for two years in South Korea, pounding English into 11-year-olds and grappling with gobbledyenglishgook in a provincial governor's office. Martin wrote all the listings chapters, and also the Transport and Directory chapters.

MARTIN'S TOP SEOUL DAY

After a bun and black coffee brekkie in a bakery, I'm off round the Insadong galleries, checking out the latest art shows – everything from Buddhist-themed art on the impermanence of life to surrealist sculptures. Then I sink a mug of quince tea in Yetchatjip, the quintessence of quaint, and stroll down to Jongno. With a couple of hours to kill, I nip into a DVD *bang* (p138) and catch up on a subtitled Korean movie. Hungry afterwards, I grab some street eats (p100) – my favourite octopus balls and a homemade sausage hotdog. I need to buy a birthday present so catch the subway to Dongdaemun and join the fashion scrum in Doota Mall (p83). Then my vegetarian friend texts about dinner. Sanchon (best atmosphere; p101) or Gamrodang (best food; p99)? Whatever. He texts back about trawling Hongdae after, Jane's Groove (p118), Tin Pan (p118). Whatever. I want to show him my latest discovery, the wondrous Dragon Hill Spa (p140). It's so good we'll probably stay all night.

Jason Zahorchak

After a completely unplanned move to Seoul after college, Jason found himself working for an English-language newspaper and exploring the city's hidden nooks with the help of some very in-the-know Seoulites. He liked his first year so much, he came back two years later, this time working for his former paper's rival. In his nearly three years in Seoul, he's lived in the city's far northeast and far northwest corners – with imposing mountains right in his backyard – and in a Hongdae 'studio', 8 *pyeong* in size (conversion: room to lie down in). He'll always be back for food – and friends. Jason wrote the introductory chapters for this book, plus the Seoul's Hidden Byways colour section.

Seoul is in many ways a casual traveller's dream: lightning-fast public transportation, English emblazoned on many signs, and generally light-on-the-wallet itineraries. To top it off, the streets are clean and crime is low.

Still, even the most intrepid explorer could require some adjustment. The often-fiery cuisine can catch you unawares, and sometimes comes only in group-sized portions. Make sure you know what you're about to tuck into. If you're staying in a *hanok* (traditional guesthouse) you'll be down on the floor with a thin mattress or blanket.

Though some planning ahead is recommended (see boxed text, p15), most things can be done on the fly and on the cheap, and work out just fine – not something that can be said too often.

WHEN TO GO

Seoul's weather leans toward the extremes. Summer is sweltering and muggy; winters are nasty, brutish and long, with Siberian winds hurtling down the peninsula.

However, spring and autumn are uniformly pleasant. Soft cherry blossoms signal the end of winter, followed by a wet, wonderful surge of green trees and colourful blooms. The autumn sky is impossibly high, with thin, wispy clouds against bright blue, and Koreans have their own word for this season's breathtaking foliage *(dampung)*, which has to be seen to be believed. Two caveats: sandstorms sometimes blow over from China between March and May, and typhoons are also a possibility from late June through to September.

No matter when you show up, there's always something to do in Seoul. Over Chuseok and New Year's (see p179), much of the city is shuttered as families travel to their ancestral homes, but there are always events planned for those who stay in town.

See p176 for climate charts, or log on to www.kma.go.kr for daily weather forecasts in English.

FESTIVALS

Seoul hosts a cornucopia of festivals throughout the year, ranging from the traditional to the high tech. The majority of celebrations take place downtown, with Seoul's beautiful palaces often showcased.

April's famed Cherry Blossom Festival is a particular highlight, with a number of areas blanketed with pale, fragrant petals. Buddha's birthday brings a kaleidoscope of light and colour, as rows of delicate paper lanterns are strung down the main thoroughfares and in temple courtyards and lighted at dusk.

Home-grown holidays and festivals follow the lunar calendar, while the rest follow the Gregorian (Western) calendar. For a list of public holidays, see p179.

January/February

LUNAR NEW YEAR

This three-day holiday is Korea's most important. Seoul empties out as locals make the trip to their home town to visit relatives, honour ancestors and eat traditional foods. That said, there are a number of events for travellers in Seoul during this time, held at the major palaces as well as the Korean Folk Village (p164), Namsangol Hanok Village (p55) and the National Folk Museum (p39). For more information visit www.visitseoul.net or www.visitkorea.or.kr. In 2010 Lunar New Year begins 14 February, and in 2011 on 3 February.

April

CHERRY BLOSSOM FESTIVAL

Nature determines the dates for this event, but early April is generally when the cherry blossoms go from first peek into full colour riot within a week. The best way to take them in is to pack a picnic and head to Yeouido's Cherry Blossom Park (Map p65), Olympic Park (Map p70) or Namsan (Map pp56–7). The blossoms are particularly beautiful – and some say most fragrant – just after the sun sets.

WOMEN'S FILM FESTIVAL IN SEOUL
www.wffis.or.kr
Featuring over 100 films from 30-plus countries, this midmonth festival attracts internationally renowned directors and some of Korea's best independent filmmakers.

May

JONGMYO DAEJE
1st Sun in May

This ceremony honours Korea's royal ancestors, and involves a parade of the royal carriage from Gyeongbokgung (p38) through downtown Seoul to the royal shrine at Jongmyo (p42), where spectators can enjoy traditional music and an elaborate, all-day ritual. Check at either location for details.

BUDDHA'S BIRTHDAY

For over a millennium, temples have honoured the Buddha's birth by adorning their courtyards with strand upon strand of resplendently coloured lanterns. Seoul's temples, such as Jogyesa (p49) and Bongeunsa (p71), are no exception. The Sunday preceding Buddha's birthday, Seoul celebrates with a huge daytime street festival and evening lantern parade (see www.llf .or.kr) – the largest in South Korea, attracting over 100,000 Buddhists and revellers. The route runs from Tapgol Park (p51) to Jogyesa. Buddha' birthday is celebrated on 21 May in 2010 and 10 May in 2011.

SEOUL WORLD DJ FESTIVAL
www.worlddjfest.com

Dozens of DJs from all over Korea and the world descend upon an outdoor arena in central Seoul for two nights and three days of nonstop partying.

SEOUL INTERNATIONAL CARTOON & ANIMATION FESTIVAL
www.sicaf.org

Half a million animation geeks can't be wrong, right? They pack auditoriums in Seoul each year to see why the city is an epicentre of animated craftsmanship (fans of The Simpsons have Korean artists to thank).

June

KOREAN QUEER CULTURAL FESTIVAL
www.kqcf.org

Lesbian, gay, bisexual, transgender, and other sexual minority communities in Seoul are represented in this series of citywide events, culminating in a parade through downtown. Usually held in conjunction with the Seoul LGBT Film Festival (www .selff.com).

DANO FESTIVAL

Held according to the lunar calendar, this festival features shamanist rituals and mask dances in many locales. At Namsangol Hanok Village (Map p55) you can ride a geunettwigi (a traditional Korean swing), gape at ssireum (traditional Korean wrestling) and receive a traditional 'shampoo' with iris-infused water. On 16 June 2010 and 6 June 2011.

BUCHEON INTERNATIONAL FANTASTIC FILM FESTIVAL
www.pifan.com

The festival brings films and filmgoers from across Asia and the world to Bucheon (Puchon), just outside of Seoul, to feast on the best in sci-fi, fantasy and horror. The all-night viewings are the ultimate challenge. Theatres are within walking distance from Songnae Station, Line 1, toward Incheon.

HELLO THERE, SEOUL

The whimsically named Hi Seoul festival has been entertaining city denizens for several years running, and has expanded into a four-part, year-long assortment of activities celebrating various features of the capital city. Go to www .hiseoulfest.org for more info.

Palace Held in early May, this part of the Hi Seoul festival features light and media shows, dance events, parades and events at Seoul's palaces, with the aim of merging Seoul's majestic past with her tech-savvy future.

Hangang Festival Held in late July and early August, this part of the festival centres on the mighty Han River. A range of concerts, water-sport opportunities and art displays lure people to the riverside.

Art Festival Held throughout October, this third phase celebrates Seoul's thriving arts community with concerts, parties and art markets.

Light Festival From mid-December through to mid-January, various locations around central Seoul are ablaze with displays of light. Ice-skating rinks and other activities take advantage of the climate.

August

SEOUL FRINGE FESTIVAL
www.seoulfringe.net
International misunderstood geniuses in all artistic media converge on the trendy Hongdae area to flee the mainstream.

September/October

CHUSEOK
The Harvest Moon Festival is a major three-day holiday when families gather, eat crescent-shaped rice cakes (get it?) and visit their ancestors' graves to make offerings of food and drink and perform *sebae* (a ritual bow). Visitors in Seoul can check the National Centre for Korean Traditional Performing Arts (p76), Namsangol Hanok Village (p55) and the National Folk Museum (p39) for activities. Begins 22 September in 2010 and 12 September in 2011.

KOREA INTERNATIONAL ART FAIR
www.kiaf.org
Nearly 70,000 art lovers descend upon COEX (p68) to gaze at the offerings of more than 200 local and international galleries and participate in a range of programs and workshops.

SEOUL MEDICINAL HERB MARKET FESTIVAL
☎ 969 4793
Held at Seoul's biggest herbal medicine market at Gyeongdong (p91), this festival offers free medicinal consultation and shamanist ceremonies, affording attendees a rare glimpse into this fascinating tradition.

SEOUL DRUM FESTIVAL
www.drumfestival.org
The Seoul Drum Festival has kept the beat going for nearly a decade early each October. While focusing on Korea's fantastic percussive legacy (see Music p25), the event brings together all kinds of ways to make a lot of noise from around the world.

HANGEUL DAY   9 Oct
This popular festival began in 1926 during the Japanese colonial period as a means of maintaining Korea's cultural identity. Many of Seoul's historic attractions feature hands-on demonstrations – it's great fun learning *hangeul* (the Korean phonetic alphabet)

under the scrutiny of local school children. Check at any of the palaces or the KTO Tourist Information Centre (Map p40) for specifics.

GUGAK FESTIVAL
www.gugakfestival.or.kr
Hip-hop *gugak*? You'd be surprised how well traditional Korean music crosses over into a modern context at this annual 10-day Seoul-wide festival.

November

KIMCHI EXPO
It wouldn't be Korea without a kimchi fete, would it? Held in early November at COEX (p68), this pungent large-scale exhibition and taste-off brings together those addicted to the red-hot national culinary symbol.

COSTS & MONEY

Seoul is a major city in a developed country, but one can enjoy good food, a warm bed and all of the major sights on a relatively low budget. Public transport, basic meals and snacks, admission prices and some accommodation are all relatively inexpensive.

That said, if you're planning to stretch your won, be sure you know exactly what you're going to get. For a dorm bed and meals purchased from cafeteria-style eateries or street vendors, plan for about W50,000 daily. Allow around W90,000 a day for two in a motel room and three big sit-down meals; for a three- or four-star stay and lavish spreads, this jumps to W300,000 (and from there to infinity).

HOW MUCH?

Litre bottle of water W1000

Small cup of coffee W3400

Pint of local beer W3000-5000

Litre of petrol W1550

Palace entry ticket free to W15,000

Souvenir T-shirt W6000-12000

One-hour bike rental W3000

Pineapple slice on a stick W1000

One bowl of *jajangmyeon* (noodles) W3500

Movie ticket W7000

ADVANCE PLANNING

Bballi! (Quick!) – you'll probably hear this cry ring out constantly on the streets of Seoul. The local stereotype is that everything – plans included – can be done hurriedly, all at the last possible minute. While this is never the best way to plan a trip, Seoul doesn't present a lot to fret about before you touch down.

Think about booking ahead if you wish to stay at a *hanok* (traditional house) as by design these old structures only house three to four rooms in total. In addition, the top-end international chain hotels can book up when conferences are in town. Hiking on the weekend can be a madhouse – all 10 million men, women and children in Seoul seem to hit the trails. If possible, consider taking a hike on a weekday instead – the same goes for skiing trips in the winter.

Call a few days ahead for the best seats at cultural events, and book the USO tour to the DMZ and the Kaesong trip to North Korea as soon as you can, as these fill up. If you're planning on leaving Seoul over any of the major holidays, you should book your bus or train travel well ahead of time.

If you're the type of traveller who likes doing things for free (rather than merely duty-free), Seoul does have some options. The city's tourism website (www.visitseoul.net) lists plenty of free events. See also the boxed text, p59.

Public galleries and museums usually charge admission fees lower than their private counterparts, and admission is free at the National Museum of Korea (p73). A guided tour at Changdeokgung (p39) is actually the cheapest option; if you want to roam freely (available Thursdays between April and November) it will set you back an extra W12,000. Look for discounts for children and the 65-and-over crowd.

INTERNET RESOURCES

About Korea (http://joongangdaily.joins.com) Check out the nifty 'About Korea' series from local paper *JoongAng Daily* on the whimsy and mystery behind Seoul's culture (it's under the 'Foreign community' tab).

Galbijim (http://wiki.galbijim.com) Fun wiki site offering detailed, often quirky information about Seoul's districts.

Korea4Expats (www.korea4expats.com) Good listings of Seoul events on this comprehensive expat-penned site.

Life in Korea (www.lifeinkorea.com) Features an overview of Seoul's tourist offerings.

Visit Korea (www.visitkorea.or.kr) Offers a handy travel planner for those who sign up.

Visit Seoul (www.visitseoul.net) The Seoul government's site gives a good background on the city's major attractions.

SUSTAINABLE SEOUL

Keeping a trip to Seoul totally eco-friendly is a challenge from the start. You can take a boat in from China or from Japan (see p173), but it is unclear how many carbon credits that would save – and you'd have to get to those places first!

Once in Seoul, however, it's easy for travellers to make a smaller impact. Seoul's public transportation system is wonderful, and thousands of buses run on low-polluting natural gas. Several 'mild-hybrid' buses are also in operation, with full-hybrid buses due to join the mix in 2011 and fuel-cell electric buses in 2013.

A city with extraordinarily high population density and soaring energy demand, Seoul has been actively recycling for years. Nearly every subway station or public building will have containers for your bottles and cans.

Bike rentals are available at many parks, though bike-rental places in the city itself are scarce, save for some services for long-term residents. Bike paths are virtually nonexistent on major roadways – and those that do exist are usually ignored by Seoul's 'creative' drivers. Wear a helmet and exercise extreme caution.

With a new 'wellbeing' movement in full swing, organic and vegetarian restaurants have been cropping up. You can buy organic food and drinks from Huckleberry Farms (p91), or hit the Beautiful Store in Hongdae (p88) and near Bongeunsa (p71) for guilt-free secondhand items.

BACKGROUND

HISTORY
A CAPITAL FOR THE AGES

The mighty walls of Korea's modern capital rose in 1394, when King Taejo, founder of the Joseon dynasty, settled the government seat in the valley of Hanyang – later to become Seoul. Nature decreed its locale: the Han River supplied Yin force and access to the sea, and the Bukhan mountain range supplied Yang energy and protection from the north.

At the new city's centre, ensconced by mountains, King Taejo built Gyeongbokgung, the Palace of Shining Happiness. The social geography of the Korean capital has changed little over the past 600 years. The seat of power – Cheongwadae (the Blue House) – rests behind Gyeongbokgung, with Seoul's central axis (now Sejongno) spread before it. Pedestrians still teem down Jongno (Bell St), but the great bronze bell, once struck each morning and evening to signal the opening and closing of the city's gates, is only rung to welcome the new year.

Korea had been unified just prior to Joseon, in AD 918 with the start of the Goryeo dynasty (from which we get the name 'Korea'). The unification would persevere – with Seoul at the centre – until the country's division following WWII, solidified by the Korean War.

INVASION AND CONQUEST

Since recorded time, external forces have cast designs upon Korea, a small peninsula among giants – Japan to the east, China and Mongolia to the west. Korea has long been caught in the middle of competing powers, with Seoul at the centre of the maelstrom. Brutal invasions – many lasting and painful – comprise the fabric of Korean history.

None weighs as heavily on the Korean psyche as the annexation by Japan just after the turn of the 20th century. Japan long had its sights on the strategic peninsula, and sought to emulate the Western powers' 'opening up' of Asian nations – a fate that had befallen Japan just decades prior. So when a large-scale peasant rebellion raged uncontrollably in Korea in 1894, Japan stepped in to 'help'. One year later, Japanese assassins would fatally stab Queen Min; King Gojong would abdicate in 1907; and in 1910 the cession would be complete.

This period marked the subjugation, and attempted eradication, of Korean identity. Locals were made to take Japanese names and were forbidden to speak their national tongue. As Japan exploited Korea's resources, only 20% of Koreans were able to even start elementary school. Though some Koreans collaborated with their colonial rulers and reaped great profit, most were unable to rise above second-class citizenship in their own land. Japanese views of this period run the spectrum, with the more politically liberal expressing regret and the more conservative pointing only to Japan's hand in Korea's modernisation – the same line among some in Korea, as well. However, for the majority of Koreans, after centuries of staving off foreign designs on their small tract of earth, this period was the ultimate humiliation.

It thus comes as no surprise that the (wary) US tolerance of the dictatorial governments that ruled the South following the Korean War yielded feelings of resentment towards the USA.

AD 1394	1592	1910
King Taejo employs geomancy, or *feng shui* (*pungsu* in Korean) to select Hanyang (Seoul) as the capital of the new kingdom of Joseon.	Seoul falls to Japan during the Imjin War. Korean forces use metal-covered 'turtle boats' to win several decisive naval battles in the eventually successful quest to expel the invaders.	After gradually increasing its power and forcing King Gojong to abdicate to the Russian legation three years prior, Japan annexes Korea, beginning 35 years of colonial rule.

Some of this resentment remains, especially among college students – it was not the first time that Koreans have felt a foreign power trying to call the shots.

WHEN BROTHER FOUGHT BROTHER

While external powers continued to knock on Korea's door, there was no shortage of internal conflict, either. The Three Kingdoms period, preceding the Goryeo dynasty, was marked by continual feuds, and peasant rebellions were commonplace throughout the Joseon era.

top picks

BOOKS ON SEOUL

- *The Dawn of Modern Korea* by Andrew Lankov – A fascinating, accessible look at early-20th-century Seoul and the cultural and social impacts of Westernisation as King Gojong tried to modernise his tradition-bound hermit kingdom.
- *Korea's Place in the Sun* by Bruce Cumings – This (somewhat Leftist) look at modern Korea tackles the whole country's history, but most of the action takes place in the capital.
- *Who Ate Up the Singa?* by Pak Wan-so – The famed writer's autobiography, recounting her childhood in Seoul under Japanese rule.
- *A Single Spark* – The collected diary writings of Chun Tae-il, the father of Seoul's 1970s labour rights movement. Chun immolated himself in a final act of protest.
- *Korea Bug* by J Scott Burgeson – A Seoul 'zine turned book, featuring interviews with a fascinating set of Seoul characters, including a shaman, a *gisaeng* (similar to a Japanese geisha), artists and directors.

The Korean War, while unique to recent historical memory, represents another such conflict along internally-riven lines – for the more agrarian South had always resented the wealthier North, and vice versa.

When the nation was at last returned to Korea with the Allied victory in 1945, the decision to divide the country into protectorates, the north overseen by the USSR and the south by the US, soon led to rival republics. On 25 June 1950, under the cover of night, North Korea marched over the mountains that rim Seoul, marking the start of the brutal civil war.

Seoul's sudden fall to the North caught the populace by surprise; the government of President Syngman Rhee fled southward, destroying the only Han River highway bridge and abandoning the remaining population to face the communists. During their 90-day occupation of the city, North Korea arrested and shot many who had supported the Rhee government.

In September 1950, UN forces led by US and South Korean troops mounted a counterattack. After an amphibious landing at Incheon, they fought their way back into Seoul. During a series of bloody battles, whole districts of the capital were bombed and burned in the effort to dislodge Kim Il Sung's Korean People's Army. When at last the UN forces succeeded in reclaiming the city, much of it lay in smouldering ruins.

Later that year, as UN forces pushed northward, the Chinese Army entered the war on the North Korean side and pushed back down into Seoul. This time the invaders found a nearly empty city. Even after the UN regained control in March 1951, only a fraction of Seoul's population returned during the two years of war that raged along the battlefront until the armistice in July 1953. Instead, they holed up in rural villages and miserable camps, slowly trickling back into the shattered capital that was once their home. Most would never hear from their northern relatives again, whether living or lost to the war.

1945	1948	1950–53
With Allied victory in WWII, Korea is liberated from Japan and divided into two protectorates – the Soviets handling the North and the US the South.	The Republic of Korea is founded in the southern part of the peninsula, with Seoul designated the capital city. The Democratic People's Republic of Korea (DPRK, or North Korea) is also founded.	Using Soviet tanks and artillery, North Korea stages a surprise invasion, triggering the Korean War. Only an armistice – still in place – brings a tenuous peace.

UNINVITED, MODERNITY ARRIVES

Ever since a brutal series of invasions not long after the capital was founded, Korea retreated inward, content to seal itself off from a harsh and dangerous world. If not for the series of events originating from forces beyond its borders, Korea might have stayed happily shuttered from the outside world.

But though the colonial period cracked open the 'Hermit Kingdom' and the Korean War upended many remaining traditional social systems, nothing served to bring Korea hurtling into the modern world more than the so-called 'miracle on the Han River' – Korea's spectacular economic rise.

After the Korean War, South Korean per-capita GDP stood at around US$100, with the North's Soviet-backed economy performing markedly better. By 1995 the GDP had broken the US$10,000 per capita mark, and by 2002 South Korea was the 11th-largest economy in the world. What was accomplished is truly breathtaking, but to call it a miracle is to ignore context: Korea's rise from the ashes began with a long period of stagnation, followed by a collaboration of big business and government under harsh authoritarian rule. A generation of workers sacrificed their quality of life to ensure Korea's affluent present.

Immediately following the war, as Seoul's population slowly returned to pick up the pieces, they found little to give them hope. Widespread hunger, disease, crime and misery comprised daily life for hundreds of thousands. On the slopes of Namsan a wretched village called Hae-bang-chon (Liberation Town) housed tens of thousands of war refugees, widows and beggars. Prostitutes lined up at the gates of the US military bases in Yongsan in a desperate effort to earn a few dollars. Even a decade after the war, average male life expectancy hovered barely above 50.

When General Park Chung-hee forcibly took the reins of the government in 1961, he quickly went to work defining national economic goals. He often followed patterns set by Imperial Japan, such as fostering big businesses (*zaibatsu* in Japanese, *jaebeol* in Korean) as engines of growth. Conglomerates such as Hyundai and Samsung achieved – and still retain – incredible economic influence.

Under Park, fear and brutal efficiency combined to deliver results. Wages were kept artificially low to drive exports, and by the mid-1970s, Seoul was well on its way to becoming a major world city. Slums were bulldozed, and the city spread in all directions. Expressways, ring roads and a subway network connected these new districts. Modernity had arrived in Seoul, but at an undeniable cost.

DEMOCRACY – AT LONG LAST

Historically, Seoul never possessed an egalitarian social setup. During the Joseon dynasty a rigid hereditary class system sharply limited social mobility. A registry from the mid-1600s suggests that perhaps three-quarters of Seoul's citizens were slaves.

Social inequality continued through the Japanese colonial period, and after the Korean War dictatorships sprang up in the South. The Syngman Rhee regime (1948–60) rigged its own re-election several times until 19 April 1960, when a popular rebellion led by unarmed students sought to overthrow him. Police opened fire on the group, which had gathered in downtown Seoul; by dusk, nearly 200 people lay dead. Rhee's right-hand man, Gibung Lee, committed suicide, as did his family. Rhee resigned a few days later and was spirited away to exile in Hawaii by the US Air Force.

1960–61	1979	1987
Popular protest ousts President Syngman Rhee; attempts at democratic rule fail – a military coup topples the unstable elected government and installs General Park Chung-hee into power.	Park Chung-hee is assassinated by the head of his own Central Intelligence Agency. The killing is considered either an attempted coup or a spontaneous act of anger.	Following sweeping national protests, with the strongest concentration in Seoul, Korea's last military dictatorship, under Chun Doo Hwan, steps down to allow democratic elections.

LONG ROAD TO FREEDOM

The past century has been one of struggle for Seoul's citizens, first with their rights stripped by Japanese colonists and then by dictatorial governments, with a brutal war in between. In 1970, 22-year-old labour activist Chun Tae-il immolated himself, crying, 'We are not machines!' A poignant statue of him stands just south of the spot where he ended his life. Several such sites are intimately tied to Seoul's unyielding quest for freedom.

Changgyeonggung (Map p40) Perhaps the most symbolic example of the Japanese subjugation of Korean culture was this beautiful palace's colonial fate – it was turned into a zoo.

Daehangno (Map p52) The main street in this district was constantly lined with student protesters from nearby Seoul National University (SNU); dissidents clogged its cafés. To quell the dissenters, Park Chung Hee moved SNU to a then-remote mountain area south of Seoul, where it remains. You can see the former main hall, now used as the headquarters of Arts Council Korea, right next to Marronnier Park.

Myeong-dong Catholic Cathedral (p59) A meeting point for many historical pro-democracy protests, the cathedral is a national symbol of democracy and human rights. Many consider outspoken Cardinal Kim the conscience of the nation.

Seodaemun Prison (p74) This sombre brick building was used to house political prisoners, first under the Japanese and then under the military dictatorships.

The flirtation with democracy following the April Revolution proved unstable and fleeting: on the morning of 16 May 1961, Seoulites awoke to news that army units had moved onto the main intersections. The city fell under direct military rule and the civilian government was removed from power.

General Park Chung-hee held an iron grip on power. During his tenure, scores of political dissidents were executed or disappeared, and he created an internal police system complete with a Central Intelligence Agency that quelled any antigovernment or pro-North movements.

Following Park's assassination in 1979, burgeoning hope was again quickly quashed when another general – Chun Doo-hwan – crushed pro-democracy uprisings all over the country (most notoriously in the southwestern city of Gwangju). But by 1987 the world was watching and the tide of popular protest was too strong. Chun stepped down and allowed democratic elections.

The sea of change finally rolled all the way in when former dissident Kim Dae-jung, a 'radical' who had survived several assassination attempts during the Park Chung-hee reign, became president in 1998. Once in power, Kim worked to achieve détente with North Korea. His presidency was followed by that of equally liberal Roh Moo-hyun.

The current president (and former mayor of Seoul), Lee Myung-bak, is a fascinating change from the previous two administrations. Formerly the hard-nosed CEO of the Hyundai construction *jaebeol,* he is known as 'Bulldozer' – derisively by those who loathe him, glowingly by his supporters – for his penchant for ramming through his policies, group opinions be damned.

STILL THE CENTRE OF IT ALL

The grand city founded over six centuries ago was and still is the nation's core. Seoul was the Joseon era's cultural headquarters, not only the home of the royal family and the *yangban*

1988	1997	2007
Seoul hosts the Olympic Summer Games, building a huge Olympic park and major expressway (while bulldozing and/or concealing slums). International showcase leads to increased trade and diplomatic relations for Korea.	Run on Thai currency sets off Asian Economic Crisis, which cripples Korean economy. International Monetary Fund offers $57 million bailout; Koreans line up to melt down jewellery to try to stabilize currency.	Former South Korean Foreign Minister Ban Ki-moon becomes the eighth Secretary-General of the United Nations.

(aristocratic) class that supported the state and its monarch, but also the centre of Korea's commerce and communications, and the pinnacle of its Confucian education system. Korean proverbs attest to the fact that anyone with any ambition needed to get to Seoul by all means. 'Even if you have to crawl on your knees, get yourself to Seoul!' was one. 'Send your ox to market but send your son to Seoul' was another.

As the seat of government, Seoul has born the brunt of bad policies during periods of lacklustre rule, but has reaped the fruits of the thinking of its wisest leaders. The greatest of these leaders was King Sejong (r 1418–50), a scholar-king of unmatched abilities who sponsored many cultural projects, consolidated border defences, and served as a model of Confucian probity. At his direction, court scholars devised the phonetic *hangeul* alphabet, a simple system of writing the Korean language that made it possible for anyone to learn to read. King Sejong's alphabet is one reason why Korea enjoys universal literacy today.

Seoulites continue to generate excellent ideas in order to build their future, while at the same time trying to work out their differences with North Korea and adjust to the emerging order in East Asia. Along the way, the face of Seoul – long one of the most homogenous cities in the world – is changing, with a recent influx of immigrants from China, South and Southeast Asia and the Middle East. All of this within the capital of the former Hermit Kingdom. It would seem that Seoul, for centuries the centre of Korea's world, is now getting used to being a major centre of the world at large.

RELIGION

Traditional and indigenous beliefs have survived in South Korea, coexisting alongside 'imported' spiritual systems, denting the myth that modernisation necessitates secularisation. As South Korea's most modern city, Seoul presents the starkest contrast between contemporary and traditional attitudes.

BUDDHISM

Korean Buddhism belongs to the Mahayana school and, since its arrival in AD 370, it has split into numerous schools. About 90% of Korean Buddhists belong to the Jogye sect, which has its headquarters in Jogyesa (p49), a large temple located near Insadong. The sect claims to have 8000 monks and 5000 nuns, and is an amalgamation of two Korean schools of Buddhism: the Seon (better known by its Japanese name, Zen) school, which relies on meditation and the contemplation of paradoxes to achieve sudden enlightenment; and the Gyo school, which concentrates on extensive scriptural study.

Approximately 28% of Seoulites are Buddhists (though not necessarily practising).

CHRISTIANITY

Korea's first exposure to Christianity was in the late 18th century. It came via the Jesuits from the Chinese Imperial court when a Korean aristocrat was baptised in Beijing in 1784. The Catholic faith took hold and spread so quickly that it was perceived as a threat by the Korean government and was vigorously suppressed, creating the country's first Christian martyrs (see p62).

Christianity got a second chance in the 1880s, with the arrival of American Protestant missionaries who founded schools and hospitals, and gained many followers.

About 25% of Koreans are Christian – 50% of Seoulites are Protestant and 15% Catholic. Gaze out of any bus or taxi window as you pass through the city at night and count the red neon crosses.

OTHER BELIEFS

Cheondogyo

Cheondogyo is a home-grown Korean religion containing Buddhist, Confucian and Christian elements that gathered momentum in the 1860s. The church was originally part of the Donghak (Eastern Learning) reform movement and embraced the idea of the equality of all human beings, a new concept in the conservative Neo-Confucian order of the time.

DOS & DON'TS

Most locals understand that visitors do not mean disrespect when they commit a minor social faux pas. But you will be even more warmly received when it is obvious that you've gone out of your way to burnish your graces, Korean style.

Shoes Off

In any residence, temple, guesthouse or Korean-style restaurant, leave your shoes at the door. And socks are better than bare feet. A pile of shoes by the entrance will usually clue you in.

Artful Bow

Though you may see members of the royal court drop to the ground to greet the king on Korean TV dramas, don't get inspired. A quick, short bow – essentially a nod of the head – is most respectful for meetings and departures.

All Hands on Deck

Give and receive any object using both hands – especially money and gifts.

Giving Gifts

When you visit someone at their home, bring along a little token of your appreciation. The gift can be almost anything – flowers, chocolates, fruit, a book, a bottle of liquor or wine, tea or something from your home country. It's also a nice gesture to gift-wrap your offering.

Your host may at first strongly refuse your gift. Don't worry: this is a gesture of graciousness. Keep insisting, and they will accept it 'reluctantly'. For the same reason, your host will not open the package immediately.

Get Over Here

Don't beckon someone using your forefinger. Place your hand out, palm down (palm up is how you call your pet), and flutter all your fingers at once.

Loss of Face

In interpersonal reactions, the least desirable commission is to somehow 'lower the harmony *(gibun)*'. A mishandled remark or potentially awkward scene should be smoothed over as soon as possible, and if you sense someone actively trying to change the subject, go with the flow. An argument or any situation that could lead to embarrassment should be avoided at all costs.

Smile, You're Embarrassed

Often, potential loss of face – say, a moment when someone realises he or she is clearly in the wrong – will result in an unlikely reaction: a wide smile. No, you're not being mocked; you've just been told, 'I'm sorry'. So if a taxi almost mows you down, only to roll down his window and flash you a big grin, he's not off his rocker – he's showing his embarrassment, which is both a form of apology and a gesture of sympathy.

The church is still going; followers support humanist principles of peace and equality. The church headquarters, Cheondogyo Temple (p52), was built in 1921 near Insadong.

Shamanism

Shamanism has long been a part of traditional Korean culture. Central to shamanism is the *mudang* (shaman), who nowadays is almost always female. Their role is to serve as the intermediary between the living and the spirit world. Mediating is carried out through a *gut*, a long ceremony that includes ecstatic dancing, singing and drumming.

Shamanism is often regarded as superstition today, yet official records show that 40,000 *mudang* are registered in South Korea (the actual figure could be closer to 100,000).

On Inwangsan (p77), a wooded hillside in northwestern Seoul, is a shamanist village where *gut* ceremonies are held.

CULTURE & LIFESTYLE

Once divided strictly along nearly inescapable class lines and hierarchical distinctions, Seoul's sensibility is now much like any modern city. People often hold loyalties to school, company and church, but egalitarianism has given way to greater individualism. The concept of family is rapidly changing, as well: nuclear rather than extended families are the norm, and birth rates are among the lowest in the developed world. Still, there linger strong traces of Korea's particular identity and remnants of its strongly Confucian past.

CONFUCIANISM

The Chinese philosopher Confucius (552–479 BC) devised a system of ethics that emphasised devotion to parents and family, loyalty to friends, justice, peace, education, reform and humanitarianism. He also urged that respect and deference should be given to those in positions of authority – a philosophy exploited by Korea's Joseon-dynasty ruling elite. Confucius firmly believed that men were superior to women and that a woman's place was in the home.

These ideas led to the system of civil service examinations (*gwageo*), where one could gain position through ability and merit, rather than from noble birth and connections (though it was in fact still an uphill battle for the commonly born). Confucius preached against corruption, war, torture and excessive taxation. He was the first teacher to open his school to all students solely on the basis of their willingness to learn.

> ### FORTUNE-TELLING
>
> These days most people visit one of the city's street tent fortune-tellers for a bit of fun, but no doubt some take it seriously. For a *saju* reading of your future, inform the fortune-teller of the hour, day, date and year of your birth; another option is *gunghap*, when a couple give their birth details and the fortune-teller pronounces how compatible they are. Expect to pay W10,000 for *saju* and double that for *gunghap*. If you don't speak the language, you'll also need someone to translate.

As Confucianism trickled into Korea, it evolved into neo-Confucianism, which combined the sage's original ethical and political ideas with the quasireligious practice of ancestor worship and the idea of the eldest male as spiritual head of the family.

The state religion of the Joseon dynasty, Confucianism still lives on as a kind of ethical bedrock (at least subconsciously) in the minds of most Koreans, especially the elderly.

Visit the spirit shrines of Joseon royalty at the splendid Jongmyo (p42). A grand Confucian ceremony honouring the deceased is held there every year.

EDUCATION

'A person without education is like a beast wearing clothes' is a proverb that nails Korea's obsession with education. Though everyone complains about this manic pursuit, it is a system hard to shake. To get into one of the top Korean universities (nearly all of which are in Seoul),

> ### HAN
>
> Difficult to describe, but its something we've all felt. Is it that particular combination of frustration and helplessness? Rage and sorrow? Locals use the concept of *han* to put into words that indescribable emotion. As for its origin, at least in Korea, some trace it back to the suppression of self under the strict traditional Confucian order, which values the group over the individual. Others say it has more to do with Korea's difficult history of subjugation under foreign powers. Wherever it stems from, *han*'s influence runs through a good deal of Korean art and culture. Of course, an attempt to pinpoint an innate 'Koreanness' risks essentialism – but there is a striking kind of sadness to some Korean songs and tales, and some local scholars point to a national 'aesthetic' of *han*. But the feeling is something that can affect us all from time to time, stemming from thoughts of why we are here and what we have had to endure. Each of us carries his or her own *han*.

GAY IN KOREA

Like many societies in which close friendships are often segregated along gender lines, it isn't unusual to see warm physical contact between two male or two female friends, including holding hands in the street. This does not mean there is general tolerance of same-sex relationships, however. Though opinions in Seoul are slowly changing and becoming more tolerant, attitudes towards gays are still years behind most of the West. Beneath a mask of modernity lurk conservative Confucian and fundamental Christian ideas. In 2001, the country's National Security Act was modified to name homosexuality as 'dangerous to youth', complete with the blocking of gay-oriented internet searches.

These moves no doubt came as no surprise to Hong Seok-chun, a popular TV personality who, upon coming out publicly in 2000, saw his career rapidly vanish amidst intense public criticism. Hong's words after the fallout: 'I expect our society will develop into a more generous society that will embrace these minorities with a warm heart.'

His hope may not have been misplaced. Two years after Hong's firing, the very network that gave him the axe aired a documentary on his story – the highest-rated program that night – and Hong's acting work has picked up once again. Seoul hosts semiregular gay film festivals and the Seoul Queer Cultural Festival (p13), with its parade attracting greater numbers each year. Several popular TV dramas have featured gay themes, and 2005–06 saw the first mainstream movies to do so (The King and the Clown; No Regrets). Though still facing harassment, gay student organisations have cropped up in greater frequency on the nation's campuses. Perhaps most notably, the English phrase 'coming out' has been hybridised into a commonly used Korean verb with the same meaning. Gay-themed internet searches are no longer banned, and in recent years there's been a flourish of Korean-language information and chat rooms online for gays and lesbians.

These are huge strides, to be sure – but for most young Koreans, revealing their personal lives to their coworkers or parents is still risky, both financially and emotionally. Though acceptance is still an uphill climb, at least these members of society know they are not alone.

Where to start: Chungusai (Between Friends; chingusai.net) – while primarily a gay men's human rights group, the site features links to several Korean lesbian groups. Sappho Korea (sappho_korea@googlegroups.com), formerly Seoul Sisters, is a mostly expat lesbian group that runs meetings, trips and parties.

high-school students go through a gruelling examination process, studying 14 hours a day, often in private cram schools at night, for their one annual shot at the college entrance test. Some retake it two or three times until they get it right.

Another phenomenon is a *girugi appa* (wild-goose father), a man who stays in Korea to work while the mother takes the children overseas for study.

ARTS

Seoul has long been the nexus of Korea's fantastic arts – in dance, music, literature, and the visual arts. Indeed, visitors will be ignoring a trove of cultural riches if they merely stick to the city's palaces and markets. Rich, colourful costumes set the scene for passionate traditional *pansori* operas. Folk dances such as *samullori,* with its whirling dervish of dancers, seamlessly meld the cacophonous and melodic. Artisans preserve the ancient art of calligraphy with their silken strokes.

Seoul takes national pride of place in the modern arts, too. Korea's film directors, including Hong Sang-soo and Lee Chang-dong, are regularly feted at international festivals such as Cannes. Fans of modern art will relish the quirky stacked-TV creations of famed local Nam June Paik at many Seoul art museums. And Asia goes gaga for Korean pop icons/eye candy Rain and BoA.

Much of the city's artistic wealth is incredibly accessible to visitors. Seoul's performing arts centres (see p136) have nightly performances offering a breathtaking smorgasbord of traditional music and dance. The flourish of galleries in Samcheong and Hongdae offers a

HANBOK

Hanbok is the striking traditional clothing that follows the Confucian principle of unadorned modesty. Women wore a loose-fitting short blouse with long sleeves and a voluminous long skirt, while men wore a jacket and baggy trousers.

As with other Confucian-based practices, times have changed. Hardly anyone puts on hanbok now except at weddings or special events, and even then it may be a more comfortable 'updated' version.

Everyday hanbok is reasonably priced, but formal styles, made of colourful silk and intricately embroidered, are objects of wonder and cost a fortune.

DUELING POETS

Seo Jung-ju (1915–2000; often spelt So Chong-ju) went by the name 'Midang' and wrote rhythmically textured, lyrical poetry full of symbolism and natural elements. His subjects were often intensely personal accounts of emotion, with a first-person narrator waxing philosophical on long-lost loves from his youth or reflecting on the nature of being a poet. Other poems mine the ancient kingdom of Silla for nostalgia surrounding a lost past. In his most famous work, 'Beside a Chrysanthemum', the narrator talks of his sister, back from 'far away byways of youth…racked with longing and lack.' So's lyrical, symbol-rich style represents the best of a generation still steeped in a more traditional aesthetic.

Shim Kyong-nim was born in 1935, the generation after So. Instead of an 'I', his poems are spoken from a collective 'we' – a move deeply shocking at the time. This 'we' was the voice of the people – the *minjung* – and Shim's poems take a hard, uncompromising look at a difficult present. His work describes poor labourers' daily delights and sorrows. It follows workers who drag their broken bodies to the local dive bar to nurse their wounded pride. It recounts the pervasive political violence in the 1960s and '70s. Shim's most famous work, 'Farmers' Dance ', uneasily tells of how young prostitutes 'lean pressed against the oil shop wall/giggling childish giggles'. Its realism is shocking even today, and represents a new kind of poetry, one advocating social involvement.

When held in comparison, the poets' work speaks volumes about the rapid shift of values in modern Korea. Wonderful collections of both poets' work are available in translation by Brother Anthony of Taize: So's *The Early Lyrics* (W8,000) and Shin's *Farmers' Dance* (W7,000).

perfect afternoon stroll through some of the best new art Seoul talent can offer. Stay in Hongdae at night to hear the latest from Seoul's vibrant indie music scene. Seoul's artists, long revered at home, have begun to arrive on the world stage.

LITERATURE

Seoul has always been a city of writers. Part of the Joseon-era government-service exam (*gwageo*) involved composing verse. During the Joseon dynasty, literature meant *sijo*, short nature poems that were hand-written (using a brush and ink) in Chinese characters, even after the invention of *hangeul* (the Korean phonetic alphabet) in the 15th century.

top picks

SEOUL LITERATURE

- *Three Generations* (1931) by Yom Sang-seop – A searing examination of class written during the Japanese colonial period.
- *The Naked Tree* (1970) by Pak Wan-so – A young woman seeks both survival and love in Korean War-era Seoul.
- *The Dwarf* (1978) by Cho Se-hui – A poetic novella about the victims of Korea's urban redevelopment.
- *A Distant and Beautiful Place* (1987) by Yang Kwi-ja – Traces the lives of the residents of a slum on Seoul's outskirts.
- *I Have the Right to Destroy Myself* (1996) by Kim Young-ha – A dark, urgent tale of modern disconnect amidst Seoul's urban landscape.

After 1945, however, there was a sharp turn away from Chinese (and Japanese) influence of any kind. Western ideas and ideals took hold, and existentialism and other international literary trends found footing, but through a unique and pervasive Korean lens.

SCULPTURE, PAINTING & CALLIGRAPHY

Seoul has an active modern art scene. Local artists tend to follow Western trends while incorporating Korean motifs and themes; the best of them combine traditional techniques with a modern vision. Top Korean artist Nam June Paik (1932–2006) has some excellent and imaginative installations in the National Museum of Contemporary Art (p75). Another icon of Korean modern art is Kim Tschang Yeul, who is obsessed with raindrops. His work can be seen at the Hoam Art Museum (p168).

Stone Buddhist statues and pagodas such as the one in Tapgol Park (p51) are among the oldest artworks in Seoul. Some marvellous examples of cast-bronze Buddhas can be seen in the National Museum of Korea (p73). Zen-style Buddhist art can be seen inside and outside Seoul's temples, Jogyesa (p49) and Bongeunsa (p71), and you'll find stone and wooden effigies of

OUTDOOR SCULPTURES

Seoul has more outdoor sculptures than any other city on the planet – really. Every high-rise building must, by law, have a sculpture outside, so keep an eye out for these often creative, often jaw-dropping feats of art. Olympic Park (p67) has an ever-expanding collection of over 200 sometimes wacky modern sculptures created by artists from around the world. Some works here are bigger than a house. The east side of the main strip in Daehangno (Map p52) is also lined with quirky modern creations. Hammering Man (p45), just west of Sejongno, is memorably disquieting.

In 2006, the city commissioned famed Swedish-US artist Claes Oldenburg and his partner Coosje van Bruggen to create a sculpture to sit at the mouth of the restored Cheonggyecheon stream that flows through the heart of Seoul. But no one told them that their mammoth, colourful swirl, Spring (Map p40), looks just like how Korean elementary-school doodlers like to render…well…poo. Best to decide for yourself just what the striking sculpture adds to Seoul's epicentre.

shamanist spirit guardians outside the National Folk Museum (p39) in the grounds of the main palace, Gyeongbokgung.

Another fascinating traditional art form is *hanji,* or Korean handmade paper. This is often dyed soft colours, and is sometimes pressed and lacquered so that it can serve as a waterproof cup or plate.

Chinese influence is paramount in traditional Korean painting. The basic tools (brush and water-based ink) are those of calligraphy, which influenced painting in both technique and theory. The brush line, which varies in thickness and tone, is the most important feature. Traditional landscape painting is meant to surround the viewer, and there is no fixed viewpoint as in traditional Western painting. A talented artist who painted everyday scenes was Kim Hong-do (1745–1816). Court ceremonies, portraits, flowers, birds and traditional symbols of longevity – the sun, water, rocks, mountains, clouds, pine trees, turtles and cranes – were popular subjects.

CERAMICS & POTTERY

Archaeologists have unearthed Korean pottery that dates back some 10,000 years, although it wasn't until the early 12th century that the art form reached a peak, with skilled potters turning out wonderful celadon pottery with a warm-green tinge. Visit the National Museum of Korea (p73) for one of the best displays. Original celadon fetches huge sums at auction, but modern copies are widely available, particularly in Insadong (p83) and Icheon (p181).

Sadly, after the 13th-century Mongol invasion the art was lost, and Koreans started to produce *buncheong*-ware, less-refined pottery decorated with simple folk designs. But it was much admired by the Japanese, and during the Imjin War in the 1590s entire families and villages of Korean potters were abducted and resettled in Japan to produce *buncheong* for their new masters. Some are still there.

MUSIC

Korean traditional music *(gugak)* is played on stringed instruments, most notably the *gayageum* (12-stringed zither) and *haegum* (two-stringed fiddle) as well as on chimes, gongs, cymbals, drums, horns and flutes. Court music *(jeongak)* is slow and stately while folk music such as *samullori* is fast and lively.

Similar to Western opera is *changgeuk,* which can involve a large cast of characters. An unusual type of opera is *pansori.* It features a solo storyteller (usually female) singing to the beat of a drum, while emphasising dramatic moments with a flick of her fan. The singing is strong and sorrowful: some say if *pansori* is done correctly, the performer will have blood in her mouth upon finishing. Only a few *pansori* dramas have survived; *Chunhyang,* the story of a woman's faith and endurance, is the most popular.

Some unusual musical instruments are on view in the Museum of Korean Traditional Music (p76), next door to the Seoul Arts Centre. Go to www.ncktpa.go.kr for information on Korean percussion, woodwind and string instruments.

Western classical music is played in a number of concert halls in Seoul, with Korean luminaries such as soprano Sumi Jo dropping in for hometown shows. Live jazz and folk bars are common, and rock, punk, hip-hop, electronic and other genres all have their followers.

BACKGROUND ARTS

ART WORLD SCANDAL

Korea's modern art community, while quite lively, does not usually make for strong gossip fodder. An exception was in 2007, when 35-year-old Shin Jeong-ah was stripped of her duties as codirector of the next year's Gwangju Biennale, by far the most internationally renowned art exhibition in Korea. It seems Shin's rapid rise proved too fast – she had lied about her credentials, forging her PhD dissertation from Yale University (she only held a high-school diploma). Always looking for some extra juice in a story, the papers ran racy photos of Shin taken by her lover – who happened to be a presidential aide, and who had used his influence to get Shin a university post. Eager readers got what they had come for: scandal and shame.

Shin was clearly talented – her stint as curator often garnered international acclaim, and landing the Gwangju spot was no mean feat for someone so young. But the modern art scene in Seoul is often one of money and connections: most of the major private galleries and museums hold affiliation with a *jaebeol* (Korea's large conglomerates), and some journalists and insiders claim that bribes and favours among an elite circle of artists and major curators is the name of the game. In this sort of culture, relying on one's talent – for artists or curators – may not be enough.

Though the student neighbourhoods of Sinchon and next-door Hongdae were the hot spots of youth music and culture in the 1980s and '90s, exploding rents and modernisation have turned them more commercial, but good indie shows are still frequent. Beatball Records (www.myspace.com/beatballmusic) is a local label that keeps an updated list of upcoming gigs on its webpage.

CINEMA & TELEVISION

After its humble resurrection following liberation and war, Korea's modern film scene, long based in Seoul's Chungmuro neighbourhood is now revered by film buffs worldwide. Key to this climb was the nixing of earlier censorship coupled with a rise in budgets. A government quota ensuring that Hollywood flicks can't push home-grown releases out of theatres hasn't hurt, either.

That said, let it be known: like many countries, Korea produces some truly awful mainstream comedies. But excellent major Korean productions don't shy away from major issues, such as the Korean War (*Taegukgi*, 2004) and its turbulent political aftermath (*The President's Last Bang*, 2005).

top picks

'FOLK' ALBUMS

- *Gayageum Masterpieces* by Chimhyang-moo – quiet and relaxing raindrop sounds.
- *Beautiful Things in Life* by Jeong Soo-nyun – haunting melodies played on the *haegum* (two-stringed fiddle).
- *The Fragrance of Bamboo* by Lee Saeng-kang – a retrospective album by a flute master.
- *A Day* by Cho Moon-young – crossover music including an Irish ballad played on a rarely heard 25-string *gayageum*.

Pervasive social issues in modern Seoul – such as the blistering pace of city life and the shifting notion of family – are tackled in films like *The Way Home* (2002) and *Family Ties* (2006), both quietly touching. *Marathon* (2005) is the inspiring true tale of a devoted Seoul mother struggling to bring up her autistic son amidst societal prejudice. Of course, there are films out there for pure entertainment: the horror films *Memento Mori* (1999) and *A Tale of Two Sisters* (2003) provide gruesome shocks for the genre aficionado, and for an action-revenge flick – something Korea excels at – nothing tops the jaw-dropping *Old Boy* (2003).

Filmmaking used to be an old-boys club. No longer: superb films by female directors are receiving greater recognition. These include Jeong Jae-eun's *Take Care of My Cat* (2001), the pitch-perfect story of five girls coming of age in the suburbs outside of Seoul, and Yim Soon-rye's *Waikiki Brothers* (2001), a sobering exploration of those left behind by Korea's economic rise. Yim's *Forever the Moment* (2008) follows the Korean women's handball team into the 2004 Olympics, offering a more reflective take than is the genre standard. Another must-see is Byun Young-joo's *The Murmuring* (1995), a subdued but shattering documentary about the fate of comfort women, Koreans forced into sexual slavery by the Japanese during WWII.

Korea's TV dramas, while popular in the rest of Asia, have not received as much international attention. This is a shame: they're often excellent (check out *Winter Sonata, Daejanggeum, My Name Is Kim Sam-soon* and *Sikgaek*).

FOUR MODERN DIRECTORS

Im Kwon-taek
- *Festival* (1996) Documenting the long and sometimes raucous funerary rites of a small-town matriarch, this moving film takes a soft-edged, wry look at fate and mortality.
- *Chihwaseon* (*Painted Fire*; 2002) Visually stunning biographical look at an extraordinarily talented – and troubled – Joseon-era painter.

Hong Sang-soo
- *Power of Gangwon Province* (1998) Challenging, disturbing exploration of a group of characters whose lives unexpectedly intersect.
- *On the Occasion of Remembering the Turning Gate* (2002) Hong's trademark ad-libbed scripting brings naturalism to this tale of one man confronting his life's quiet disappointments.

Bong Joon-ho
- *Memories of Murder* (2003) Set in the late 1980s, just as Korea's military dictatorship was in its last throes, this story of Korea's first serial murder case is a flawless, riveting meditation on the country's modern history.
- *The Host* (2006) This symbol-laden paean to classic monster movies is somehow able to juggle poignancy and heart-stopping action.

Lee Chang-dong
- *Oasis* (2002) A difficult, powerfully acted tale of the unexpected love that develops between a sociopath and a severely disabled girl.
- *Secret Sunshine* (2007) Jeon Do-hyeon took the acting award at Cannes for her portrayal of a mother confronting loss in this stunning meditation on forgiveness and faith.

Korean films are occasionally shown with English subtitles in cinemas, but the best way to see them is on DVD at one of Korea's numerous DVD *bang* (rooms that offer small private rooms with comfortable armchairs and a large screen).

A top resource for Korean cinema is www.koreanfilm.org, which covers all aspects of the industry and features scads of reviews. Seoul Selection (p83) has a great selection of Korean DVDs.

THEATRE

Seoul has a thriving theatre scene based mainly around Daehangno, where more than 50 small theatres put on everything from rock musicals and satirical plays to opera and translations of Western classics. Nearly all shows are in Korean but drama fans should still enjoy the experience.

DANCE

Modern dance is active in Seoul, with at least two annual modern dance festivals (see the boxed text, p136). *Contemporary Dance Scenes of Korea* (2001) is a comprehensive, chronological study of Seoul's modern dance scene.

Korean folk dances include dynamic *seungmu* (drum dances), satirical and energetic *talchum* (mask dances) and solo improvisational *salpuri* (shamanist dances). Most popular are *samullori* dance troupes, who perform in brightly coloured traditional clothing, twirling a long tassel from a cap on their heads. Try this at home: participants dance, head twirl and beat a drum or gong at the same time. See p136 for details on traditional dance venues. Every year, elegant court dances accompanied by an orchestra are performed in front of Jongmyo (p42) on the first Sunday in May.

ARCHITECTURE

Seoul's skyline – dominated by mammoth skyscrapers and endless high-rise apartments – at first suggests no building has survived the war and economic modernisation. But a treasure trove of architecture from all periods of Seoul's history remains, resulting in a juxtaposed hodgepodge that at times finds a quirky harmony.

MIXED MEDIA

Seoul's print media is dominated by a trio of major conglomerates – the Chosun, JoongAng, and Dong-a dailies – known locally as *chojungdong*, an amalgam of their names and a testament to their encompassing collective hold. Because of their influence and ties to Korea's *jaebeol* (large conglomerates), along with the fact that they thrived under Korea's military dictatorships, some Koreans harbour residual mistrust toward 'the big three'.

Offering a challenge to this media triumvirate, a new player entered the fray after Korea's democratisation. Several reporters fired for their political beliefs banded together to start the *Hankyoreh* newspaper, which focused on providing a missing left-wing angle to the news. More recently, Korea's position as number one in the world for online access and citizen cyber-participation yielded another lefty media player: OhmyNews! (www.ohmynews.com), a web-based guerrilla news operation reliant upon reader-journalists for its content.

Each side of the media debate is criticised by the other for biased reporting and influence-peddling, but nothing was as interesting as (normally) liberal-leaning then-President Roh Moo-hyun's declaration that all media – right and left – was out to get him, upon which he cut off reporters' access to his cabinet members! The press, it seems, may never be truly free.

TRADITIONAL ARCHITECTURE

Traditional Korean architecture takes seriously humankind's contract with the natural world. Colour, line and scale are meant to meld with surrounding hills, rivers and forests. Korean palaces and temples are of modest size, not meant to impose themselves upon the people who enter their walls. (In contrast, try to not feel intimidated when standing before, say, the Forbidden City in Beijing.)

There are three main types of traditional architecture found in Seoul: palaces, temples and homes. They are all primarily made of wood, with no nails used – a system of braces and brackets holds the elements together. They were (and sometimes still are) heated using an ingenious system of circulating underfloor smoke tunnels called *ondol*.

Palaces

During the Joseon era, five main palaces were constructed in the royal capital of Seoul. These were cities unto themselves, massive complexes with administrative offices, residences, pleasure pavilions and royal gardens, all hemmed in by imposing walls. A prominent feature is the roof of these structures, which is made from heavy clay tiles with dragons or other mythical beasts embossed on the end-tile. The strikingly bold, predominantly green and orange paintwork under the eaves is called *dancheong*. Ceilings are often intricately carved and coloured.

Because of centuries of invasion and war, Seoul's palaces have all been painstakingly rebuilt countless times, sometimes changing their shape altogether. Gyeongbokgung, for example, stands at a fraction of its original size.

Temples

Korean temples, like palaces, are painted in natural colours. Outside murals depict the life of Buddha or parables of self-liberation; inside the shrines are paintings of Buddhist heavens – and occasionally hells. Look for intricately carved lattice in the Buddhist shrines, and for a *sansingak*, or Mountain God Hall, which contains an image of the deity in question and represents the accommodation of Korean Buddhism to Korea's pre-existing shamanist beliefs.

Keeping watch over temple entrance gates are paintings or statues (sometimes both) of the fierce-looking guardians of the four directions who protect Buddhists from harm.

Sadly, due to Joseon-era persecution of Buddhism, few old temples are extant in Seoul.

Homes

Traditional houses, often called *hanok*, are complex in design yet masterfully understated. Unlike palaces and temples, Korean homes are left unpainted, their brown and tan earth tones giving off a warm, intimate feel. The tiled roofs hold a layer of mud and rice straw that both insulates and ventilates.

Social rank dictated the decorations, beam size, roof pitch and number of rooms – rules not relaxed until the 1930s. Confucianism had the largest impact on the interior layout, decreeing that males and females should not sit close after the age of seven. Thus, the traditional home was divided into two sections, the *sarangchae* for men and the *anchae* for women. In larger homes, these comprised different buildings, surrounded by walls and gates. In the *anchae,* the women of the family raised children, did the cooking and ran the household. The *sarangchae* housed the library, an ancestral shrine and rooms in which to receive guests, who seated themselves on comfortable low cushions and enjoyed a tea service.

Traditional homes look out onto a central courtyard, or *madang,* often with a simple garden. See the Samcheong-dong walk (p47) for a look at some *hanok.*

EARLY MODERN AND COLONIAL ARCHITECTURE

In the late 19th century, the Western world pressed to open Korea, and Western and Japanese missionaries, traders and diplomats flooded into the Hermit Kingdom. This period is often regarded as 'colonial' architecture, although some of it represents purely Korean attempts to modernise along Western lines. Churches were usually designed by French, American or British missionaries, including wonderful examples of Gothic and Romanesque styles, but much of Seoul's early modern architectural heritage was built by the Japanese – including the massive Government-General building, built on part of Gyeongbokgung and finally torn down in 1996.

Japanese colonial architects often emulated Western Renaissance and neo-baroque architectural styles, although you'll also find the occasional art nouveau or other modernist style thrown in.

MODERN ARCHITECTURE

Though the needs of post–Korean War reconstruction required a focus on more utilitarian concerns, much of Korea's modern architecture is distinct, usually following one of two trajectories: either an attempt to reinterpret traditional Korean architecture in concrete and steel, or to communicate Seoul's cutting-edge technological prowess.

First and perhaps foremost of Korea's postindependence architects was Japanese-trained Kim Swoo-geun, whose early work reflected the influence of Le Corbusier and Kenzo Tange. He is responsible for the curving lines of the Olympic Stadium (Map p70). Another architectural great is Kim Chung-up, whose work includes the soaring Peace Gate at Olympic Park (p67).

ENVIRONMENT & PLANNING

During South Korea's postwar economic rise, little thought was given to the environmental impact of so much rapid construction. Things slowly began to improve after democratisation in the late 1980s, but with 1997's economic crisis, standards were relaxed in order to help drive development. Environmentalists continue the fight to get stronger standards in place.

Architecture on Display

- Traditional: For palaces, don't miss Gyeongbokgung (p38) and Changdeokgung (p39). Jogyesa (p49) is one of Seoul's most beautiful temples. For *hanok,* Namsangol Hanok Village (p55) and Samcheong-dong (p47) have the best examples.
- Early Modern: Myeong-dong Cathedral (p59) features beautiful, high-vaulted ceilings, whereas Chung-dong First Methodist Church has a more spare aesthetic. Seoul Anglican Cathedral may be the most spectacular, a Romanesque stone structure incorporating a number of Korean traditional elements. (The latter two can be seen on the Deoksugung walk, p45.) Impressive Japanese colonial architecture includes the neo-baroque Seoul Station with its Byzantine dome (Map pp56–7) and the Renaissance-style Seoul City Hall, with its imposing grey facade (Map40).
- Modern: The gold-tinted 63 Building (p62) on Yeouido, and the downtown Jongno Tower (Map p50) are two not to miss. Also check out the National Theatre (p137), the Sejong Centre for the Performing Arts (p137), and the presidential mansion of Cheongwadae (p44).

In the last decade, the Seoul government has made an effort to increase civic involvement in reducing waste. The public response has been strong – recycling is popular and composting is the norm, and a new home-grown 'wellbeing' movement embraces more environmentally sound practices.

THE LAND

Seoul is a city of craggy peaks – eight major ones in total. Namsan, the proud sentinel, overlooks the Han River, which cleanly bisects the city. The hills of Seoul kept the king safely ensconced in power in the centre of the city, and they served to divide neighbourhoods along socio-economic lines, creating class rifts that still smoulder.

The peaks have helped Seoul's various religious sects, particularly Buddhism and shamanism, commune with nature. Buddhist temples cling to all of Seoul's mountains, and shamanist rituals are still practiced high up in the rocky folds of Inwangsan, though development encroaches year by year.

Seoul's mountains also serve an important social and health function – weekends see city dwellers heading in droves to enjoy the outdoors. See p78 and p164 for some lofty options.

top picks

SEOUL ARCHITECTURE BOOKS

- *Hanoak – Traditional Korean Houses* (1999) is a fully illustrated book on the exterior and interior design of Korea's traditional one-storey wood-and-tile houses.
- *Joseon Royal Court Culture* (2004) by Shin Myung-ho gives the facts about the unique Confucian royal-court lifestyle. Based on primary sources, the superbly illustrated book gives a human context to the now-empty palaces.
- *Seoul's Historic Walks* (2008) by Cho In-Souk and Robert Koehler offers eight tours around Seoul, illustrating the transition from traditional to modern architectural styles. Features maps and plenty of photographs.

GREEN SEOUL

With one of the highest population densities in the world, and the highest per capita energy consumption in Asia, Seoul isn't a particularly 'green' burg. But the city has made some strides in recent years. Air quality is generally decent and improving, and natural gas buses are helping a great deal (the lion's share of Seoul's air pollutants is from buses and trucks). However, the pollution blowing in from China is gradually worsening, cutting into some of the gains.

To increase 'greenspace', Seoul has recently begun a massive, 25-neighbourhood urban renewal project. In October 2005 the first link was opened – the Cheonggye Stream Project, restoring a paved-over streambed and lining it with walking paths. Proponents insist the stream will provide a much-needed greenspace chain for recreation and parks (Seoul has plenty of large, lovely parks; most just aren't where anyone lives) and moderate the city's radiant heat from buildings and concrete. Detractors point out that for the sake of a few fountains and fanfare for then-mayor (and now president) Lee Myung-bak, some of the funkiest 'real Seoul' neighbourhoods – such as the traditional Cheonggye Market area along the old streambed – fell to the wrecking ball, and that the renovation actually worsened traffic.

For information on how visitors can reduce their impact, see Sustainable Seoul (p15).

URBAN PLANNING & DEVELOPMENT

With such a large population, Seoul has no choice but to continue expanding outward in all directions. Unfortunately, this hasn't resulted in more affordable housing, as land speculation and a real-estate pricing bubble have kept prices soaring for the past several years; prices are only now beginning to wane. In fact, some of these suburbs have become the highest-priced addresses in the entire country.

To combat this problem, the city government has built several low-cost housing units in several neighbourhoods, but the issue is far from solved, as even these homes remain out of reach for many families.

NEIGHBOURHOODS

top picks

- **Gyeongbokgung** (p38)
  Seoul's grandest palace includes two museums
- **Changdeokgung** (p39)
  A unique World Heritage garden adjoins the palace
- **Deoksugung** (p42)
  Includes a tea pavilion and two art galleries
- **Jongmyo** (p42)
  Confucian shrines honouring 500 years of Joseon royalty
- **National Museum of Korea** (p73)
  Ancient treasures displayed in a modern setting
- **War Memorial & Museum** (p73)
  A wonderful exhibition brings the Korean War to life
- **Seodaemun Prison** (p74)
  Torture chambers and an execution room
- **Jogyesa** (p49)
  Colourful temple with Buddhist art-and-crafts lessons
- **Olympic Park** (p67)
  200 wacky sculptures, five stadiums and three museums
- **World Cup Stadium** (p75)
  With a park, cinema, mall, spa and more

What's your recommendation? lonelyplanet.com/seoul

NEIGHBOURHOODS

Seoul's main historical and sightseeing area is bustling downtown Gwanghwamun, which includes a handful of feudal-era palaces and museums as well as artsy-crafty Insadong and Samcheong-dong. Seoul Plaza, outside City Hall, and the Cheonggyecheon Plaza frequently host events in a city with more festivals than days in the year. To the north lies Bukhansan National Park, with a cobweb of hiking trails that lead up through densely wooded hillsides to picturesque Buddhist temples and granite peaks. The park is packed with hikers at week-

'The majestic Han River (Hangang) winds through the city, its banks dotted with cycleways, swimming pools and parks.'

ends, so it's best to come during the week and avoid queuing for the summits. Seoul is surrounded by mountains, which is why King Taejo chose the city as the capital 600 years ago.

To the east is the student and theatre district of Daehangno, which has street sculptures and murals, a jazz academy and a very lively drama scene. Over 50 small theatres compete for business, covering the neighbourhood with posters advertising their shows. Further east is an eclectic band of traditional markets that sell clothes and collectables, accessories and antiques, Asian health foods and medicines. The reopening of the Cheonggye stream means you can walk along it from downtown to Dongdaemun Market.

To the south, within walking distance of City Hall and downtown, is the ever-popular fashion shopping and entertainment area of Myeong-dong, which lures thousands of young people and tourists every evening. Brand names aimed at young and old hang out here, and you can lose yourself for hours in the latticework of narrow, quiet streets, the underground shopping arcades and the four-in-a-row Lotte department stores.

Just over the road the huge Namdaemun Market is very traditional, from the lack of price tags to the pork-hock meals and the money-changing grannies sitting outdoors on stools. Further south, walk or take the cable car up Namsan (South Mountain) and visit the landmark N Seoul Tower, jutting from the mountaintop, for another perspective on Seoul. Namsan used to be a Japanese enclave during the colonial era, but the area is being returned to nature and this splash of green is becoming popular with early morning joggers.

South of Namsan is the busy tourist shopping and expat entertainment area of Itaewon – a different atmosphere to the rest of the city. It's a UN of eating establishments and gay and hostess bars, with street stalls blocking up the pavements and lots of foreigners walking around.

To the west, just a short subway ride from downtown, is the buzzing student neighbourhood made up of Hongdae, Sinchon and Ewha. Hongdae has the indie bands, clubbing and quirky cafés, Sinchon has the restaurants, bars and love motels, and Ewha has the fashion and beauty shops, including a street of designer wedding dresses with starkly contrasting styles, all extravagant.

The majestic Han River (Hangang) winds through the city, its banks dotted with cycleways, swimming pools and parks. In the river is the island of Yeouido, a financial and administrative hub that is home to the stock exchange and the National Assembly.

South of the river, the upmarket residential and business neighbourhood of Gangnam includes Apgujeong, with global and local brand-name boutiques, plush department stores and luxury hotels. Garosu-gil is an interesting Euro-Korean street of bistros and boutiques, while a galaxy of restaurants, bars and shops clusters around Gangnam station. Further east is Jamsil where the giant COEX Mall and Conference Centre, the multifaceted Lotte World and the sculpture-filled Olympic Park are located. These all represent modern Seoul, while the atmospheric temple Bongeunsa and a trio of royal tombs in a rare patch of greenery are reminders of the past.

The excellent foreigner-friendly subway system brings the many attractions beyond central Seoul within easy reach, including the parks and mall at the World Cup Stadium, a massive zoo, must-see museums and art galleries, a horse-racing track and Ttukseom Seoul Forest Park.

Migum-si

Jungnang-gu

Han River (Hangang)

Gangdong-gu

Hanam-si

Gwangjin-gu

Songpa-gu

Seongbuk-gu

Dongdaemun-gu

Seongdong-gu

GANGNAM & JAMSIL (p67)

Gwacheon-si

Hyoja-dong

GWANGHWAMUN (p38)

INSADONG & DAEHANGNO (p49)

MYEONG-DONG, NAMSAN & ITAEWON (p55)

Jung-gu

Seocho-gu

Han River (Hangang)

Seodaemun-gu

Yongsan-gu

Yeongdeungpo-gu

Dongjak-gu

Gwanak-gu

Mapo-gu

HONGDAE, SINCHON & YEOUIDO (p62)

Han River (Hangang)

3 km

2 miles

0
0

ITINERARY BUILDER

It's best to mix up sights and activities each day – a palace, a museum, a market, a cycling trip or park, and in the evening head to an entertainment district for a restaurant, a traditional music-and-dance show and a bar before relaxing in a spa. You can flit easily and quickly from one neighbourhood to another on the subway or by taxi, although visiting south of the river takes longer.

ACTIVITIES	Sights	Shopping	Eating
Gwanghwamun	Gyeongbokgung (p38)	Dongdaemun Market (p83)	Gamrodang (p99)
	Changdeokgung (p39)	Kyobo Bookshop (p83)	Tosokchon Samgyetang (p99)
	Jongmyo & Changgyeong-gung (p42)	Seoul Selection (p83)	Solmoemaeul (p99)
Insadong & Daehangno	Jogye Temple (p49)	Ssamzie (p85)	Sanchon (p101)
	Unhyeongung (p51)	Kukjae Embroidery (p84)	Gogung (p101)
	Cheondogyo Temple (p52)	Filipino Sunday Market (p85)	About Shabu (p103)
Myeong-dong, Namsan & Itaewon	Deoksugung (p42)	Namdaemun Market (p86)	Korea House (p105)
	Namsangol Hanok Village (p55)	Lotte Department Store (p86)	Baekje Samgyetang (p106)
	N Seoul Tower (p55)	Migliore Mall (p86)	Zelen (p106)
Hongdae, Sinchon & Yeouido	63 Building (p62)	Noryangjin Fish Market (p89)	63 Buffet Pavilion (p107)
	Jeoldusan Martyrs Museum & Chapel (p62)	Free Market (p88)	Busan Ilbeonji (p107)
	Yeouido Full Gospel Church (p64)	Record Forum (p90)	Teolbogodoeni (p109)
Gangnam & Jamsil	Lotte World (p69)	Galleria (p90)	Gorilla in the Kitchen (p110)
	Olympic Park (p67)	COEX Mall (p90)	Hanmiri (p109)
	Seolleung Park Royal Tombs (p72)	Huckleberry Farms (p91)	Nolboo Yuhwangorijin-heukgui (p110)
Greater Seoul	Seodaemun Prison (p74)	Yongsan Electronics Market (p92)	Gwangjang Market (p83)
	National Museum of Korea (p73)	Janganpyeong Antiques Market (p91)	
	War Memorial & Museum (p73)	Gyeongdong Market (p91)	

AREA

HOW TO USE THIS TABLE

The table below allows you to plan a day's worth of activities in any area of the city. Simply select which area you wish to explore, and then mix and match from the corresponding listings to build your day. The first item in each cell represents a well-known highlight of the area, while the other items are more off-the-beaten-track gems.

Drinking & Nightlife	Sports & Activities	The Arts
Buck Mulligan's (p115)	City Hall Plaza Ice-skating (p141) Baseball Hitting Practice (p141)	Sejong Centre for the Performing Arts (p137) Nanta Theatre (p137) Chongdong Theatre (p136)
Live Jazz Club (p132) Top Cloud Bar (p115) Bier Halle (p115)	Hidinck Pool (p142)	Sarang Ticket Office (p137) Hakchon Green Theatre (p137) Cine Castle DVD (p138)
Gecko's Terrace (p117) 3 Alley Pub (p117) Grand Ole Opry (l)	Namsan & N Seoul Tower Walk (p59) LCI Bowling (p142) Chunjiyun Spa (p140)	Korea House (p137) National Theatre (p137)
Club FF (p132) M2 (p131) Tin Pan Music Bar (p118)	Cycling (p141) Namugeuneul Foot Spa (p118) Yeouido Swimming Pool (p142)	Sangsangmadang (p66)
Once in a Blue Moon (p133) Oktoberfest (p119) Dublin (p119)	Spa Lei (p141) Cycling (p67) Olympic Coliseum Golf (p141)	Seoul Norimadang (p138) COEX Mall Megabox (p138)
Samcheong-dong Walk (p47) Wandering Around Deoksugung (p45)	Dragon Hill Spa (p140) Horse Racing (p143) Inwangsan Shamanist Hillside Walk (p77)	Seoul Arts Centre (p138) Yeakdang Theatre (p138)

GREATER SEOUL

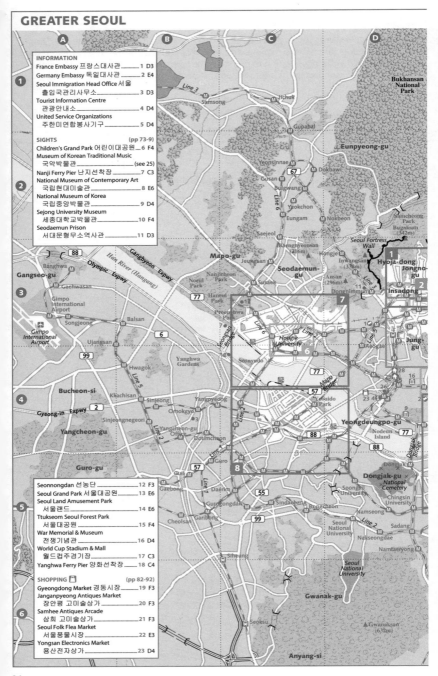

INFORMATION

France Embassy 프랑스대사관	1 D3
Germany Embassy 독일대사관	2 E4
Seoul Immigration Head Office 서울 출입국관리사무소	3 D3
Tourist Information Centre 관광안내소	4 D4
United Service Organizations 주한미연합봉사기구	5 D4

SIGHTS (pp 73–9)

Children's Grand Park 어린이대공원	6 F4
Museum of Korean Traditional Music 국악박물관	(see 25)
Nanji Ferry Pier 난지선착장	7 C3
National Museum of Contemporary Art 국립현대미술관	8 E6
National Museum of Korea 국립중앙박물관	9 D4
Sejong University Museum 세종대학교박물관	10 F4
Seodaemun Prison 서대문형무소역사관	11 D3

Seonnongdan 선농단	12 F3
Seoul Grand Park 서울대공원	13 E6
Seoul Land Amusement Park 서울랜드	14 E6
Ttukseom Seoul Forest Park 서울대공원	15 F4
War Memorial & Museum 전쟁기념관	16 D4
World Cup Stadium & Mall 월드컵경기장	17 C3
Yanghwa Ferry Pier 양화선착장	18 C4

SHOPPING (pp 82–92)

Gyeongdong Market 경동시장	19 F3
Janganpyeong Antiques Market 장안평 고미술상가	20 F3
Samhee Antiques Arcade 삼회 고미술상가	21 F3
Seoul Folk Flea Market 서울풍물시장	22 E3
Yongsan Electronics Market 용산전자상가	23 D4

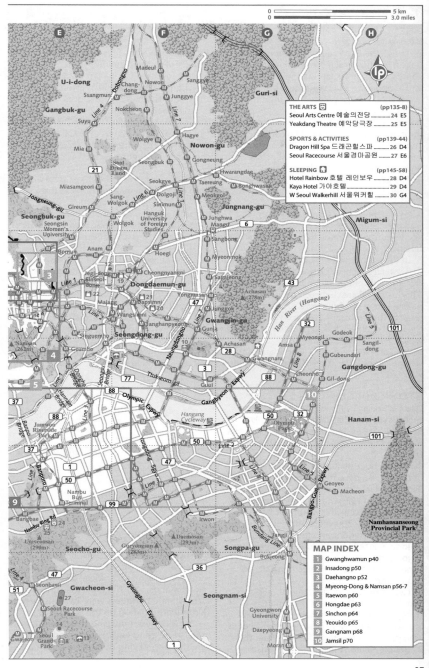

0 ————— 5 km
0 ————— 3.0 miles

THE ARTS (pp135-8)
Seoul Arts Centre 예술의전당 24 E5
Yeakdang Theatre 예악당극장 25 E5

SPORTS & ACTIVITIES (pp139-44)
Dragon Hill Spa 드래곤힐스파 26 D4
Seoul Racecourse 서울경마공원 27 E6

SLEEPING (pp145-58)
Hotel Rainbow 호텔 레인보우 28 D4
Kaya Hotel 가야호텔 29 D4
W Seoul Walkerhill 서울워커힐 30 G4

MAP INDEX
1 Gwanghwamun p40
2 Insadong p50
3 Daehangno p52
4 Myeong-Dong & Namsan p56-7
5 Itaewon p60
6 Hongdae p63
7 Sinchon p64
8 Yeouido p65
9 Gangnam p68
10 Jamsil p70

37

Shopping (p82), Eating (p99), Sleeping (p148)

Although their size and splendour have been greatly reduced by wars, fires and Japanese colonial policy, Seoul's royal palace compounds contain a variety of restored buildings that offer visitors glimpses of Korea's fascinating feudal past. The palaces followed Confucian ideals of frugality and simplicity – they're unique, but don't expect the opulent grandeur of Western palaces.

Today the large palace buildings are mostly empty but the maze of corridors, courtyards, buildings and gardens used to be thronged with government officials and scholars, eunuchs and concubines, soldiers, servants and slaves. The natural historian Isabella Bird was very impressed when she visited Gyeongbokgung in 1895: 'What with 800 troops, 1500 attendants and officials of all descriptions, courtiers and ministers and their attendants, secretaries, messengers and hangers-on, the vast palace enclosure of Gyeongbokgung seemed as crowded and populated as the city itself.'

The grand formal buildings, where government business was carried out, contrast with the smaller, more informal living quarters, divided into male and female sections as dictated by Confucian principles.

Gyeongbokgung, Changdeokgung and Deoksugung are all worth a visit, and are within walking distance of each other. Changgyeonggung can be visited free along with World Heritage Jongmyo, a Confucian memorial shrine to the Joseon kings and queens and their loyal retainers.

In the warmer months, free concerts and historical re-enactments are held in the palaces.

Between the palaces, stroll around the Samcheong-dong district (p47) for designer hats, a living treasure jade craftsman, a room filled with 2000 owls and Seoul's best vegetarian restaurant. This historical area between the palaces was where the *yangban* (aristocrats) lived in their tiled houses, some of which have survived. Ordinary folk lived in thatched houses to the south, but none of their houses have survived. Jongno was the main street of the walled city north of the river, but ordinary folk kept to the narrow, twisting alleyways. Markets still exist near the gates, which were closed every night.

Around Deoksugung is where early missionaries built Seoul's first Protestant churches and schools, and a fascinating collection of buildings they are – see them on the Around Deoksugung walk (p45).

GYEONGBOKGUNG Map p40

Palace of Shining Happiness; ☎ 732 1931; http://english.cha.go.kr; adult/child/teenager W3000/free/1500; ⏱ 9am-5pm Wed-Mon Mar-Oct, to 4pm Wed-Mon Nov-Feb; ◉ line 3 to Gyeongbokgung, Exit 5

Originally built by King Taejo, the founder of the Joseon dynasty, the grandest of Seoul's palaces served as the principal palace until 1592, when it was burnt down during the Japanese invasions. It lay in ruins for nearly 300 years until Heungseon Daewongun, regent and father of King Gojong, started to rebuild it in 1865. King Gojong moved in during 1868, but the expensive rebuilding project virtually bankrupted the government.

Two of the grandest architectural sights in Seoul are here. The first is the ornate two-storey Geunjeongjeon, the main palace building, where kings were crowned, met foreign envoys and conducted affairs of state. With its double-tiered stone platform, flagstone

top picks

GWANGHWAMUN

- Gyeongbokgung (left)
- Changdeokgung (opposite)
- Deoksugung (p42)
- Jongmyo (p42)

courtyard and surrounding open-sided corridors, Geunjeongjeon is an impressive sight.

Then walk left to Gyeonghoeru, a large raised pavilion resting on 48 stone pillars and overlooking an artificial lake with two small islands, which is almost as grand a scene. State banquets were held inside and kings went boating on the pond.

Behind these imposing structures are smaller meeting halls, and behind them are the king's living quarters, with a mas-

TRANSPORT: GWANGHWAMUN

An alternative to walking, taxis and the subway is provided by the Seoul City Tour Bus (p181), which provides a convenient above-ground introduction to the city.

ter bedroom the size of a ballroom, surrounded by eight small rooms that were used by ladies-in-waiting, concubines, servants, slaves and guards. Altogether the palace consisted of 330 buildings and had up to 3000 staff, including 140 eunuchs, all serving the royal family.

On the right is Gyotaejeon, the separate but large living quarters for the primary queen, and behind that is a terraced garden, Amisan, with *ondol* (underfloor heating) chimneys decorated with longevity symbols. Also on the eastern side is Jaseondang, the quarters for the Crown Prince, who spent his mornings, afternoons and evenings reading, studying and listening to lectures. But at night he could relax with his wife and his concubines, who were graded into four ranks (the king, of course, had more and they were graded into six ranks). One canny tutor married the Crown Prince off to his daughter and put family members into top government positions.

At the rear, King Gojong built more halls for his own personal use and an ornamental pond with an attractive hexagonal pavilion on an island, where a heron can sometimes be spotted.

It was near here on 8 October 1895 that Queen Myeongseong (Queen Min) was killed in her bedroom by Japanese assassins who then burnt her body. It is said only one finger survived the fire. Four months later King Gojong fled from the palace to the nearby Russian legation building and never returned.

During Japanese colonial rule, most of the palace was destroyed. The Japanese governor general's ugly office block was built inside the walls, but was demolished in 1996, and work on restoring the palace to its former glory will take decades more.

An audio commentary and a free guided tour (at 11am, 1.30pm and 3.30pm) are available to learn more about this unique, Korean-style palace. Soldiers in Joseon-era uniforms stand guard and there are regular changing of the guard ceremonies, as well as a re-enactment of the government service examination (see p48).

The National Folk Museum (☎ 3704 3114; www.nfm.go.kr; admission free with entry to the palace) takes at least an hour to walk around. This major museum, built in 1939, has modern displays divided into three large sections and uses models, varied film techniques, photos of Korea now and a century ago, and apartment mock-ups to illustrate social life during the ages. Listen to *yangban* children rote learning (as children still do) and watch a shamanist ceremony called a *gut*. See an amazingly colourful funeral bier (it looks like a fantasy Noah's Ark) – these were used to give the deceased a great send-off. Screened on the wall above is footage of these old-style funerals. The Confucian notion of filial piety was tough. Children had to mourn their parents for three years – making daily food offerings and wearing white mourning clothes. See the website for details of free music and dance performances on weekend afternoons.

The new National Palace Museum (☎ 3701 7500; free with the palace entry ticket; 9am-5pm Tue-Sun) has royal artefacts that highlight the wonderful artistic skills of the Joseon era – royal seals, illustrations of court ceremonies, and the gold-embroidered *hanbok* (traditional clothing) and exquisite hairpins worn by the queens and princesses – but very little English signage. Note this museum closes on a different day to the palace and that a small admission charge of W2000 may be reintroduced.

CHANGDEOKGUNG Map p40

Palace of Illustrious Virtue; ☎ 762 9513; www.cha.go.kr; entry by guided tour in English adult/child W3000/1500; tours 11.30am, 1.30pm & 3.30pm Tue-Sun Dec-Mar, Tue, Wed & Fri-Sun Apr-Nov; line 3 to Anguk, Exit 3

Generally, you can only look around this World Heritage palace on a 90-minute guided tour. However, on Thursdays between April and November, you can visit unescorted (adult/child W15,000/7500; 9.15am-6.30pm Apr-Nov, last entry 4.30pm). It's much better going around at your own speed, plus you can see more of the palace and grounds than on the tour. An audio guide can be borrowed free of charge.

Changdeokgung was originally built in 1405 as a secondary palace, but when

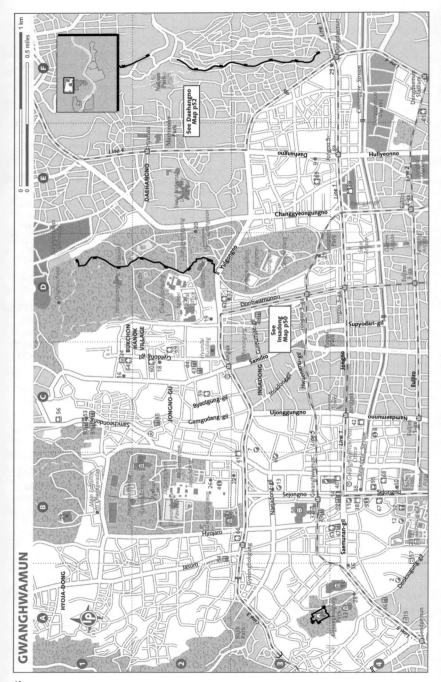

GWANGHWAMUN

GWANGHWAMUN

Gyeongbokgung (Seoul's principal palace) was destroyed during the Japanese invasion in the 1590s, Changdeokgung became the primary palace until 1896. Like all Joseon palaces, it has a mountain behind it and a small stream in front – good *pungsu* (feng shui).

Enter through the imposing gate Donhwamun, turn right and cross over the stone bridge (built in 1414) – note the guardian animals carved on its sides. On the left is the beautiful main palace building, Injeongjeon. It sits in harmony with the paved courtyard, the open corridors and the trees behind it. Its size and design are perfect – elegant and colourful but also stately. The electric lights inside are a reminder that Changdeokgung was used as a palace well into the 20th century.

Next door are the government office buildings, including one with a blue-tiled roof. Further on are the private living quarters of the royal family. Peering inside the partially furnished rooms, you can feel what these Joseon palaces were like in their heyday – a bustling beehive buzzing round the king, full of gossip, intrigues and whispering. Don't miss the white-tiled kitchen. Round the back is a terraced garden with decorative *ondol* chimneys. Over on the right is something completely different – Nakseonjae, built by King Heonjong (r 1834–49) in an austere Confucian style using unpainted wood. Royal descendants lived here until 1989.

Walk through the dense woodland and suddenly you come across a serene glade among the large, ancient trees. This is the highlight, Biwon (Huwon), the Secret or Hidden Garden. Here are pavilions on the edge of a square lily pond, with other halls and a two-storey library. The board out the front, written by King Jeongjo, means 'Gather the Universe'. Joseon kings relaxed, studied and wrote poems in this tranquil setting. The all-important civil service examination, *gwageo*, took place outdoors here (see the boxed text, p48).

Further on are a couple more ponds and Yeongyeongdang, a typical *yangban* house, originally built in 1828 as a place for the Crown Prince to study. Continuing on are more pavilions and ponds, and finally Ongnyucheon, where a rock has three Chinese characters inscribed on it by King Injo in 1636: *ong-nyu-cheon*, which means 'jade flowing stream'. A poem composed in Chinese characters by King Sukjong (r 1674–1720) was carved into the rock in 1690:

> 'The stream flows away endlessly
> And the waterfall plummets down from the sky
> These remind me of a white rainbow, thunder and light flooding the valleys.'

A channel was also carved into the rock where the kings and their scholar officials would sail their rice wine cups while writing similar *sijo* poetry and carousing.

DEOKSUGUNG Map p40

Palace of Virtuous Longevity; ☎ 771 9951; http://english.cha.go.kr; adult/child/youth W1000/ free/500; 🕑 9am-9pm Tue-Sun; ◎ line 1 or 2 to City Hall, Exit 2

Originally an aristocratic villa, Deoksugung became a palace in 1593 when King Seonjo moved in after all of Seoul's other palaces were destroyed during the Japanese invasion. Despite two kings being crowned here, it became a secondary palace from 1615 until 1897 when King Gojong moved in after leaving the nearby Russian legation.

Although he was forced by the Japanese to abdicate 10 years later, Gojong carried on living here in some style until he died in 1919. His son, Sunjong, reigned as a puppet emperor until 1910 when he too was forced to abdicate by the Japanese, who then annexed Korea, bringing the Joseon dynasty to an undignified and abrupt end after more than 500 years.

The palace used to be three times as big as it is now, but it still contains small gardens and ponds amid an extraordinary potpourri of contrasting architectural styles. Behind a grand wooden audience hall in traditional Korean style is a fusion-style tea pavilion Heonggwanheon designed by a Russian architect. The tea pavilion has pillars, a veranda and metal railings decorated with deer and bats – both auspicious creatures. This is where King Gojong drank the soothing beverage while discussing current affairs and poetry with his visitors.

The stone mythical creatures in the main courtyard are *haetae*, which are supposed to protect the palace from fire, but in 1904 they must have fallen asleep – the palace burnt down.

King Gojong's living quarters, Hamnyeongjeon, was where he died in 1919, an event which sparked off nationwide protests against Japanese rule.

The earlier of the two Romanesque buildings is Seokjojeon (built between 1900 and 1909 and designed by a British architect), which now houses art and craft exhibitions (usually free admission). The other one (designed by a Japanese architect and built in the late 1930s) houses the Deoksugung Museum of Art (☎ 368 1414; admission free-W10,000). With four large galleries on two levels, the exhibitions include major international art shows.

The changing of the guards (🕑 10.30am, 2pm & 3pm Tue-Sun 15 Feb-31 Dec) is an impressive ceremony involving 50 participants, who dress up as Joseon-era soldiers and bandsmen.

Free guided tours of the palace (in English) take place at 10.30am on weekdays and at 1.40pm at the weekend. The ticket office (Map pp56–7) is at the southwest corner of the palace.

JONGMYO & CHANGGYEONGGUNG
Map p40

☎ 765 0195, 762 4868; adult/child W1000/500; 🕑 9am-5pm Wed-Mon Mar-Oct, to 4.30pm Wed-Mon Nov-Feb; ◎ line 1, 3 or 5 to Jongno 3-ga, Exit 11

Surrounded by dense woodland, the impressive buildings of World Heritage Jongmyo (www.cha.go.kr) house the spirit tablets of the Joseon kings and queens and some of their most loyal government officials. Their spirits are believed to reside in a special hole bored into the wooden tablets.

DONHWAMUNNO STROLL

For a peak into typical scenes of Seoul neighbourhood life, take a slow stroll down the pleasant tree-lined Donhwamun St, which runs south from Changde-okgung (p40). Check out shops selling artworks, Shamanist deities, antiques and *hanbok* (traditional clothing) as well as small workshops and an eel restaurant. Enjoy the bustle of the local community as Seoulites go about their everyday business. At the end of the street is a cinema district, where you can take the subway, or walk along Jongno (Bell St) – famous for its jewellery shops and street eats. Or why not walk along the narrow alleyway that runs parallel to the main street – in the past peasants used this alley to avoid having to keep bowing to the *yangban* (aristocrats) walking along Jongno.

Near the entrance are two ponds, both square (representing the earth) with a round island (representing the heavens). The shrines are where earth meets the heavens, where the royal spirits come and go. The triple paths were originally built for the king, the crown prince and the spirits.

On the right are buildings which were used to store ritual vessels and incense. They now contain an exhibition about the ceremonies that were conducted here – in fact they still take place once a year when the Yi clan, descendants of the Joseon kings, re-enact the ceremony. They make lavish offerings of food and drink to the spirits of their royal ancestors, who are regaled with solemn music and dance. It takes place on the first Sunday of May and lasts seven hours.

The main shrine, Jeongjeon, constructed in 1395, is a very long, stately and austere building with a large stone-flagged court-yard in front of it. Inside are 49 royal spirit tablets in 19 small windowless rooms which are usually locked. On the right-hand side of the main entrance is Gonsindang, which houses the spirit tablets of 83 meritorious subjects. They served their kings well and were rewarded with their spirit tablets sharing the royal compound – the highest honour they could hope for. On the left side are shrines to Chilsa, the seven gods who aid kings.

The smaller shrine, Yeongnyeongjeon (Hall of Eternal Peace), built in 1421, has 34 spirit tablets of lesser kings in six rooms. These include four ancestors of King Taejo (the founder of the Joseon dynasty) who were made kings posthumously.

From Jongmyo, walk over the footbridge to Changgyeonggung (Palace of Flourishing Gladness). An English-speaking tour guide (free) should be available at 11.30am and 4pm at the main gate. This palace was originally built in the early 15th century by revered King Sejong for his parents. Like the other palaces it was destroyed twice by the Japanese – first in the 1590s and then during the colonial period from 1910 until 1945, when the palace suffered the indignity of being turned into a zoo. Only a fifth of the palace buildings survived or have been rebuilt. The oldest surviving structure is the 15th-century stone bridge over the stream by the main gate.

The main hall, Myeongjeongjeon, with its latticework and ornately carved and decorated ceiling, dates back to 1616. The stone markers in the courtyard show where the different ranks of government officials had to stand during major state ceremonies. The smaller buildings behind the main hall were where the kings and queens lived in their separate households.

Further away were rice fields (tended occasionally by the king) and an archery range where the military trained. Behind the ponds is Daeonsil, a botanical glasshouse, which was built in 1909 and is still full of plants. It takes around 25 minutes to walk from here back down to the entrance to Jongmyo.

In the small park at the entrance to Jongmyo, male pensioners often gather to talk about life, read the newspaper, play *baduk* (go) and *janggi* (a variation of Chinese chess), picnic, nap and even dance to *trot* music.

KOREAN COMFORT WOMEN PROTEST
Map p40

http://comfortwomen.wordpress.com; Outside Japanese Embassy, Jungbuhakdong-gil; ⊗ noon Wed; ⊙ line 3 to Anguk, Exit 6

Every week a handful of elderly Korean comfort women, who were forced into prostitution as teenagers during WWII, gathers outside the Japanese embassy. Together with their supporters they wave placards and shout slogans. Although their government has refused to apologise, groups of Japanese tourists come and apologise to these very determined ladies. Less than 100 Korean comfort women are still alive but one of them, Hwang Geum-joo, says she will never give up: 'Our numbers are dwindling every year, but we are still full of anger and they should apologise for what they did to us!'

The protests started in 1992 and they represent the dogged Korean spirit that never gives up. Read dramatic personal testimonies on the website, which also has details of monthly tours to the House of Sharing, where some of the ladies live.

CHEONGWADAE Map p40
Blue House; ☎ 737 5800; www.president.go.kr; ◎ line 3 to Gyeongbokgung, Exit 3

The Blue House is Korea's answer to America's White House. Back in 1968 a squad of 31 North Korean commandos was caught just 500m from the Blue House on a mission to assassinate President Park Chung-hee. The threat from the North has diminished but security remains tight. To see Cheongwadae, visitors must join a free 80-minute tour, which does not venture inside any important buildings – it only visits the palatial grounds and Chilgung, small locked shrines that contain the spirit tablets of seven royal concubines whose sons became kings during the Joseon dynasty.

Tours (Korean language only, passports required) run from Tuesday to Saturday at 10am, 11am, 2pm and 3pm. You must pre-book online and pick up the tickets at the ticket booth (◎ 9am-3pm tour days) in Gyeongbokgung. A tour bus takes you the short distance from the car park to Cheongwadae.

SEOUL MUSEUM OF HISTORY Map p40
☎ 724 0114; www.museum.seoul.kr; adult/child/student W700/free/300; ◎ 9am-8pm Tue-Fri, 10am-6pm Sat & Sun; ◎ line 5 to Gwanghwamun, Exit 7

The museum displays interesting artefacts, old photographs, movie films and music. Unfortunately it's marred by poor design and a lack of English descriptions. Many aspects of Seoul are world-class but this museum is lagging behind.

GYEONGHUIGUNG Map p40
Palace of Shining Celebration; ☎ 724 0274; admission free; ◎ 9am-6pm Tue-Sun; ◎ line 5 to Gwanghwamun, Exit 6

This detached palace was completed in 1623 and used to consist of a warren of

courtyards, buildings, walls and gates spread over a large area. But it was destroyed during the Japanese annexation and a Japanese school was established here. Only the main audience hall, Sungjeongjeon, and the smaller official hall behind it along with a few paved courtyards, walls and corridors, have been restored. The entrance gate, Heunghwamun, has toured around Seoul, including a stint outside the Hotel Shilla, but was moved to its present site in 1988. Recently, outdoor performances of *Daejanggeum*, a musical based on the popular TV series about a royal cook, have been held in the palace courtyard.

AGRICULTURE MUSEUM Map p40
☎ 2080 5727; admission free; ◎ 9.30am-5.30pm Tue-Sun; ◎ line 5 to Seodaemun, Exit 5

A new museum that has imaginative displays such as glass floors, a mock-up of a painted tomb, and a traditional village complete with voices. It's a worthy effort but has no chance of persuading the young generation that farming is fun, so the outlook for the industry is bleak despite the upbeat tone of the museum. Few Koreans want to be a farmer – or a farmer's wife.

ANGLICAN CHURCH Map p40
☎ 738 8952; ◎ line 1 or 2 to City Hall, Exit 3

An imposing Renaissance-style church built in the shape of a cross with Korean-style tiles on the roof – it's a fine example of architectural fusion. Work on the church began in 1922 but the full design was not completed until 1996.

SEJONG GALLERY Map p40
☎ 399 1111; www.sejongpac.or.kr; Sejongno; admission free; ◎ 10am-5pm; ◎ line 5 to Gwanghwamun, Exit 8

Next to the famous theatre and concert hall is this less famous gallery, but the changing exhibitions are generally worth a look as modern Korean artists often display wonderful work in the four gallery rooms. There's a relaxing garden out the back.

SEOUL MUSEUM OF ART ANNEXE
Map p40
☎ 2124 8800; http://seoulmoa.seoul.go.kr; admission free; ◎ 10am-5pm; ◎ line 1 or 2 to City Hall, Exit 2

Two large, white, hangarlike structures make up this unusual art gallery with ever-changing exhibitions that cover everything from traditional brush and ink to modern angst.

DIA GALLERY Map p40

☎ 742 6030; Gyedong-gil; admission free; ☯ 9.30am-6pm; ◉ line 3 to Anguk, Exit 3

The building is traditional but the puzzling experimental digital art on display is anything but. Just like the universe, the definition of art is expanding…

BUKCHON CULTURE CENTRE Map p40

☎ 3707 8270; admission free; ☯ 9am-6pm Mon-Fri; ◉ line 3 to Anguk, Exit 3

A small exhibition about *hanok* (tradtional houses) in Bukchon, housed appropriately enough in a Bukchon *hanok*. These houses reflect the core Confucian values of frugality, simplicity, oneness with nature and separation of the sexes.

DONGDAEMUN Map p40

Great East Gate; Heunginjimun; ◉ line 1 or 4 to Dongdaemun, Exit 6

Seoul's eastern fortress gate dates back to the 14th century, but the existing structure was built in 1869 and had to be renovated after being severely damaged during the Korean War when Seoul changed hands four times. Dongdaemun Market (p83) starts at this gate.

STATUE OF HAMMERING MAN Map p40

◉ line 5 to Gwanghwamun, Exit 6

The moving metallic shadow of a hammering man towers five storeys above the street. Funded by a local insurance company, the superman of a blacksmith has been silently hammering since 2002. It was made out of 50 tonnes of steel by American artist Jonathan Borofsky, whose art is humanist but mechanical, simple but thought-provoking. Is work just a meaningless ritual that dominates our lives?

ADMIRAL YI SUN-SIN'S STATUE Map p40

Sejongno; ◉ line 5 to Gwanghwamun, Exit 4

This statue is a downtown landmark. Seoul-born Yi Sun-sin (1545–98) designed a new type of metal-clad warship called *geobukseon* (turtle boats), and used them to help achieve a series of stunning victories over the much larger Japanese navy that attacked Korea at the end of the 16th century. A *geobukseon* replica can be seen in the War Memorial & Museum (p73).

STROLLING AROUND DEOKSUGUNG
Walking Tour

The area alongside Deoksugung is called Jeongdong and is where foreigners lived in the 1880s after King Gojong lifted the ban on Christianity and foreign residents as part of an effort to modernise Korea, the still-feudal Hermit Kingdom. The great powers established embassies here, and missionaries built Korea's first Western-style churches and schools.

1 Seoul Museum of Art From Exit 1, turn right and then go left along Deoksugung wall. It's a pleasant walk with shady trees and little traffic, and romantic enough to have had a Korean song written about it. Stop for a look inside the Seoul Museum of Art (p58) on the left.

2 Paichai Hakdang Come out of the gallery and turn left to the red-brick school building, the 'Hall for Rearing Useful Men', constructed in 1916. The school originally opened in 1885 with two pupils. The modern museum inside reveals a great deal about the lives of the early missionaries in Seoul.

3 Chungdong First Methodist Church At the roundabout sits this quaint red-brick church, built in 1897 by American missionaries in a style that makes it look like it's been transported from an English village. Go round the back and the caretaker should let you see inside. A hundred worshippers attend the 2pm Sunday services.

4 Simpson Hall Walk past the subterranean Chongdong Theatre and on the left is a top school founded by missionaries in 1886, Ewha Girls High School. It was a radical move in

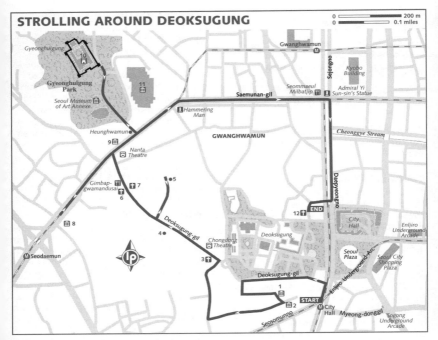

STROLLING AROUND DEOKSUGUNG

WALK FACTS

Start Subway line 1 or 2 to City Hall station, Exit 1
End Anglican Church
Distance 2km
Time 3 hours plus
Exertion Easy
Fuel stops Gimbapgwamandusai, Seommaeul
Milbatjip

a country where only boys went to school. Simpson Hall, built in 1915, was being turned into a museum at the time of writing.

5 Russian Legation Tower Turn right to see a white tower, all that remains of the large Russian Legation Building, where King Gojong sought refuge for a year in 1896 after Japanese agents assassinated his wife, Queen Min, in Gyeongbok Palace.

6 Chinese Christian Church Further on is the unusual Chinese Christian Church, founded in 1912 by American missionary Mrs Deming, pastor Li Kwoh-feng and Cheh Tao-hsin.

7 Franciscan Chapel Across the road is the Franciscan Chapel. Walk into the education centre and down the steps on the left to the wonderfully atmospheric semicircular, stonewall chapel adorned with modern sculptures.

8 Agriculture Museum If you need fuel, you'll find a budget diner, Gimbapgwamandusai (p100), on the left. Further up, turn left along the main road to visit the recently revamped Agriculture Museum (p44), which is like a small folk village inside.

9 Police Museum Across the road from the Nanta Theatre (p137) is the Police Museum (☎ 735 2519; admission free; ⏱ 9.30am-5.30pm Tue-Sun), which has some surprisingly fun exhibits as well as interesting old photographs.

10 Gyeonghuigung Past Heunghwamun (p44), a traditional gate, are two large white hangars that house the Seoul Museum of Art Annexe (p44) and a small palace complex, Gyeonghuigung (p44).

11 Seoul Museum of History Next door is the history museum (p44), and opposite is the giant statue of a shadowy Hammering Man (p45), Seoul's most impressive public artwork.

12 Anglican Church Carry on past Seommaeul Milbatjip (p100) and Admiral Yi Sun-sin's Statue (p45) on the left, and turn right to walk down to the impressive Anglican Church (p44), a very fine example of a Renaissance-style Asian fusion building with a touch of the Byzantine.

SAMCHEONG-DONG WALK
Walking Tour

This walk is shaded by trees most of the way, avoids crossing major roads and covers a conservation area that is filling up with intriguing shops, galleries and small museums (many close on Mondays). Samcheong-dong is like Insadong but less swarming with tourists.

1 Art Gallery Street Turn right along the main road until you reach Dongsipjagak, a Joseon-era watchtower built in 1865, and then turn right past Seoul Selection (p83). Further on along this road are three leading art galleries, Gallery Hyundai, Kumho Museum of Art and Kukje Gallery.

2 Yejibong Fork right and explore small shops, including Yejibong (예지봉), which sells the work of master jade craftsman, Kim Yeong-hee.

3 Samcheong Park Past Sipjeondaebotang (p115), a goblin-sized traditional teashop, turn right and on the left over the road is the green oasis of Samcheong Park, where a short walk takes you through attractive woodland.

4 Owl Museum Cross back over the road to look round one lady's magnificent obsession, a one-room museum (☎ 3210 2902; adult/child W5000/3000; ✆ 10am-7pm Tue-Sun) with 2000 owl objects at the last count. Further down the road on the left is feathered competition in the shape of the Chicken Art Museum (☎ 276 3995; adult/child W3000/2000; ✆ 10am-6pm Tue-Sun).

5 Viewpoint Turn right down Bukchon-hanok-gil and at Bee Soap you can watch soap being made. Follow the alley through a quiet neighbourhood of traditional *yangban* houses hiding behind high walls. At the end of the alley turn left and walk uphill to a splendid viewpoint of tiled rooftops that hasn't changed much in the past 70 years.

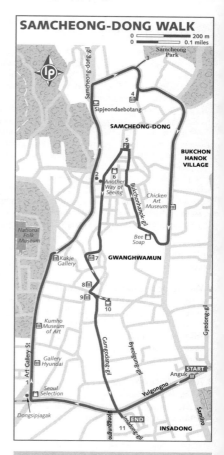

SAMCHEONG-DONG WALK

6 You & Me Carry on and turn left at the public bath chimney and on the left is You & Me, a tiny shop where two sisters painstakingly stitch wonderful examples of *bogaji*, traditional Korean wrapping cloths adorned

EXAMINATION HELL

It's not just recently that Korean students have had to study 12 hours or more every day to squeeze themselves into a high-status job. In the past, *yangban* (aristocratic) sons had to learn Chinese characters and memorise Confucian classics in order to pass the *gwageo*, the examination that gave them access to the all-important government jobs. From over 10,000 hopefuls, only the top 30 or so were offered high-ranking posts. A re-enactment of the examination takes place in Gyeongbokgung every October.

The kings took a personal interest and role in the exam, and the final stage – lasting from 8am until sunset – was held in the secluded palace garden of Biwon (p42). The scholar-king Sejong even set some of the questions: Are identification tags a good idea? How should a census be organised? Should the number of slaves be limited? Students who passed returned to their hometown in triumph like an Olympic gold medallist.

The civil exam had the highest status because Joseon society valued the scholar above the soldier (with unfortunate consequences when samurai-dominated Japan attacked in the 1590s). For military protection, the kings relied on regional superpower China to help them when necessary. There was, however, a military exam, *mugwa*, which included horse-riding and archery (a high-status sport that kings took part in and in which Koreans excel today). The third exam, *japgwa*, was for technical specialists such as doctors, astronomers, lawyers, linguists and accountants. Their status was lower, but they were far better off than the *sangmin* (peasants), the *chonmin* (slaves) or the despised *paekchong* (untouchables), such as butchers, who could never escape their low-born status.

with embroidery that can take three months to complete.

7 World Jewellery Museum Just down the road on the right is Another Way of Seeing, an art workshop for the blind. Turn left at the end of this alley and you reach the World Jewellery Museum (adult W5000; ⏰ 10am-7pm Tue-Sun), whose well-lit displays prove that small is beautiful.

8 Tibet Museum Another private museum, the Tibet Museum (adult/child W5000/3000; ⏰ 10am-7pm) has a small but interesting collection of Tibetan items and Chinese teapots.

9 Artsonje Center At the crossroads this centre (⏰ 11am-7pm Tue-Sun) is a trailblazing art gallery that's always worth a visit.

10 Yeondu Café Turn left at Artsonje for this café (연두; ☎ 736 5001; ⏰ 10am-11pm), one of the new, serious-about-coffee places where organic, global, fair trade coffee beans are lovingly roasted and prepared amid a delicious coffee aroma.

11 Insadong-gil Retrace your steps to Gamgodang-gil and walk past more dinky restaurants and cute shops. At the main road, turn left to return to Anguk subway station or cross the road to visit Insadong-gil.

INSADONG & DAEHANGNO

Shopping (p83), Eating (p101), Sleeping (p150)

Insadong is the country's craft capital. Paper made by hand from mulberry bark, stunning lacquer ware, hand-painted fans, exquisite embroidery, pale-green celadon pottery, beautiful antique furniture, *hanbok* clothing boutiques – Insadong is a hit with tourists and locals alike. Mixed in with tourist tat, the art and craft spills out of the main street into surrounding side alleys and even into Anguk subway station.

Insadong's glorious blending of old and new is exemplified by the fortune tellers, some of whom now use a laptop to help with their predictions. A hundred private art galleries showcase the best of modern and traditional Korean art. Don't be shy about going to the art galleries – you might have to visit quite a few before you come across something wonderful, but don't doubt that you will. It may be a simple ink painting of mountains, it may be a brash, in-your-face modernist statement or a gentle, beautiful picture, awash with Buddhist philosophy about the impermanence of life. Shows by major foreign artists appear regularly (Chinese modern art is selling well at present) and the local art is as varied and as good as you can see in any other city.

Hidden down the alleyways are great restaurants (Insadong is a gastronomic centre of excellence too) and atmospheric teashops, but don't come here for exciting nightlife. Insadong has a handful of bars but the area is dead by 10pm. However, Insadong-gil is closed to traffic from 2pm to 10pm on Saturday and from 10am to 10pm on Sunday when pedestrians take over the street. The area takes on a festival feeling on warm weekend evenings with crowds enjoying the street stalls, street eats and even the occasional busker playing a tuba, a banjo or a Korean flute.

A short subway or taxi ride away, in Daehangno, magic, mime and musical shows at one of the many small theatres can be enjoyable, even if you don't know a single word of Korean. The youthful theatre scene is packed with energy, attitude and talent, and you can expect a high-quality show. The larger theatres such as Arko, Hakchon Green and Dongsoong Arts Centre put on major shows, but the 50 intimate, fringe-style venues with 100 or less seats are often fun and exciting too. A musical *Hamlet* for example, or *A Midsummer Night's Dream* on roller-skates.

Street sculptures can be found along the eastern side of the main street, Daehangno, all the way to where the lively Filipino market is held every Sunday. This main street was a hotbed of demonstrations against the military dictatorships that ruled South Korea after the Korean War, but nowadays the drama is limited to inside the area's many small theatres.

There's no shortage of cafés with names like A Twosome Place, With Me, Dandelion Garden and Angel-in-us. Try to visit Daehangno at the weekend when shady Marronnier Park becomes a hive of activity and entertainment, particularly on warm afternoons. From Marronnier Park it's only a 30-minute walk up to Naksan Park and part of Seoul's ancient, often renovated fortress wall, which offers a splendid viewpoint over the city.

JOGYESA Map p50

☎ 725 6641; Ujonggungno, Insadong; ☽ 4am-9pm; ◉ line 3 to Anguk, Exit 6

Within the grounds of this temple is Daeungjeon, the largest Buddhist shrine in Seoul. It was built in 1938, but the design followed the late-Joseon-dynasty style. Murals of scenes from Buddha's life and the carved floral latticework doors are two of its attractive features. Inside are three giant Buddha statues: on the left is Amitabha, Buddha of the Western Paradise; in the centre is the historical Buddha, who lived in India and achieved enlightenment; on the right is the Bhaisaiya or Medicine Buddha, with a medicine bowl in his hand. The small 15th-century Buddha in the glass case was the main Buddha statue before he was replaced by the much larger ones in 2006. On the right-hand side is a guardian altar with lots of fierce-looking

top picks

INSADONG & DAEHANGNO

- Jogyesa (left)
- Unhyeongung (p51)
- Tapgol Park (p51)
- Cheondogyo Temple (p52)

INSADONG

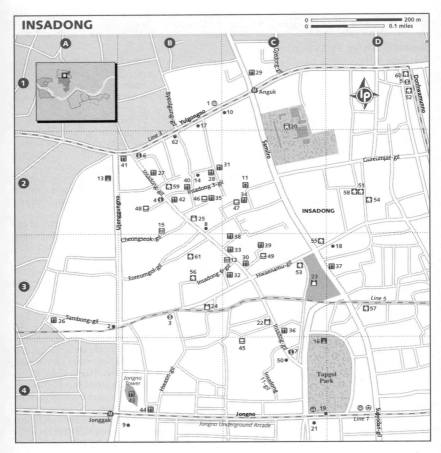

guardians in the painting behind, and on the left side is the altar used for memorial services (white is the funeral colour).

Believers who enter the temple bow three times, touching their forehead to the ground – once for Buddha, once for the *dharma* (teaching) and once for the *sangha* (monks), 20 of whom serve in this temple. Outside there are candles (like Buddha they light up the world, dispelling darkness and ignorance) and incense sticks (the smoke sends wishes up to heaven).

Behind the main shrine is the modern Amitabha Buddha Hall, where funeral services are held. The statues are the 10 judges who pass judgement, 49 days after someone's death, to decide if they go to heaven or hell.

The belfry houses a drum to summon earthbound animals, a wooden fish-shaped gong to summon aquatic beings, a metal cloud-shaped gong to summon birds and a large bronze bell to summon underground creatures. They are banged 28 times at 4am and 33 times at 6pm.

The new Central Buddhist Museum (☎ 2011 1960; adult/child W2000/1000; ❧ 9am-6pm Tue-Sun) has three galleries of antique woodblocks, symbol-filled paintings and other Buddhist artefacts. In one corner is a teashop, Namu (☎ 732 5292; teas W3000-5000; ❧ 10am-7pm Mon-Sat). In another corner is the Information Centre for Foreigners (☎ 732 5292; ❧ 10am-5pm), staffed by English-speaking Buddhist guides. Making lanterns and prayer beads, doing woodblock printing, painting and drinking green tea are usually possible. The activities are free but donations are welcome. Ask about having a meditation

INSADONG

lesson and a four-bowl Buddhist monk meal (W30,000). A temple stay (p176) can also be arranged.

UNHYEONGUNG Map p50
Cloud Hanging Over the Valley Palace; ☎ 766 9090; Samilro, Insadong; adult/youth W700/300; ⏰ 9am-7pm Tue-Sun Mar-Oct, to 5pm Tue-Sun Nov-Feb; Ⓜ line 3 to Anguk, Exit 4
The modest and plain natural-wood design of this minor palace reflects the austere tastes of Heungseon Daewongun (1820–98), King Gojong's stern and conservative father, whose policies included massacring Korean Catholics, excluding foreigners from Korea, closing Confucian schools

TRANSPORT: INSADONG & DAEHANGNO
For Insadong take the subway to Anguk or Jongno 3-ga and for Daehangno take the subway to Hyehwa. After that, walking is the only way to get around these small districts with their mazes of narrow alleyways.

and rebuilding Gyeongbokgung. Gojong was born and raised here until 1863 when he ascended the throne aged 12 with his father acting as regent.

Rooms are furnished and mannequins display the dress styles of the time, giving some idea of how people here used to live. As was the custom, women were hidden away in their own separate quarters.

An hour-long re-enactment of the marriage of King Gojong to Queen Min is held here every year, where the actual event took place in 1867 when he was 15 and she 16.

TAPGOL PARK Map p40
Jungno, Insadong; admission free; ⏰ 9am-6pm; Ⓜ line 1 or 5 to Jongno 3-ga, Exit 1 or 5
Opened in 1897, Tapgol is a symbol of Korean resistance to Japanese rule. On 1 March 1919, Son Byeong-hui and 32 others signed and read aloud a Declaration of Independence (a copy in English can be read on the memorial plaque). Many of them were high-school teachers, 16 were Cheondogyo followers, 15 were Protestant Christians and two, including poet-monk

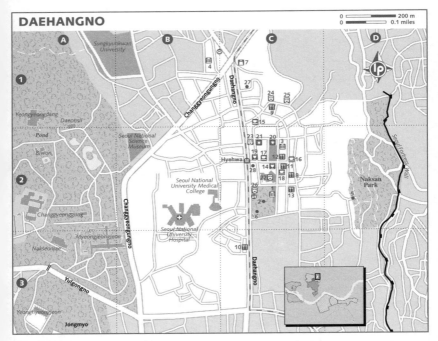

DAEHANGNO

0 ⊏——————⊐ 200 m
0 ■——————⊐ 0.1 miles

Young-un, were Buddhists. All were arrested and locked up in the notorious Seodaemun Prison (p74). A torrent of protest against Japan followed in Seoul and throughout Korea, but the *samil* (1 March) movement was ruthlessly suppressed. Hundreds of independence fighters were killed and thousands arrested. In the park, 10 murals depict scenes from the heroic but unsuccessful struggle.

The park's other outstanding feature is the 10-tier, 12m-high stone pagoda that once graced Wongaksa, a nearby Buddhist temple destroyed in 1504 on the orders of the Confucian king. Buddhists were forced out of the cities into the mountains, where Korea's great temples still stand today. The pagoda, a treasure of Buddhist art, has wonderful carvings all over it. Unfortunately it's encased in a glass box, somewhat reducing its impressiveness.

CHEONDOGYO TEMPLE Map p50
☎ 735 7579; Insadong; ☽ 9am-6pm; ⊙ line 3 to Anguk, Exit 6

The architectural fusion of East and West in this superb temple building echoes the East-West fusions of Cheondogyo's ideal-

istic philosophy (see p20). Designed by a Japanese architect and constructed in 1921, this is a handsome baroque-style, red-brick and stone temple with a tower. Inside, the wood panelling, lines of chairs and plain decoration create an impression of a lecture theatre, although there are stained-glass windows.

A pamphlet on this indigenous religion, known as the Heavenly Way, is available in English. It's members were key figures in the Donghak rebellion and the independence movements opposed to Japanese rule. The founder, Great Master Suun (1824–64), was executed for being a radical reformer. Followers believe that God is within everyone. Services (featuring lots of bowing) are held every Sunday at 11am, attended by 100 mainly middle-aged worshippers. Men sit on the left and women on the right.

MARRONNIER PARK Map p52
Daehangno; ⊙ line 4 to Hyehwa, Exit 2

This free performance area in Daehangno usually has something happening on warm weekend afternoons. Student artists draw portraits in one corner while rappers rap,

DAEHANGNO

B-boys break-dance and high-school rock bands crank it up on the outdoor stage. A *samullori* troupe bangs their drums and gongs while dancing around under the chestnut trees. 'Mr Guitar', a musician and comedian, regularly performs in front of a large and appreciative audience. Couples play badminton, people in wheelchairs play basketball, and yo-yo geeks spin their toys.

MOKIN MUSEUM Map p50
☎ 722 5066; Cheongseok-gil, Insadong; adult/child W5000/3000; ⏰ 10am-7pm; ◉ line 3 to Anguk, Exit 6

Mokin are carved and painted wooden figures and decorative motifs that were used to decorate *sangyeo* (funeral carriages). Carved by humble village craftsmen, they are a unique folk art drenched in Buddhist and shamanist beliefs. Carved flowers represent wealth and yearning for a perfect world, while birds represent messengers from this world to the next, fish symbolise life and learning (as they never close their eyes), and tigers and goblins scare evil spirits away.

HWABONG GALLERY Map p50
☎ 737 0057; Insadong; admission free; ⏰ 10am-7pm; ◉ line 3 to Anguk, Exit 6

Cutting-edge Korean art is usually on show in two of the galleries, while the third contains a couple of fascinating books – the smallest book in the world (no more than a dot), as well as the largest book.

ARKO ART CENTRE Map p52
☎ 760 4724; www.arkoartcenter.or.kr/english; Marronnier Park, Daehangno; ⏰ 11am-8pm; ◉ line 4 to Hyehwa, Exit 2

I'M LOST!

Most streets in Seoul have no name. If they do, there is usually no sign and hardly anyone knows its name (*no or ro* means road, while *gil* is a lane). Using street names and consecutive numbers is a Western idea that has not been adopted, so the traditional system is still used.

Seoul is divided into 25 large districts (*gu*) and 522 smaller neighbourhoods (*dong*). Every building has an official number, but they are assigned as they are built, so building 27 could be between building 324 and building 19. The building number usually has the street name on it, but is written in *hangeul* (the Korean phonetic alphabet).

So a typical address like 104 Itaewon-dong, Yongsan-gu, means building 104 in the Itaewon neighbourhood of the Yongsan district. However, you could wander around Itaewon for hours in search of this building with no hope of finding it. Only the postmen have maps with all the building numbers on it. So do what the locals do – make a phone call to the place you are looking for and ask for directions (hopefully they speak a language you understand!).

This guide gives street names where useful, indicates the nearest subway station and which exit to take, and gives directions to places that are tricky to find. Every visitor gets lost sometimes unless they're a human compass. Don't worry about it and don't be afraid to ask. Try to navigate around Seoul using landmarks rather than street names and numbers, just as the locals do. Always check the neighbourhood map on the wall at every subway exit to orientate yourself before venturing out.

Avant-garde art of all genres is assembled here in a couple of galleries overlooking Marronnier Park.

MOKKUMTO GALLERY Map p52
☎ 764 0700; admission free; ⏱ 10am-7pm Mon-Fri, to 6pm Sat; Ⓜ line 4 to Hyehwa, Exit 2
Like most of the theatres in Daehangno, the art up here on the 3rd and 4th floors is on the fringe. The 4th floor also has craft.

MUSEUM OF KOREAN STRAW HANDICRAFTS Map p52
☎ 743 8787; Daehangno; admission W3000; ⏱ 10am-5pm; Ⓜ line 4 to Hyehwa, Exit 4
The masks, human figures, torches, bird catchers, bags, mats, cradles, chicken nests, rope, egg holders, and human and cattle shoes are all made of straw.

BOSINGAK Map p50
Jongno, Insadong; Ⓜ line 1 to Jonggak, Exit 4
Situated in Jongno (Bell St), Seoul's main street during the Joseon period, this pavilion houses a modern copy of the city bell – the original, forged in 1468, is in the garden of the National Museum of Korea. The bell is rung only at New Year, when crowds gather here to celebrate. In Joseon times, the great bell was struck 28 times every night at 10pm to ask the heavens for a peaceful night and to signal the closure

top picks

BIRD'S EYE VIEWS
- N Seoul Tower (opposite)
- 63 Building (p62)
- Inwangsan (p77)
- Western Namhansanseong (p78)

of the gates and the start of the nightly curfew, which was enforced by club-wielding watchmen. It was struck 33 times for the 33 Buddhist heavens at 4am, which signalled the start of the new day when the gates were reopened. It also sounded when fire broke out, as often happened with so many wooden and thatched buildings.

POETS CORNER Map p50
Yulgongno, Insadong; Ⓜ line 3 to Anguk, Exit 6
By the North Gate entrance to Insadong is a miniature park, where poems by three different poets (from the 12th, 15th and 20th centuries) who all wrote in the traditional *sijo* style are on plaques on the wall, in Korean and English. *Sijo* poetry is short, simple and usually about nature and the lessons to be learnt from it.

Shopping (p85), Eating (p104), Sleeping (p151)

Adjacent to downtown Gwanghwamun, the delightful, almost traffic-free streets and alleyways of Myeong-dong are Seoul's top spot for youth fashion culture. Every evening mainly female crowds flock to this compact district to shop for brand-name clothing and beauty products. Ever-changing stores cater to every youthful style tribe. Cafés, restaurants, department stores and high-rise shopping malls with food courts, spas and cinema multiplexes have made this area mega-popular with young locals and Japanese visitors. It's a fun atmosphere with street stalls and outdoor performances.

Next door is Namdaemun Market, an even more bustling shopping magnet, and to the south lies 226m Namsan, with its iconic N Seoul Tower and panoramic views over the entire city. To the east is Namsangol Hanok Village, a historical site that's popular with Korean film-makers. Namsan was a Japanese zone during colonial times and Koreans were forced to worship at the Shinto shrine there. Nothing of the zone remains, and the area is being returned to nature with walking trails.

Itaewon has a very different atmosphere and character to all the other Seoul neighbourhoods. The main expat area in the city, it's full of foreigners and foreign restaurants. You might hear more English being spoken here than Korean. The US forces that used to be stationed at nearby Yongsan are being relocated south of Seoul, but Itaewon continues to be a lively expat entertainment zone with bars and clubs aplenty, both gay and straight. Market stalls line the main street and the district comes to life in the evening. Come here for suit and shirt tailors, hip-hop clothing, large sizes, cowboy boots and eel-skin bags.

Itaewon is going upmarket and now has a prestigious art museum as well as fine dining restaurants and a smart new hotel on the main strip. These days the antique shops probably outnumber the hostess bars.

N SEOUL TOWER Map pp56-7

☎ 3455 9277; Namsan; adult/child/youth W7000/3000/5000; ⏰ 9am-midnight; ⓜ line 1 or 4 to Seoul Station, Exit 10

As iconic as kimchi, N Seoul Tower offers panoramic but hazy views of the immense metropolis created almost from scratch after the Korean War. Daytime views are great, but if you come at sunset you can watch the great city morph into a galaxy of twinkling stars. Perched atop Namsan, you can eat in the budget Food Court (meals W7000; ⏰ 10am-10pm) at ground level or in the more elegant Italian bistro, Sweetree (meals W5000-25,000; ⏰ 10am-10pm), one floor up. The Beer

Garden (⏰ 5-11pm Mon-Fri, noon-11pm Sat & Sun) is another option. High up the tower is Hancook for Korean food and N Grill for expensive Western-style nouveau cuisine served in a revolving restaurant. See p59 for details about walking up Namsan to N Seoul Tower or taking the cable car. Yet another option is to take yellow bus 2 outside Exit 4 of Chungmuro subway station (Line 3 or 4).

NAMSANGOL HANOK VILLAGE
Map pp56-7

☎ 2266 9101; Namsan; admission free; ⏰ 9am-8pm Wed-Mon May-Sep, to 6pm Wed-Mon Oct-Apr; ⓜ line 3 or 4 to Chungmuro, Exit 4

Five differing yangban stone, wood and tile houses from the Joseon era have been moved here from different parts of Seoul. The architecture and furniture are austere and plain, and conjure up the lost world of Confucian gentlemen scholars, who wielded calligraphy brushes rather than swords. Scenes from the movie Untold Scandal, a 2003 Korean take on Dangerous Liaisons, were filmed here.

Weavers, cooks, calligraphers and kite-makers can be spotted at the weekend, while rice-wine brewing and traditional music take place some evenings. At

top picks

MYEONG-DONG, NAMSAN & ITAEWON

- N Seoul Tower (above)
- Namsangol Hanok Village (right)
- Leeum Samsung Museum of Art (p58)
- Seoul Museum of Art (p58)

MYEONG-DONG & NAMSAN

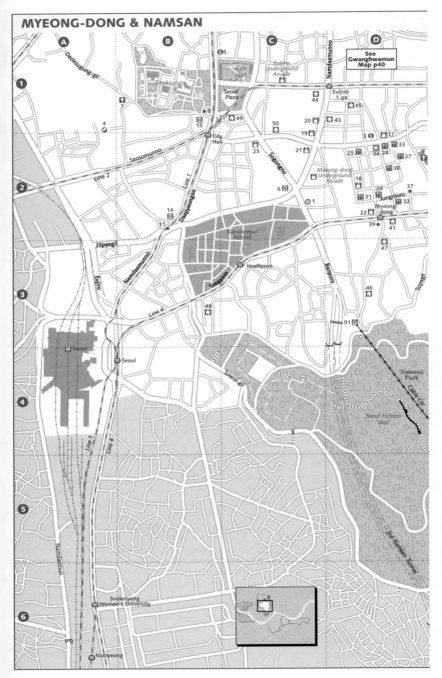

See Gwanghwamun Map p40

Deoksugung-gil

Deoksugung

City Hall

Seoul Plaza

Euljiro Underground Arcade

Euljiro 1-ga

Seosomunno

Line 2

Line 1

Daepyeongno

Sogongno

Jilpaegil

Namdaemunno

Eulliro

Myeong-dong Underground Arcade

Namdaemun Market

Toegyero

Hoehyeon

Line 4

Myeong-dong

Jungmuro

Sopaegil

Namsan Park

Cable Car

Seoul Fortress Wall

Sowol-gil

Seoul

Seoul

Sukmyung Women's University

Namyeong

Banporo

3rd Namsan Tunnel

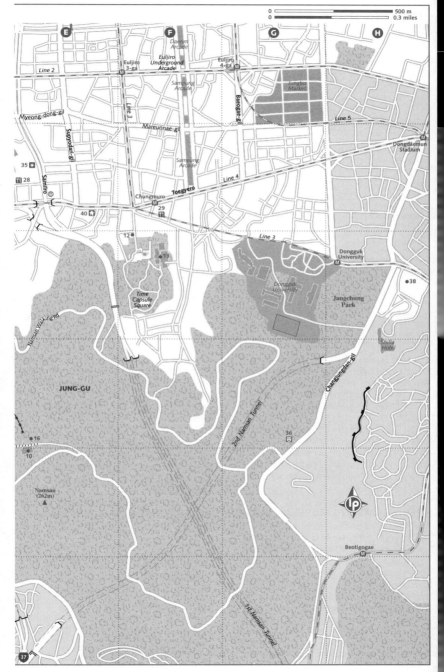

0   500 m
0   0.3 miles

E **F** **G** **H**

Daelim Arcade

Euljiro
3-ga

Euljiro
Underground
Arcade

Euljiro
4-ga

Line 2

Sampung
Arcade

Jungbu
Market

Line 5

Baogae-gil

Myeong-dong-gil

Line 3

Mareunnae-gil

Dongdaemun
Stadium

Supyodan-gil

35

28

Samilro

Sampung
Arcade

Line 4

Toegyero

Chungmuro
29

40

Line 3

Dongguk
University

38

12

13

Dongguk
University

Jangchung
Park

Time
Capsule
Square

Namsan Walking rd

JUNG-GU

Changjungdan-gil

Shilla
Hotel

2nd Namsan Tunnel

36

16

10

Namsan
(262m)

Beotigogae

1st Namsan Tunnel

37

57

MYEONG-DONG & NAMSAN

Chuseok (Harvest Festival) half of Seoul squashes in here for the traditional performances and festival atmosphere. At the time of writing, a new *hanok*-style theatre named Namsan Gugakdang was being built here.

On the right of the entrance gate is an office that provides English-speaking tour guides (10am to 5pm) on most days. The guides can tell you all about the *yangban* lifestyle and the different types of *hanok* they used to live in.

LEEUM SAMSUNG MUSEUM OF ART
Map p60
☎ 2014 6901; http://leeum.samsungfoundation.org/eng; Itaewon; adult/child W10,000/6000; ☻ 10.30am-6pm Tue-Sun; ⊕ line 6 to Hangangjin, Exit 1
In Museum 1 visitors start on the 4th floor and descend a white staircase, a decor that contrasts with the black galleries, where the ancient Korean ceramic metal and art treasures are superbly lit to bring out their inner beauty. Museum 2 has an entirely different look, with outdoor lighting, natural

construction materials and a collection of 20th-century Korean and international art. Museum 3 is reserved for special exhibitions. An audio guide costs W2000. Tours in English (free) start at 3pm on Saturday and Sunday.

SEOUL MUSEUM OF ART Map pp56-7
☎ 2124 8800; http://seoulmoa.seoul.go.kr; Myeong-dong; adult/child/youth W700/free/300; ☻ 10am-9pm Mon-Fri, to 6pm Sat; ⊕ line 1 or 2 to City Hall, Exit 2
Ultra-modern, bright galleries hide behind the forbidding brick-and-stone facade of the 1927 Supreme Court building. Opened

---

TRANSPORT: MYEONG-DONG, NAMSAN & ITAEWON

Walking to Myeong-dong and Namdaemun Market from Gwanghwamun is possible, but you can take a taxi or use the subway. If you don't fancy walking up 262m Namsan, take the cable car or hop on the frequent and handy yellow bus 2. Take the subway to Itaewon and then walk around.

in 2002, the gallery hosts top-notch exhibitions that are always worth a visit. Check the website for painting classes and other details.

BANK OF KOREA MUSEUM Map pp56-7
Currency Museum; ☎ 759 4888; Myeong-dong; admission free; ⏰ 10am-5pm Tue-Sun; ⦿ line 4 to Hoehyeon, Exit 7
The granite, chateaulike Bank of Korea, built in 1912, is an outstanding example of Japanese colonial architecture both inside and outside. The exhibits here include fascinating old coins such as knife money, WWI pottery coins, seashell money from Yap Island and Korean coins dating back 2000 years. Upstairs there are specimen notes from around the world.

MYEONG-DONG CATHOLIC CATHEDRAL Map pp56-7
☎ 774 1784; Myeong-dong; ⦿ line 4 to Myeong-dong, Exit 6
This elegant, red- and grey-brick Gothic-style cathedral was built between 1894 and '98 by Chinese bricklayers. Inside, the traditional vaulted ceiling and stained-glass windows contrast with the modern air-conditioning and the TV screens. The cathedral provided a sanctuary for student and trade-union protestors during the long period of military rule after the Korean War, and is now a national symbol of democracy and human rights. Come at 9am on Sunday for English-language worship in the chapel.

NAMDAEMUN Map pp56-7
Great South Gate, Sungnyemun; Myeong-dong; ⦿ line 1 or 4 to Seoul Station, Exit 3
Originally constructed in 1398, this landmark gate has been reconstructed many times throughout history, including the present day – it was burnt down and rebuilt in 2008. The famous day-and-night Namdaemun Market (p86) starts at the gate.

RODIN GALLERY Map pp56-7
☎ 2259 7783; Myeong-dong; admission approx W5000; ⏰ 10am-6pm Tue-Sun; ⦿ line 1 or 2 to City Hall, Exit 8
This unusual glass pyramid building has two large sculptures by French sculptor Rodin on permanent display, plus changing contemporary art exhibitions in two galleries.

top picks

IT'S FREE

- **Namsangol Hanok Village** (p55) Tour traditional houses where long-haired, pipe-smoking aristocrats once lived.
- **Jogyesa** (p49) and **Bongeunsa** (p71) Check out two contrasting Buddhist temples.
- **Walking tours** (p77 and p78) Head into and up the hills around Seoul.
- **Olympic Park** (p67) Explore 200 outdoor sculptures and the Mongchon Museum.
- **Agriculture Museum** (p44) Dig down to Korea's rural roots.
- **Bank of Korea Museum** (left) Explore the root of all evil.
- **Yeouido Full Gospel Church** (p64) Sing along with the huge congregation on Sunday – better than Lloyd-Webber.
- **Art Galleries** Visit 30 galleries, then visit 30 more, then...

NAMSAN & N SEOUL TOWER
Walking Tour
1 Cable car station From the subway exit walk for 15 minutes up to the cable car station (☎ 753 2403; one-way/return W6000/7500; ⏰ 10am-11pm). Take the cable car (a queue can form at weekends) if you don't feel like walking uphill to Namsan.

2 Namsan walking road If you're going to walk, cross the road and go up the steps to Namsangongwon-gil, Namsan walking road. This road is now pedestrians-only and even has a rubberised surface to make walking easier. The walking road continues to the National Theatre of Korea (3km away).

3 Waryongmyo Walk left for 5 minutes to reach the very unusual shrine, Waryongmyo, dedicated to Zhuge Liang (AD 181–234), a semimythical Chinese statesman and general, a 'hidden dragon' revered for his intelligence. A crane feather fan is his symbol. The Buddhist/Taoist/shamanist shrine is drenched in atmosphere and history, and serves as a reminder that Koreans used to revere Chinese (rather than Western) culture.

4 Viewpoint Return the way you came, and continue on to an exercise trail. Turn left up

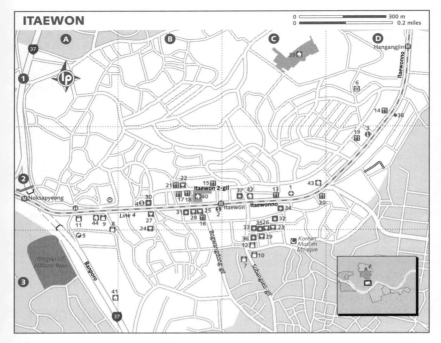

ITAEWON

the steps and after 10 minutes or so the first wonderful panoramic view of Seoul spreads out below your feet.

5 Seoul Fortress Wall On the right is a section of Seoul's fortress wall. Look over the top to see just how big the wall is. Over 100,000 workers built the original wall in the 1390s. It snaked for 19km across the hills around Seoul, and included the major gates Namdaemun and Dongdaemun. More than 10km of it has been restored.

6 Signal beacons In the Joseon era long lines of beacons (over 600 of them) radiated out from Namsan in five directions to all parts of the country, providing an early-warning system to the King in Seoul. One lit fire meant all was well, two to four fires lit meant an enemy was approaching, and five lit fires meant fighting had started.

7 N Seoul Tower Finally you reach the tower (p55), an iconic landmark that's visible from all over the city. It's a 20-minute uphill walk from the bottom of the steps by the

UP NAMSAN & N SEOUL TOWER

WALK FACTS

Start Subway line 4 to Myeong-dong, Exit 4
End Namsangol Hanok Village
Distance 3km
Time 2½ hours
Exertion Moderate
Fuel stop N Seoul Tower

ITAEWON

exercise trail. Here you can eat and drink with a billion-won view, 243m up in the sky, then take an elevator up the tower, another 236m higher.

8 Green Namsan Walk on down to the bus stop, turn almost 360° sharp right and walk down the nearly traffic-free road. On the way is a sign for a nature trail, if you want to explore more of green Namsan, away from the urban clutterscape. Otherwise it's a 20-minute walk to the bottom of the hill.

9 Ahn Junggeun Museum At the bottom of the hill, turn right into the street with parked cars on one side, past the quince trees and plastic deer to a tree-lined square. The museum (☎ 771 4195; adult W1000; ♡ 9am-5pm) is dedicated to a Korean independence fighter (1879–1910) who assassinated Ito Hirobumi,

the Japanese governor-general of Korea, in 1909 and was executed the following year.

10 Seoul Science Park On the other side of the square is this science park (☎ 311 1262; admission free; ♡ 10am-5pm Mon-Fri), a fascinating rabbit warren of a children's science museum with hands-on, discover-for-yourself exhibits and special exhibitions.

11 Statues Walk down the steps to another square with two statues commemorating independence fighters Kim Koo (1876–1949), who was sent to Seodaemun Prison (p74), and Lee Si-yeong (1869–1953).

12 Namsangol Hanok Village Walk back to the bus stop and the yellow bus 2 (W800; every 10 minutes, 7.30am to midnight) will drop you near Namsangol Hanok Village (p55) and Chungmuro subway station.

Shopping (p88), Eating (p107), Sleeping (p154)

Hongdae is packed with hole-in-the-wall restaurants, boutiques and CD shops. The weekend craft markets, the indie live-music dens, the techno, Latin American and hip-hop dance clubs and the street murals all reflect the artistic and alternative slant that the Hongdae neighbourhood represents. At its heart is Hongik University (known as Hongdae), Korea's leading art and design centre.

Here you can find extraordinary pubs, like the baronial Castle Praha, and cafés with spa foot pools, where 'doctor fish' nibble and rejuvenate aching feet. Sangsangmadang is Hongdae's new symbol – an extraordinary 'butterfly wing' concrete-and-glass structure that houses fringe art, music and movies.

Hongdae morphs into Sinchon, another student area with masses of bars and budget restaurants, not to mention all the love motels, pool halls and DVD, karaoke and internet rooms. Then Sinchon morphs into Ewha, where female 20-somethings are the predominant customers, and the characteristic demure feminine style never goes out of fashion. Don't miss the street of rococo wedding outfits, Seoul's top free fashion show.

In complete contrast, Yeouido is a 3km-long and 2km-wide island in the Han River which used to be a sandy airfield but has been transformed into a rather soulless business centre. Skyscrapers house the headquarters of media, finance and insurance companies. The Stock Exchange and the National Assembly are on the island, too, but the gold-tinted 63 Building is the main attraction for tourists. Singing along with the world's largest church congregation is a Sunday must-do at Yeouido Full Gospel Church.

Along the southeastern side of the island, Cherry Tree Park is popular in mid-April when the cherry trees blossom, while the Han River's park and cycleway are packed with cyclists, walkers, rollerbladers and picnicking families on warm weekends. Why not hire a bicycle, or take a boat trip along the Han River from the pier?

63 BUILDING Map p65

☎ 789 5663; www.63.co.kr; Yeouido; ☿ 10am-9pm; ⊖ line 5 to Yeouinaru, Exit 4

One of the tallest and most stylish skyscrapers in Seoul, the 63 Building has recently been given a makeover. A 15-minute walk from the subway, it has three major attractions: Sea World (adult/teenager/child W15,000/13,000/11,000; ☿ 10am-10pm), an aquarium that has penguin feeding at 3.30pm and seal, sea lion and diving shows hourly; IMAX (adult/teenager/child W8000/7500/6500; ☿ movies 10am-9pm), showing hourly movies on a gigantic screen with English-language commentary in an earphone; and Sky Art (adult/teenager/child W9000/8000/7000; ☿ 10am-midnight), which combines a 60th-floor observation deck with changing art exhibitions. A triple ticket (adult/teenager/child W26,000/W23,000/W20,000) makes for a big day out, especially if it includes the 63 Buffet Pavilion – see p107).

JEOLDUSAN MARTYRS MUSEUM & CHAPEL Map p64

☎ 2126 2299; Nr Sinchon; museum admission by donation; ☿ 9.30am-5pm Tue-Sun; ⊖ line 2 or 6 to Hapjeong, Exit 7

Jeoldusan means 'Beheading Hill' – this is where up to 2000 Korean Catholics were executed in 1866 following a decree, signed by Regent Heungseon Daewongun (King Gojong's father), to kill all Catholics. The victims' bodies were thrown into the nearby Han River, and only 40 of their names are known.

The museum has books, diaries and relics of the early Catholic converts, some of whom were martyred and became saints. The displays have English descriptions. Downstairs are mementoes of Pope John Paul II's visit here in 1984.

Steadfast early Christian converts faced waves of government persecution, but they refused to recant their new faith.

top picks

HONGDAE, SINCHON & YEOUIDO

- 63 Building (left)
- Jeoldusan Martyrs Museum & Chapel (left)
- Yeouido Full Gospel Church (p64)

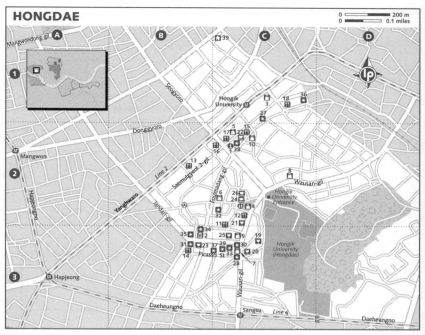

HONGDAE

INFORMATION

Tourist Information Centre
관광안내소 **1** C2

SIGHTS (pp62-6)
Sangsangmadang 상상마당 **2** B3

SHOPPING 🛍
Beautiful Store 아름다운가게 **3** C1
Free Market 홍대프리마켓 **4** C2
Kodak Photo Shop 코닥포토샵 **5** C2
Lush 러쉬 **6** C2
Napkin 냅킨 **7** C3
Purple Record 퍼플레코드 **8** C2
Record Forum 레코드포럼 **9** C3
Volkswagen 폭스바겐 **10** C2

EATING 🍴 (pp93-112)
Agio 아지오 **11** C3
BaB 밥 **12** C2

Baengnyeon Samgyetang
백년토종삼계탕 **13** B2
Castle Praha 캐슬프라하 **14** B3
Naniwa 나니와 **15** C2
Nolboo 놀부 **16** C2
Richemont Bakery
리치몬드제과점 **17** C2
Samtong Chicken 삼통치킨 **18** C1

DRINKING 🍷🍺 (pp113-20)
360@ 360알파 **19** C3
Jane's Groove
제인스그루브 **20** C2
Labris 라브리스 **21** C2
Namugeuneul 나무그늘 **22** C2
OG Bar 오지 **23** B3
Princess 프린세스 **24** C2
Tin Pan Music Bar
틴팬뮤직바 **25** C2
Zibe 지베 **26** C2

NIGHTLIFE ✦ (pp121-6)
Bahia 바히아 **27** C1
Club Evans 클럽애반스 **28** C3
Club FF 클럽에프에프 **29** C3
Club Hooper 클럽후퍼 ....(see 30)
Club Saab 클럽사브 **30** C3
DGBD 디지비디 **31** B3
Free Bird 프리버드 **32** C2
Joker Red 조커레드 **33** C3
Luxury Noraebang
럭셔리노래방 **34** B2
M2 엠투 **35** B3
Macondo 마콘도 **36** C1
Sk@2 스카이2 ....**37** C3
Soundholic 사운드홀릭 **38** C2
ta 타 ....(see 29)

SLEEPING 🛏 (pp145-58)
Lee & No Guesthouse
리앤노게스트하우스 **39** C1

Inside Catholic churches, *yangban* nobles
and ordinary folk sat together as equals in
the sight of God, an act that challenged
the rigid Confucian hierarchy of Joseon
society.

Outside the museum are gruesome
details of the tortures early Catholics were
subjected to by the government, who
regarded them as dangerous heretics. Their

arms and legs were bent and broken, they
were beaten with heavy sticks and hung up
in trees by their long hair (in those days all
Korean males wore their hair long and tied
up in a topknot).

Next to the museum is a stark, white
memorial chapel. Masses are held at 10am
daily and also at 3pm except on Mondays.
The singing is beautiful.

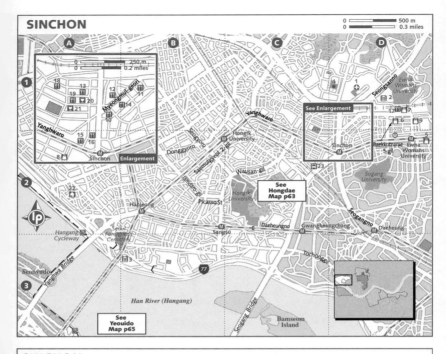

SINCHON

INFORMATION

International Clinic (Severance Hospital)
세브란스병원국제진료센터 1 D1

SIGHTS (pp62-6)

Ewha Womans University Museum
이화여자대학교박물관 2 D1

Jeoldusan Martyrs Museum & Chapel
절두산순교박물관 3 B3

Yonsei University
연세대학교 4 D1

SHOPPING (pp81-92)

Ahyeon-dong Wedding Street
아현동 웨딩거리 5 D2

Baekkotnarae 5-gil
배꼿나래 5 길 6 D1

Eunha 은하 7 D1

Jaeraesijang 재래시장 8 A2

Papaya 파파야 9 D1

EATING (pp93-112)

Bonghee Seleongtang
봉희설렁탕 10 A1

BSD Dubu House LA
북창동순두부 11 B1

Chuncheon Myungdong
춘천명동닭갈비

Chuncheonjip 춘천집 13 A1

Happy Table 해피테이블 14 B1

Hwedra Ramyeon 훼드라 라면 15 A2

Red Mango 레드망고 16 A2

Shanghai 중화요리상하이 17 D1

Teolbogodoeni 털보고된이 18 A1

DRINKING (pp113-20)

Beatles 비틀즈 19 A1

Flower 꽃 20 A1

Woodstock 우드스탁 21 A1

SLEEPING (pp145-58)

Kims' Guesthouse
킴스 게스트하우스 22 A2

TRANSPORT (pp171-5)

Sinchon Bus Terminal
신촌시외버스터미널 23 C2

Walk down to the garden from the museum and turn right towards the Han River. Go down the steps and turn right to see the cliffs that the dead bodies of the martyrs were thrown from. The river was higher in those days. Carry on past the cliffs, turn right up the steps and on the right is a memorial sculpture.

From the subway exit, take the second turn left and follow the covered railway line for 700m – it's less than a 10-minute walk.

YEOUIDO FULL GOSPEL CHURCH
Map p65

☎ 783 4135; www.fgtv.org; Yeouido; ⊙ line 5 to Yeouinaru, Exit 1

The Full Gospel Church was founded by Assembly of God pastor David Cho in 1958, and the existing church building was opened in 1973. Visit on a Sunday to experience 15,000 people, young and old, crowded into this circular, cathedral-sized church, with thousands more overflowing into the side chapels. Everything is mega –

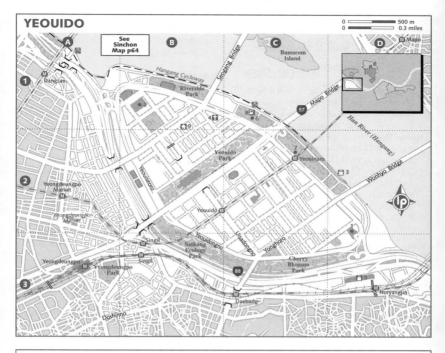

YEOUIDO

huge screens by the altar show TV-news-style programs about the church; it takes five minutes for the 150-member choir and the orchestra to file in; and hundreds of coaches are parked outside to bring the faithful to prayer.

Ask one of the white-coat-wearing ushers for directions to the foreigners' section, where headphones provide a translation of the service. Seven services are held every Sunday. This is Christianity Seoul-style, altogether a-ma-zing.

HAN RIVER FERRIES Map p65

☎ 785 4411; Yeouido; adult/child W11,000/5500; ⏱ 11.30am-9.30pm; Ⓜ line 5 to Yeouinaru, Exit 3
Take a trip from Yeouido pier to any of the Han River ferry piers or take a one-hour round trip back to Yeouido. The four other piers are at Yanghwa (Map pp36–7), Nanji (Map pp36–7), Ttukseom (Map p70) and Jamsil (Map p70). A concert boat (adult/child W16,000/8000; ⏱ 7.30pm Tue-Sun) leaves from Yeouido pier and includes a BBQ buffet and live music.

TRANSPORT: HONGDAE, SINCHON & YEOUIDO

Taking the subway is the best way to reach these neighbourhoods. On Yeouido hire a bicycle to take advantage of the excellent cycleways that run along both sides of the Han River, or take a ferry to a number of riverside piers.

top picks

FOR CHILDREN

- Lotte World (p69) A mainly indoor Disneyland-ish amusement park with scary rides and musical parades. The complex also includes an ice-skating rink, ten-pin bowling and lots more.
- Seoul Grand Park (p75) A huge zoo, acres of greenery and a fun dolphin-and-seal show. A large amusement park with adrenaline rides is next door.
- Children's Grand Park (p76) A zoo, camel rides, a chimpanzee, parrot-and-seal show, an amusement park, eco areas and more.
- 63 Building (p62) The Sea World Aquarium is next door to an IMAX theatre.

EWHA WOMANS UNIVERSITY MUSEUM Map p64

☎ 3277 3151; Sinchon; admission free; ☯ 9.30am-5pm Mon-Sat, closed 1-31 Aug & 21 Dec-1 Mar; ◉ line 2 to Ewha Womans University, Exit 2
The exhibits spread over three floors conjure up the extinct world of the *yangban* (aristocratic) elite with wonderful examples of their refined taste in ceramics, art, furniture and clothing, that have now all been swept away.

SANGSANGMADANG Map p63

☎ 330 6205; Eoulmadang-gil, Hongdae; ☯ noon-10pm; ◉ line 2 to Hongik University, Exit 5
This new 'butterfly wing' arts building (funded by ginseng and tobacco profits!) typifies Hongdae culture, with a cinema showing independent films (look out for ones with English subtitles), a concert space (hosting top indie bands) and art galleries that focus on experimental, fringe exhibitions.

NATIONAL ASSEMBLY Map p65

☎ 788 2865; www.assembly.go.kr; Yeouido; admission by tour free, no English; ☯ 9am-5pm Mon-Fri; ◉ line 5 to Yeouinaru, Exit 1
The pillared National Assembly building with a green roof was completed in 1975. The tours take about 30 minutes but are not always available. Entry is via the tours only – you can't wander about by yourself.

Shopping (p90), Eating (p109), Sleeping (p154)

Gangnam is a modern business district south of the Han River, more noted for its numerous bars and restaurants than its tourist sights, but further east in Jamsil there are half a dozen top attractions. Teheranno is the heart of Seoul's thriving IT industry, while Jamsil is a sea of office and apartment blocks surrounding an ancient Buddhist temple and a trio of 500-year-old royal tombs. The COEX Mall, Lotte World and Olympic Park are the other big sites in Jamsil.

Gangnam is an upper-crust residential area, and the celebs and debs pour into Apgujeong, with its global and Korean brand-name stores and small designer boutiques. The designer stores are very spread out, so expect a fair amount of footslogging. It's Seoul's high-class fashion centre with photographic studios and model agencies next door to cosmetic surgery clinics. Come here to spot local media darlings in celebrity-owned restaurants, suss out brand-name goods from Stussy to Tiffany, buy organic food and check out fashion accessories for pets. The look of the whole area is not high class, but the prices in the designer stores certainly are.

To the west of Apgujeong, Garosu-gil is a thriving new street filled with chic stores, euro-style cafés, quirky bars, quality bakeries and varied restaurants packed into one small area.

OLYMPIC PARK Map p70

Jamsil; ⊙ **line 8 to Mongchontoseong, Exit 1**

This very large, green park with wilderness areas, lakes and other interesting features is best visited by bicycle, though bicycles are not available for hire in the park itself. Otherwise make use of the car-tram if it's running.

A massive 2.7km Baekje-dynasty earth fortification, Mongchontoseong, built in the 3rd century AD, runs through the park. The Mongchon Museum (☎ 424 5138; admission free; 🕙 10am-8pm Tue-Fri, to 6pm Sat & Sun) has some precious golden relics of the Baekje kings, a seven-pronged sword and the usual dull pots. The history of human settlement here goes way back.

Attractions built for the 1988 Seoul Olympics include the indoor swimming pool (sometimes open to the public), tennis courts, three gymnasiums (gymnasium 1 hosts major concerts) and the velodrome.

The latter is now used by punters who gamble on bicycle and even motor boat races. On Wednesdays and Thursdays between March and December, motor boats race three times round a 600m course at Misari (20km east of Seoul) while gamblers watch the races on screens.

Scattered like buckshot around the park are over 200 sculptures, some larger than a house. Designed and made by sculptors from around the world, most of the artwork is puzzling even after reading the artists' descriptions of their work. Groups picnic among the art and the trees.

The bunkerlike Soma Museum of Art (☎ 425 1077; www.somamuseum.org; admission W1000-10,000; 🕙 10am-6pm Tue-Sun) has a tempting café and shop, a permanent display of Olympics-themed video art by Nam June Paik and five galleries for special exhibitions.

The Olympic Museum (☎ 410 1051; adult/teenager/child W3000/2000/1500; 🕙 10am-6pm Tue-Sun) has screens showing the exciting highlights of the 1988 Seoul Olympics, together with a brief history of the Olympics.

Fast food, a convenience store and the excellent Fresh House (p110) are at the World Peace Gate near the main entrance, where rollerbladers glide along on warm evenings and weekends.

Cycling around the extensive Olympic Park is the best way to visit. Take subway line 2 to Sincheon, leave by Exit 7 and walk straight for 10 minutes. Cross over the road and walk up and then down the steps under the Olympic Expressway. Walk

top picks

GANGNAM & JAMSIL

- Olympic Park (above)
- COEX Mall (p68)
- Lotte World (p69)
- Bongeunsa (p71)
- Seolleung Park Royal Tombs (p72)
- Garosu-gil (p72)

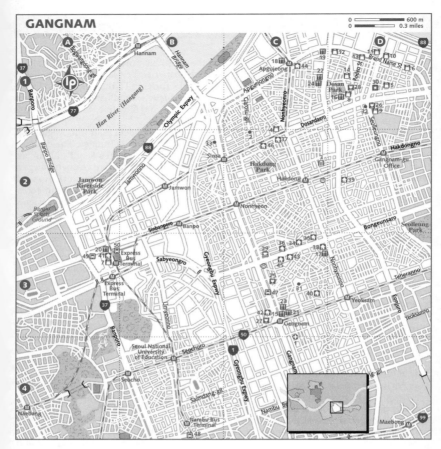

to the river and then left to the boat pier and the bicycle hire stall (p141). ID deposit is required. Bring your own padlock if you have one.

Cycle north along the Han River for 15 minutes. Just after the second bridge turn right and go under the two bridges and along a stream. Carry on along the left bank for 10 minutes before crossing over the stream and then turning left into Olympic Park. It's a cycleway all the way.

COEX MALL Map p70
☎ 6002 5312; www.coexmall.com; Jamsil;
⏲ 10am-10pm; ⊖ line 2 to Samseong, COEX Exit
This vast underground maze of a mall is a top shopping and entertainment attraction that incorporates food courts, a department store, four hotels, the COEX Conven-

tion Centre, World Trade Centre and much more.

The COEX Aquarium (☎ 6002 6200; www.coex aqua.com; adult/teenager/child W15,500/13,000/10,000; ⏲ 10am-8pm, last entry 7pm) is the largest in Seoul, with thousands of fish and other sea creatures in 90 tanks. You can see live coral, sharks, turtles, rays and evil-looking piranhas swimming around in large tanks. Exquisite small creatures such as pulsating jellyfish, glass fish and sea horses are

TRANSPORT GANGNAM & JAMSIL
Use the subway or taxis to travel to and around Gangnam and Jamsil – the neighbourhood is too large and spread-out to walk around.

GANGNAM

also on display. Feeding takes place daily (sharks at 1.30pm).

The small **Kimchi Museum** (B2; adult/teenager/child W3000/2000/1000; 🕑 10am-6pm Tue-Sun) sings the praises of pickled, peppery cabbage and its wondrous health benefits. The museum is almost impossible to find – go down the steps near the 7-Eleven convenience store.

The 17-screen **Megabox** (☎ 6002 1200; movies W7000; 🕑 8am-midnight) is always buzzing. If you're more into reading, **Bandi & Luni's** (☎ 6002 6090; 🕑 9.30am-10.30pm) has English books (section B1) and magazines (section A1), while next door **Evan Records** (☎ 6002 1000; 🕑 10.30am-11pm) has CDs, DVDs, Blu-ray discs and listening posts.

The **Hyundai Department Store Food Court** (meals W4000-9000; 🕑 10.30am-8pm) has something for everyone at reasonable prices, which means it's always super-busy. Try the Asian-Spanish fusion paella or the giant hamburger with wedges. Which of seven flavours of waffle do you want? With so many temptations, choosing what to eat is tough.

LOTTE WORLD Map p70
☎ 411 4921; www.lotteworld.com; Jamsil; 🕑 9.30am-11pm; 🚇 line 2 or 8 to Jamsil, Exit 3

This huge complex includes an amusement park, an ice-skating rink, a cinema multiplex, department store, folk museum, shopping mall, hotel, restaurants and more. Kids and adults alike love Lotte World, and couples can arrange to meet at Lotte's own Trevi Fountain. Visit at the weekend to see a free traditional show at nearby **Seoul Norimadang** (p138) at 3pm.

Lotte World Adventure & Magic Island (day pass adult/teenager/child W35,000/30,000/26,000; 🕑 9.30am-11pm) is a mainly indoor Korean version of Disneyland, complete with 'flying' balloons, 3D films, laser and music shows, screen rides, fantasy parades and thrill rides that go down very fast or round and round and up and down very fast. The scarier the ride, the longer the queue on busy days. The outdoor Magic Island is in the middle of Seokchon Lake, and that part may close in bad weather. The carousel has been popular with dating couples since it starred in the TV drama series *Stairway to Heaven*.

The indoor **ice-skating rink** (B3 fl; per session adult/child W13,000/12,000, skate rental W4500; 🕑 10am-10pm) is in a fairyland setting, but watch out for tiny speedsters training to become future Winter Olympic champions.

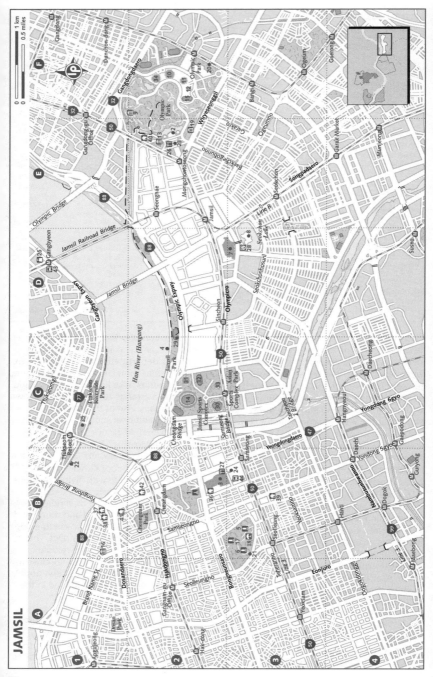

JAMSIL

1 km
0.5 miles

70

JAMSIL

Nearby is a bowling alley (B3 fl; adult/child
W3600/3200, shoe rental W1400; 🕙 10am-midnight)
next to a pool hall (B3 fl; pool/3 ball/4 ball per hr
W6800/9600/10,800; 🕙 10am-10pm). Or why not
don a flak jacket and steel helmet and fire
off some rounds in the shooting range (B3 fl; 10
bullets W20,000-30,000; 🕙 9am-8pm)?

The Folk Museum (3rd fl; adult/teenager/child
W5000/3000/2000; 🕙 9.30am-8pm) uses imaginative techniques like dioramas, scale models and moving waxworks to bring scenes
from Korean history to life. The price is
included in the day-pass ticket for Lotte
World Adventure & Magic Island.

Outside is the Charlotte Theatre (www.charlotte
theater.co.kr), which presents big musical
shows such as Cats.

There are the usual shops, fast-food
outlets and restaurants including Pizza Hut,
Marché and Sizzlers. The Lotte Department Store
(🕙 10.30am-8.30pm) has upmarket fashions
but reasonably priced food in its basement
food court, most of it freshly made on the
spot. Choose from nine real fruit juices, and
then decide between the lobster, a-meal-
in-a-pumpkin or asking an Indian chef to
toss a savoury, paper-thin roti onto the
hotplate.

BONGEUNSA Map p70

☎ 3218 4827; Jamsil; ⊙ line 2 to Samseong, COEX
Exit 5

Just north of the COEX Mall and Convention Centre, the shrines and halls of this
Buddhist temple are spread among a
forested hillside and have a quieter, more
secluded atmosphere than Insadong's
Jogyesa (p49). Founded in AD 794, the buildings have been rebuilt many times over the
centuries.

Entry to the temple is through Jinyeomun
(Gate of Truth), protected by four fierce
guardians. On the right is a charity shop,
Beautiful Store (🕙 10.30am-6pm Tue-Sun). On the
left is a small hut where an English-speaking
volunteer guide is usually available.

Make an effort to visit on Thursday
because from 2pm to 4pm, monks and
volunteers offer a temple program in
English that costs only W10,000 and
includes lotus-lantern making, dado (tea
ceremony), a temple tour and Seon (Zen)
meditation.

The main shrine, Daewungjeon, last renovated in 1982, has lattice doors and is decorated inside and out with Buddhist symbols
and art that express Buddhist philosophy
and ideals. A small 14th-century bell is

hidden in one corner. On the right is the funeral hall, while behind are smaller shrine halls and a massive standing statue – the Maitreya (Future) Buddha.

Nearby is the oldest hall, Panjeon, constructed in 1856, which houses over 3000 150-year-old woodblocks with Buddhist scripture and art carved into them. The building is only open from around 10am every day – check with the volunteer guide at the entrance.

SEOLLEUNG PARK ROYAL TOMBS
Map p70

Seongjongneung Park; ☎ 568 1291; Jamsil; adult/teenager W1000/500; ☉ 6am-5.30pm Tue-Sun Mar-Oct, 6.30am-8pm Tue-Sun Nov-Feb; ◎ line 2 or Bundang Line to Seolleung, Exit 8

The spirit tablets of the Joseon kings and queens are in Jongmyo, but their tombs are scattered all around Seoul. The tombs are elaborate but mostly underground, and were the scene of regular ceremonies to remember and honour the dead.

Walk over to the first tomb, that of King Seongjong (r 1469–94), who was a prolific author and father – he had 28 children by 12 wives and concubines. He died in Changdeokgung. Go around the side and you can walk up to the tomb for a closer look. The statuary includes human and animal guardians – some of the latter look like sheep. The stone lanterns are to guide the king's spirit home.

It's a short walk to the second tomb, that of King Seongjong's second wife, Queen Jeonghyeon Wanghu, where you can also get a close-up look.

A 10-minute walk further on through the thickly wooded park is the tomb of King Seongjong and Queen Jeonghyeon's second son, King Jeongjong (r 1506–44). Although he ruled for 38 years he was a weak king and court factions held the real power, as they often did during the Joseon period. At this tomb you can see the full layout – the gateway and the double pathway to the pavilion where memorial rites were carried out – but you can't go near to the tomb.

From subway Exit 8 walk straight ahead for 500m and the entrance is on the right.

GAROSU-GIL Map p68

Gangnam; ◎ line 3 to Apgujeong, Exit 5

This tree-lined street is filling up with more and more cute fashion boutiques, art galleries, music bars and cafés. French food, wine and style is much in evidence, but mixed in with the usual Italian and Asian styles. The street's trendy newcomers are now spilling over into the side streets.

Recommended places to pop into include La Cuba Latin Music Pub, Pain de Papa (unique breads), King Kong Steak (a reasonably-priced, stylish diner), Lone Costume (fashionista styles with attitude), bloom & goûté (real French choux pastry in a flower-scented pavement café), and Grandmother (Arabian Nights fantasy bar).

From Apgujeong subway station exit 5, walk straight for 10 minutes to arrive at the northern end of Garosu-gil. It's a 10-minute walk to Sinsa subway station (Line 3, Exit 8) from the street's southern end.

OPERA GALLERY Map p70

☎ 3446 0070; Brand Name St, Jamsil; admission free; ☉ 10am-7pm; ◎ line 3 to Apgujeong, Exit 2

The only gallery in Seoul to see work by famous-name, cutting-edge Western artists and sculptors. Artists nowadays are a kind of brand, so Brand Name St is a suitable location for this always impressive gallery.

MUSEUM OF KOREAN EMBROIDERY
Map p68

☎ 5155 1114; 4th fl, Sajeon House, Gangnam; admission free; ☉ 10am-4pm Mon-Fri; ◎ line 7 to Hak-dong, Exit 10

A tiny one-room museum with painstaking examples of a neglected and unheralded female craft and embroidery books to browse. In the good old days nearly everything was embroidered – clothes, shoes, boxes, pillow-ends, screens, pin cushions, toys and thimbles. Delicate patchwork *pojagi* (wrapping cloths) had many uses and some were made out of silk or *ramie* (cloth made from pounded bark). From the subway exit turn left and then take the second alley on the right.

Shopping (p91), Sleeping (p157)

Some of Seoul's best attractions lie outside the city centre, but they can be easily and quickly reached by subway. The nearest of them is Seodaemun Prison, which is just one subway stop east of Gyeongbokgung. Also to the east is the World Cup Stadium & Mall, which is surrounded by large, green parks. To the south of Namsan near Itaewon, two major museums – the new National Museum and the War Memorial & Museum – are highlights. On the northern bank of the Han River, Ttukseom Seoul Forest Park is a very pleasant spot to relax and cycle around.

Out in the southern suburbs, the Seoul Arts Centre (p138) promotes traditional and modern culture, both Korean and Western. In the hills further south is a huge zoological garden within walking distance of an exciting amusement park and a major art gallery. Just one subway station north is the horse-racing track (p143).

NATIONAL MUSEUM OF KOREA
Map pp36–7

☎ 2077 9000; www.museum.go.kr; admission free; ⏰ 9am-6pm Tue-Sun; ⊖ line 1 or 4 to Ichon, Exit 2

The grand, marble-lined, modernist building cleverly channels plenty of natural light to show off Korea's ancient treasures. The museum took eight years to construct, finally opening in October 2005. The gardens on the right of the reflecting pond, with ancient stone pagodas, the original Bosingak bell and Dragon Falls – perhaps the most picturesque spot in Seoul – are worth a visit.

Pick up a ticket from the office in the left-side section, which also houses the Yong Theatre, special exhibitions and the children's section. Enter the huge atrium foyer and work your way down the right-hand side, passing through the various ruling dynasties, from simple comb-design pots and dolmens to the skilful and imaginative Baekje-era incense holder and the intricate gold work of the Silla dynasty crowns and necklaces. Based in Gyeongju, the Silla dynasty was a Korean renaissance, when artisans decorated just about everything. Cross over to the other side for the straight-laced Joseon era with its stodgy government bureaucracy of reports, official portraits, royal rituals, ID tags, scholarly aristocrats, slaves and peddlers.

top picks

GREATER SEOUL

- National Museum of Korea (left)
- War Memorial & Museum (below)
- Seodaemun Prison (p74)
- World Cup Stadium & Mall (p75)
- Seoul Grand Park (p75)
- Ttukseom Seoul Forest Park (p76)

If your time and stamina is limited, skip the 2nd floor (donations and paintings) and head to the wonderful ancient ceramics that Korea is famous for (3rd floor). Don't miss the outstanding 6th-century statue of the Pensive Bodhisattva and the large Buddhas, also on the 3rd floor.

Restaurants, cafés and a teashop provide places to revive and relax. The museum is a 15-minute walk from the subway station. Follow the signs to Exit 2 before exiting through a ticket banner.

WAR MEMORIAL & MUSEUM
Map pp36–7

☎ 709 3139; www.warmemo.co.kr; adult/child W3000/2000; ⏰ 9.30am-6pm Tue-Sun; ⊖ line 4 or 6 to Samgakji, Exit 12

This huge museum documents the history of warfare in Korea and has an especially good section on the Korean War (1950–53). It takes at least three hours to browse the whole place, so arrive before 3pm. Only snacks are available. Don't try to cover this museum and the National Museum of Korea in one day.

On the 1st floor are paintings and panoramic displays illustrating many fierce battles

TRANSPORT: GREATER SEOUL

The subway is the best way to visit the sights in Greater Seoul. Some sights are a 15-minute walk from the subway, but you can always hop on a shuttle bus (Seoul Arts Centre), take a tram train or chairlift (Seoul Grand Park), ride in a horse and carriage (Seoul Racecourse) or jump in a taxi (Ttukseom Seoul Forest Park).

THE FORGOTTEN WAR?

During the Korean War 21 countries took part in the UN operation to save South Korea after it was attacked by the North, including five countries which sent medical teams. North Korean and Chinese troops suffered huge casualties, estimated at 215,000 and 400,000 respectively. Civilian casualties on both sides added up to two million.

It was a massive conflict involving millions of troops and many desperate battles, yet it is often referred to as the 'Forgotten War' – the name of a book (and film) on the Korean War. Nowadays few people know much about the war, and many Korean War veterans feel that they have been forgotten. According to figures at the War Memorial Museum (p73), the Republic of Korea had 152,279 soldiers killed in action, America 33,642, UK 1086, Turkey 724, Canada 516, Australia 332, France 269, Colombia 213, Greece 186, Thailand 130, Netherlands 124, Ethiopia 122, Philippines 112, Belgium 106, New Zealand 43, South Africa 35, Luxembourg 2 and Norway 2.

fought against invading Mongol, Japanese and Chinese armies. Many items are only vaguely dated, but there is a replica of one of Admiral Sun-sin's famous iron-clad turtle warships (called *geobukseon*), which he used to defeat the Japanese navy in the 1590s.

Upstairs, visitors can view heaps of black-and-white documentary footage (with English commentary) of the main battles and events of the Korean War. Along with photos, maps and artefacts, the films give a fascinating insight into what the war was like: the surprise 4am attack from the North (spearheaded by 240 Russian-made tanks), the build-up of UN (mainly US) forces in Busan, the daring amphibious landing at Incheon, the sweep north followed by the surprise Chinese attack – all of which took place in 1950.

On the left of the museum entrance are the names of UN soldiers killed during the war (see the boxed text, above).

On the 3rd floor the Combat Experience Room is just that, and lasts five minutes (every 30 minutes from 9.30am to 4.30pm). Other displays cover Korea's involvement in the Vietnam War (4700 Koreans died), North Korean attacks on the South since 1953, and Korea's UN peacekeeping roles.

Children love playing on the large military hardware outside – tanks, helicopters, missiles and planes, including a B52 bomber.

Every Friday at 2pm from April to June and in October and November a military band performs, and a marching parade culminates in an awesome display of military precision and weapon twirling by the honour guard.

SEODAEMUN PRISON Map pp36–7
☎ 303 9750; adult/child/teenager W1500/500/1000; ⊗ 9.30am-6pm Tue-Sun Mar-Oct, to 5pm Tue-Sun Nov-Feb; ◉ line 3 to Dongn-immun, Exit 5

The prison, built in 1908, is a symbol of Japanese cruelty and oppression during their colonial rule of Korea from 1910 until 1945. The main hall has three floors of exhibitions, including lifelike re-creations of torture scenes in the nightmarish interrogation cells in the basement. Photographs of the prison and prison conditions are on view along with video footage. Not everything is translated into English.

Visitors can look around and go inside the original prison cell blocks where the independence fighters were held. Built to house 500 prisoners, up to 3500 were packed inside during the height of the anti-Japanese protests in 1919. There was no heating and the food was just rice, barley and beans.

The factories where prisoners were forced to make bricks and military uniforms have gone, but some of the red prison-made bricks with Chinese characters stamped on them have been used to make the pavements.

In another building you can experience what the prisoners suffered. Firstly the torture scenes – look at the spikes in the box which prisoners were put inside; next the court finds you guilty, and you sit down on the execution chair to be hanged – be warned: the chair drops down!

An outdoor memorial lists the names of 90 Koreans known to have died in the prison, but around 300 to 600 nameless others died here from torture, execution, malnutrition and disease.

The most famous victim was Ryu Gwan-sun, an 18-year-old Ewha high school student, who was tortured to death in 1920. The female prisoners were kept in underground cells.

The execution building (1923) is chilling. Behind it is a 200m tunnel to a hillside cemetery where the bodies were buried.

Next to the prison is Dongnimmun Park, with an impressive Western-style granite archway. Built by the Independence Club in 1898, it stands where envoys from Chinese emperors used to be officially welcomed to Seoul. A tribute of gold, tiger skins, green tea, ginseng, horses, swords, *ramie* cloth, straw mats and eunuchs would be handed over by the Koreans. This ritual symbolised Chinese suzerainty over Korea, which only ended when King Gojong declared himself an emperor in 1897. The two stone pillars in front of the gate are all that remain of Yongunmun, the gate that stood near Mohwagwan, the Guest Hall for Cherishing China, where Chinese envoys stayed on their regular visits to Seoul.

WORLD CUP STADIUM & MALL
Map pp36-7
☎ 2128 2002; Ⓜ line 6 to World Cup Stadium, Exit 1

Costing US$151 million, the spectacular 64,000-seat World Cup Stadium was built to stage the opening ceremony and some of the matches of the 2002 World Cup soccer finals, which Korea co-hosted with Japan.

The Seoul World Cup Museum (adult/child W1000/500; ⏲ 9am-6pm) relives the highs and lows of the 2002 cup on screen, along with souvenirs and a couple of virtual soccer games. Nearby is the tour office (☎ 2128 2000; adult/child W1000/500; ⏲ 9am-6pm) for trips behind the scenes to the changing-rooms that the soccer superstars used.

The stadium is also home to a CGV cinema multiplex, a popular fashion store called Homever, a food court and spa. Around the stadium are large parks that have been cleverly reclaimed from landfill sites and returned to a natural state. To arrive by bicycle, see p141.

SEOUL GRAND PARK Map pp36-7
☎ 500 7114; www.grandpark.seoul.go.kr; adult/child/teenager W3000/1000/2000; ⏲ 9am-7pm Mar-Oct, 9am-6pm Nov-Feb; Ⓜ line 4 to Seoul Grand Park, Exit 2

This zoo park is so large and spread out that a visit here is also a hiking trip. Walk straight ahead from the subway Exit 2 for five minutes to a large glass building. Here either walk for 15 minutes, take a tram train (adult/teenager/child W800/600/500) or turn right to catch the sky chairlift (adult/teenager/child W4500/3000/2500) to the zoo entrance.

Another 15-minute walk from the zoo entrance takes you to the National Museum of Contemporary Art (below) or to Seoul Land Amusement Park (below).

Seoul's best zoo is set among forested hillsides, and families picnic along the shady banks of a stream that runs through the park. It's easy to spend all day here. The zoo is home to a long list of exotic creatures, including the ever-popular African ones. A huge aviary contains cranes, swans, pelicans and other large birds, and an indoor botanic garden houses a forest of cacti, numerous orchids and carnivorous pitcher plants. Ants and swimming beetles are on display in the insectarium. A very entertaining dolphin-and-seal show (adult/teenager/child W2000/1500/1000) is held at 11.30am, 1.30pm, 3pm and 4.30pm in summer but only at 1.30pm and 3pm in winter.

SEOUL LAND AMUSEMENT PARK
Map pp36-7
☎ 504 0011; http://eng.seoulland.co.kr; day pass adult/child/teenager W29,000/22,000/25,000; ⏲ 9.30am-10pm summer, to 6pm winter; Ⓜ line 4 to Seoul Grand Park, Exit 2

Keep the children happy all day at this Disney look-alike family amusement park with five themed areas, special shows and the main attraction: thrill rides that spin you like a top or drop you like a stone. The rollercoaster is long and scary but the most popular thrill, Sky X flying on a wire, costs W15,000 extra. An art gallery (below) and a zoo (left) are a 15-minute walk away, or take the tram train.

NATIONAL MUSEUM OF CONTEMPORARY ART Map pp36-7
☎ 2188 6000; www.moca.go.kr; admission free, special exhibitions adult/child W3000/1500; ⏲ 10am-6pm Tue-Sun Mar-Oct, to 5pm Tue-Sun Nov-Feb; Ⓜ line 4 to Seoul Grand Park, Exit 2

A large and impressive art gallery spread over three floors, this museum also has sculptures in the garden. The outstanding exhibit is *The More the Better* – a 1988 installation of 1000 flickering TV screens piled up into a pagoda shape by leading Korean video artist Nam June Paik. Viewing this exhibit is like channel hopping without a remote. Other exhibits by the same artist include a piano jukebox – log onto www .paikstudios.com to learn more about this artistic pioneer. The international section contains a sculpture made of dice and another one utilising squashed petrol cans.

Overall, the permanent collection of Korean modern art is disappointing, a mishmash of pictures with no real stand-outs or themes or styles, but the special exhibitions can be more worthwhile.

TTUKSEOM SEOUL FOREST PARK
Map pp36-7

☎ 3708 2588; admission free; ☻ 24hr; ⊚ line 2 to Ttukseom, Exit 8

This relatively new park, a 15-minute walk from Ttukseom station (don't get off at Ttukseom Resort station!), is a very pleasant area to enjoy some time in natural surroundings. It's large, so it's best to hire a bicycle or rollerblades from the rental stall (bicycles/rollerblades per hr W3000/5000; ☻ 9am-10pm) located by Gate 1. Lockers cost W500.

The park used to be a hunting ground in Joseon times, then became a horse-racing track and sports fields, but is now a regenerating forest. Among the trees and lakes are deer enclosures, eco areas, an insect exhibition, a plant nursery, a Lotteria overlooking a pond and fountains that shoot up from the ground, which kids love playing in. You can also cycle through a tunnel down to the Han River and along the cycleway that follows the river in both directions.

CHILDREN'S GRAND PARK Map pp36-7

☎ 2290 6114; admission free; ☻ 5am-10pm; ⊚ line 7 to Children's Grand Park, Exit 1

Ask for a free map at the entrance to this large shady park, which features a rose garden, flower beds and fountains, and plenty to keep children busy. The amusement park (rides cost extra) has fear-factor experiences for all ages. The zoo (☻ 10am-6pm) areas include exotic animals such as tigers, elephants, jaguars, meerkats, penguins and a mob of monkeys. Pony and camel rides cost W5000 for adults, W4000 for children.

A glasshouse botanical garden has cacti up one end, and a tropical jungle and bonsai trees at the other end. A wetland eco area has a boardwalk. The 30-minute Anistory Show (☎ 4566 1911; www.anistory21.co.kr; adult/child W5500/4000; ☻ shows 11.30am, 1pm, 2pm, 3pm, 4pm, 5pm & 6pm) is fun and features a cute parrot, a chimpanzee act and eager performing seals.

SEJONG UNIVERSITY MUSEUM
Map pp36-7

☎ 3408 3077; admission free; ☻ 10am-noon & 1-3pm Mon-Fri; ⊚ line 7 to Children's Grand Park, Exit 6

Sejong has a superb collection, especially the *hanbok* display, which takes up an entire floor and includes outstanding royal clothing. Rarely visited, the museum should be more popular – the furniture arranged into rooms, the wooden, leather and silk shoes worn by the different social classes present vivid images of Korea's feudal past. A poem displayed at the museum praises it as 'a place of wisdom, beauty and virtue' where visitors can 'listen to the thousand-year-old ancestors whispering quietly'.

MUSEUM OF KOREAN TRADITIONAL MUSIC Map pp36-7

☎ 580 3130; admission free; ☻ 9am-6pm Tue-Sun; ⊚ line 3 to Nambu Bus Terminal, Exit 5

Next door to the Seoul Arts Centre, the National Centre for Korean Traditional Performing Arts (NCKTPA; ☎ 580 3300; www.ncktpa.go.kr) is home to this museum, where visitors can see and listen to traditional Korean musical instruments that are rarely heard today. The *eo* is shaped like a tiger and played by banging its head with a stick and then running the stick over the notches on its back. Check the NCKTPA website for music lessons for foreigners. See p138 for shows at the Yeakdang Theatre.

SEONNONGDAN Map pp36-7

⊚ line 1 to Jegi-dong, Exit 1

The altar is not worth visiting except for one day in April (which varies with the lunar calendar): the re-enactment of the ceremony when Joseon kings came here to pray for a good harvest. A royal procession heads to the altar, where food offerings are laid out in special brass containers. Musicians in red robes play traditional instruments, and after the Confucian ceremony the onlookers tuck into *seolleongtang* (beef soup) and *makgeolli* (fermented rice wine) free of charge, just as in Joseon days. From the subway exit, walk straight as far as the notice board and turn right. When you come to a fork, go right. The altar is a 300m walk on the right.

INWANGSAN SHAMANIST HILLSIDE WALK
Walking Tour

On this hillside walk you can see Seoul's most famous shamanist shrine, small Buddhist/shamanist temples and part of Seoul's medieval fortress wall, and enjoy a bird's-eye view of Seoul from Inwangsan (White Tiger Mountain). The area has a special atmosphere because of the outdoor shamanist ceremonies that invoke the spirits of the departed. All visitors should treat the area and people with respect, and remember that taking a photograph could interfere with an important ceremony.

1 Entrance Gate From subway Exit 2 turn down the first small alley on your left. At the five-alley crossroads, fork right up the steps and you'll soon reach the colourful gateway to the shamanist village. It's a 15-minute walk from the subway.

2. Buddhist/shamanist temples Turn left where houses and small temples cling to the rocky hillside. The temples have colourful murals of birds and blossom on their outside walls, and wind chimes clink in the breeze. One mural depicts the parable of the ox, which represents man's mind being tamed.

3. Bongjeonwonsa Back on the main path is a shop and a temple, Bongjeonwonsa. If you are invited inside, three shamanist deities – Sansin (mountain god), Dokseong (river god) and Chilseong (the seven stars of the Big Dipper) share the altar with Buddha. Buddhism and shamanism have coexisted peacefully for over 1500 years.

4 Guksadang Up the steps is Guksadang. Originally built on Namsan peak in the 1390s, the Japanese demolished it in 1925, so Korean shamanists secretly rebuilt it on Inwangsan. Inside the shrine are paintings of shamanist gods, and the altar is often loaded with rice cakes, fruit and a pig's head – food offerings for the spirits.

5 Zen rocks Walk left and up some steps to the extraordinary Zen rocks (Seonbawi), which look like a Salvador Dali painting – two large rocks have been so eroded that they look like two robed monks. At the altar in front of the rocks, women still come to pray for a son.

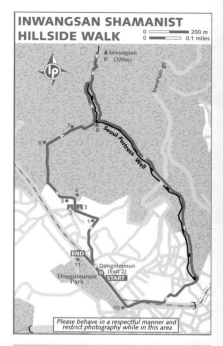

INWANGSAN SHAMANIST HILLSIDE WALK

Please behave in a respectful manner and restrict photography while in this area

WALK FACTS

Start Subway line 3 to Dongnimmun station, Exit 2

End Seodaemun Prison

Distance 3-4km

Time 3 hours

Exertion Moderate

Fuel Stop Pack a picnic for the peak

6 Shamanist altar Eroded rocks create an eerie atmosphere and in small crevices are candles, incense sticks and offerings. Climb up the hill for five minutes to an unlikely exercise trail, and after another five-minute uphill walk is a shamanist altar, surrounded by flowers. A small Buddha is carved into the rock on the left above the altar.

7 Shamanist ceremony area Shamanists have been coming to this sacred area for thousands of years. One rock embodies the spirit of a famous general, while another is where children's spirits shelter. You may see an old lady is bowing and waving five different coloured flags to attract the spirits, or a young girl is drumming and meditating.

8 Seoul Fortress Wall Turn right, past small rock altars with offerings of dried fish, *makgeolli* and sweets, to reach the renovated Seoul fortress wall. Turn left to walk up to the start of the wall for amazing views of an amazing city.

9 Inwangsan peak Carry on for another 15 minutes to reach the best view of all from atop Inwangsan peak at 338m. Feel how vast Seoul is at this wonderful picnic spot. After lunch, head back down the other side of the fortress wall to the road.

10 Independence Gate Walk across the road and through the green gate for a woodland stroll alongside more of the fortress wall. Twenty minutes later you reach a road and the end of the wall. Turn right along the road for 10 minutes until you reach Independence Gate, across the road.

11 Seodaemun Prison Cross the road for the not-to-be-missed Seodaemun Prison (p74).

WESTERN NAMHANSANSEONG WALK
Walking Tour

This is a great walk, 'bathing in nature' out in the lush green hillsides that surround Seoul. It runs along part of a colossal fortress that guarded the southern approaches to Seoul. The 10km wall was built by hand, with few tools or equipment, and has a dramatic history.

1 Namhansanseong Entrance From Exit 1, walk 200m to the bus stop. Every bus stop to the park entrance (Namhansanseong *ipgu*), and bus 9 goes to Jungro Village inside the mountain fortress. Otherwise grab a taxi, unless you want to try the 2km walk to the park entrance, which is under a bridge.

2 Daewonamsa At the entrance on the right is a handicraft shop and the first of many natural springs. After walking uphill for 15 minutes, take a 200m detour to Daewonamsa (대원암사), a typically tiny monastery/temple with five residents.

3 Baekryeonsa A little further on is another temple, Baekryeonsa. Its founder loved flow-

ers as a symbol of purity and beauty, and the temple is surrounded by them.

4 Nammun Fork right at the big signboard and you'll soon reach Nammun, the imposing south gate of the fortress. Its origins go back a millennium, but the wall was rebuilt in 1626. It hugs the contours of the land, winding around the hillsides for 10km, varying between 3m and 7m in height.

5 Yeongchunjeong Turn left along the inside of the fortress wall, which soon offers extensive views of Seoul city. Look out for birds, butterflies and the occasional striped squirrel. It's a 15-minute climb to Yeongchun-

WALK FACTS

Start Subway line 8 to Namhansanseong, Exit 1
End Jungro Village
Distance 4km
Time 2 hours
Exertion Easy to Moderate
Fuel Stops Coffee Relax, Jangseong

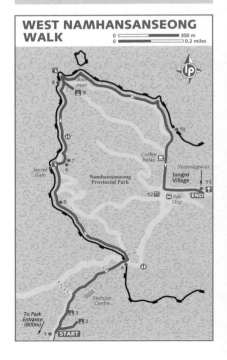

WEST NAMHANSANSEONG WALK

SHAMANIST CEREMONIES

Ceremonies called *gut* usually take place outdoors or inside a plastic-sheet tent. They involve contacting departed spirits, which are attracted by music, chanting, waving flags and lavish offerings of food and drink. During some *gut* drums are beaten and the *mudang* (female shamanist priest) dances herself into a frenzied state that allows her to communicate with the spirits and be possessed by them. Another *gut* helps to guide the spirit of a recently departed person to find peace in the other world. Resentments felt by the dead can haunt and plague the living and cause them all sorts of misfortune, so upset or angry spirits need placating. For shamanists death does not end relationships, they simply take another form. Smartly dressed couples come to Guksadang shamanist shrine to ask for good fortune with a business project, make contact with a deceased relative or cure an illness.

jeong, a pavilion used in the feudal days by garrison soldiers.

6 Cheongnyangdae Ten minutes further on is a secret gate, one of 18 scattered around the walls along with the four main gates. Nearby is Cheongnyangdae, the shrine to Yi Hoe who was executed after false accusations were made that he had embezzled funds meant for the fortress's construction. His wife and concubine both subsequently committed suicide.

7 Sueojangdae Alongside is Sueojangdae, a pavilion from where King Injo conducted the defence of the fortress in 1636 when Korea was attacked by a large Manchu army from China. After a 45-day siege, King Injo surrendered and his son was kept hostage in Beijing for the next eight years.

8 Seomun Another 10-minute walk away is Seomun, the West Gate. Go out this gate and walk along the more impressive-looking outside of the wall to Am-mun, another gate with a panoramic view.

9 Gukcheongsa A short detour goes to Gukcheongsa, one of the nine temples that used to be inside the fortress. In those days the toughest, most feared soldiers were Buddhist monks, who were not pacifists when the nation was in danger.

10 Bungmun Continue on round the wall for 20 minutes to reach Bungmun, the North Gate. From here, walk down to the village of restaurants past Coffee Relax, a rustic café offering rest and refreshment.

11 Namhansanseong Church From here it's a five-minute stroll down to Jungro Village. Turn left to see another military pavilion, Yeonmugwan. Just beyond is an outstanding example of a fusion-style church in a land that should be world famous for its extraordinary Christian churches.

12 Jangseong On the roundabout, Jangseong (장성; ☎ 031-743 6600; meals for 2-3 W45,000; ☸ 10am-10pm) is a restaurant with small, rustic-style private rooms. Be sure to try the *tokkitang* (a spicy rabbit stew with vegetables). Afterwards, bus 9 (W900, 15 minutes, hourly) can drop you near Namhansanseong subway station.

top picks

- **Namdaemun Market** (p86)
- **Dongdaemun Market** (p83)
- **Galleria** (p90)
- **COEX Mall** (p90)
- **Lotte Department Store** (p86)
- **Migliore Mall** (p86)
- **Ssamzie** (p85)
- **Janganpyeong Antiques Market** (p91)
- **Yongsan Electronics Market** (p92)
- **Free Market** (p88)

SHOPPING

Seoulites love shopping. The traditional markets, electronics emporiums, underground arcades, upmarket department stores and glitzy malls are all bursting at the seams with more goodies than Santa's sack. Three of the best general malls are at COEX, Central City and the World Cup Stadium. World-class department stores include Lotte (in Myeong-dong and Lotte World), Hyundai (in Sinchon, COEX Mall and Apgujeong), Shinsegae (in Namdaemun Market and Central Mall) and Galleria (in Apgujeong). They all have regular sales with heavily discounted prices.

For clothing, shoes, accessories or fabrics you can't beat Dongdaemun Market; children's clothes, spectacles and cameras are best bought at Namdaemun Market. Larger sizes in clothes and shoes, souvenir T-shirts, leather jackets and hip-hop gear, together with tailor-made clothing, can be found in Itaewon, where English is widely understood. For electronic gizmos drop into Yongsan Electronics Market or Techno Mart. For Asian teas, health foods and medicines go to Gyeongdong Market. Antique-lovers can browse the Janganpyeong arcades or Insadong, Itaewon and the new permanent flea market where stalls sell antiques, reproductions and collectables. For brand-name boutiques head to Myeong-dong, but Westerners can struggle to find their size, fit and style.

Souvenirs and gifts such as macramé and embroidery, boxes made of handmade paper *(hanji)*, wooden masks, fans, painted wedding ducks, lacquer ware boxes inlaid with mother-of-pearl or ox horn can be found in the craft shops of Insadong. More expensive items include pale-green celadon pottery, reproduction Joseon-dynasty furniture and elegant *hanbok* (traditional clothing). Shirts or blouses made of lightweight, see-through *ramie* (cloth made from pounded bark) make an unusual fashion gift. Ssamzie in Insadong or the weekend afternoon Free Market in Hongdae are the places to find one-off hand-crafted items. The many types of Korean tea – made of anything from grains such as barley, corn and burnt rice to fruits like quince, red dates and *omija* berries – are another popular buy.

Ginseng, the wonder root, turns up everywhere. You can chew it, eat it, drink it or bathe in it. Ginseng chewing gum, ginseng chocolate, ginseng tea, ginseng wine, ginseng soup, ginseng rice porridge, ginseng soap and ginseng bath salts are all ways to benefit from its health-giving properties.

Most shops open daily from 10am to around 9pm, but some are closed on Sunday. Department store opening hours are 10am to 7.30pm daily, although some close one day a week or two days a month. Market times vary, but some stalls stay open even on days when a market is generally closed.

Before venturing into the markets or buying from street stalls, get a handle on approximate prices by looking in a department store, supermarket or regular fixed-price shop. Some stallholders start off with a very inflated price, whereas others quote only a slightly inflated figure. You can expect a discount of around 30%, but this is an average figure only and varies case by case. Walking away is the best way of achieving a lower price. Bargaining is part of the way of life in Seoul, so even when shopping in boutiques and opticians you can always request a discount if you feel it's justified or if you are buying more than one item.

GWANGHWAMUN

Downtown is famous for huge bookshops, which have sizeable English-language book and magazine sections. The historical Samcheong-dong district area is a hot new shopping attraction with unique boutiques and craft workshops springing up among the small art galleries, cafés and museums. Kilometres of underground shops are hidden beneath the main east/west thoroughfares, Jongno and Euljiro.

Above ground Jongno features a cluster of glittery jewellery shops around Tapgol Park. Use the underground Euljiro arcade to walk east to the iconic Dongdaemun Market or else walk alongside the newly rediscovered Cheonggye stream. Marvel at the scale of Doota Mall where hundreds of small fashion stores cover floor after floor of this high-rise mall or walk round the Dongdaemun Shopping Complex, which must have the most amazing display of fabrics anywhere in the world.

YOUNGPOONG BOOKSHOP

Map p40 Books

☎ 399 5656; ⏰ 9.30am-10pm; Ⓜ line 1 to Jonggak, Exit 1

A major downtown bookstore with cafés, English-language magazines and a ticket office on the top floor, plus English-language books in the H2 and H3 sections downstairs.

SEOUL SELECTION Map p40 Books & DVDs

☎ 734 9565; www.seoulselection.co.kr; ⏰ 9.30am-6.30pm Mon-Sat; Ⓜ line 3 to Anguk, Exit 1

Come here to buy books on Korean culture in English, along with Korean CDs and Korean movies and drama series on DVD (with English subtitles). Staff speak English and can recommend titles. Secondhand books are also for sale. Stay for a drink (W3000 – try the homemade citron tea) and free internet surfing. Check out the website for an excellent monthly newsletter about what's on in Seoul.

KYOBO BOOKSHOP Map p40 Books & Music

☎ 3973 5100; B1, Kyobo Bldg, Jongno; ⏰ 9.30am-10pm; Ⓜ line 5 to Gwanghwamun, Exit 4

A wide selection of English-language books is in section F of this large and famous bookstore that also sells English-language magazines (section J), CDs and gifts.

DONGHWA DUTY-FREE SHOP

Map p40 Brand-Name Goods

☎ 399 3100; ⏰ 9.30am-7.30pm; Ⓜ line 5 to Gwanghwamun, Exit 6

This extensive shop is packed with the usual duty-free brand-name goods that you can buy at the airport. You need to take your passport and tickets, but shopping here can avoid a rushed, last-minute shop at the airport.

DONGDAEMUN MARKET Map p84 Market

Ⓜ line 1 or 4 to Dongdaemun, Exit 5 or 7, or line 2, 4 or 5 to Dongdaemun Stadium, Exit 1

Where to begin in this colossal market? Many shoppers start at Doota Mall (☎ 3398 2386; ⏰ 10.30am-5am Tue-Sat, to 11pm Sun, 7pm-5am Mon), a leading fashion icon full to the brim with domestic brands. Besides floors dedicated to adult clothing, it has a floor of accessory shops, a bag and shoes floor, a children's floor, a brand-name floor and

a food-court floor. Migliore Mall (☎ 339 3001; ⏰ 10.30am-4.30am Tue-Sun) is another fashion mall next door. Others in this area also have cinemas and saunas.

The multistorey Dongdaemun Shopping Complex (☎ 8am-7pm Mon-Sat) has an unbelievable range of fabrics and trimmings of every conceivable kind.

Other parts of the market specialise in shoes, pets (some are shockingly overcrowded in their cages) and street stalls. Soccer shirts are in the Euljiro underground arcade. The other market buildings sell all types of clothing and accessories, both retail and wholesale. Some shops have prices, but many don't, so bargaining is the name of the game.

Russian and Central Asian companies import clothing from Dongdaemun Market and have offices and restaurants nearby.

GWANGJANG MARKET Map p40 Market

⏰ 9am-10pm Mon-Sat; Ⓜ line 1 or 4 to Dongdaemun Stadium, Exit 8

This rabbit warren of a market has been frozen in time: everything is still traditional and unmodernised. Look out for the food stalls with workers grinding mung beans – they sell crispy, thick *bindaetteok* (mung-bean pancake) for W4000 that are big enough to be shared by two.

INSADONG & DAEHANGNO

Seoul's most fascinating and popular shopping street, Insadong-gil, is traffic-free on Saturday from 2pm until 10pm and on Sunday

VAT REFUNDS

Global Refund (☎ 776 2170; www.globalrefund.com) offers a partial refund (about 5% to 8%) of the 10% value added tax (VAT). Spend more than W30,000 in any participating shop and you can later claim a refund. The retailer hands over a special receipt, which must be shown to a customs officer at Incheon International Airport. Go to a Customs Declaration Desk (near the check-in counters) before checking in luggage – the customs officer will want to see the items before stamping the receipt. After going through immigration, show the stamped receipt at the relevant refund desk, next to the duty-free shops, to receive the won refund in cash or by cheque.

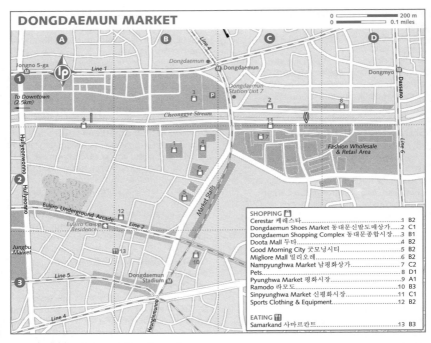

DONGDAEMUN MARKET

from 10am until 10pm. It's well worth visiting more than once. Insadong is the centre of Seoul's commercial art world, with over 50 small private art galleries displaying and selling the work of Seoul's top artists, potters and sculptors. Masses of small shops sell pottery, antiques, calligraphy brushes, handmade paper, embroidery and souvenir knickknacks. The reproduction Goryeo-dynasty celadon pottery looks just like the real thing. Don't forget to try some of the special snacks sold mainly from street stalls. Buddhist items, such as cassettes of monks chanting, incense sticks, and monk's and nun's clothing, can be bought in shops near the Buddhist temple, Jogyesa. Over in Daehangno, the cheerful, chatty Filipino Sunday Market in is a fun place to forage for lunchtime snacks.

BANDI & LUNI'S Map p50   Books
☎ 2198 3000; B2 Jongno Tower, Insadong;
🕙 10am-10pm; 🚇 line 1 to Jonggak, Exit 3
A large bookshop with an excellent range of English books in section D2, English magazines in A1. There's plenty of seats to relax in while you read a book in comfort (with or without buying it).

SABEE Map p50   Clothing
☎ 722 2426; Hwaenamu-gil, Insadong;
🕙 9.30am-8.30pm; 🚇 line 3 to Anguk, Exit 6
Another unique Insadong store, the only outlet for these traditional *hanbok*-style clothes for men and women. The orange colour comes from a special Korean technique of using persimmon dye that uses all parts of the tree – flowers, bark, leaves and seeds. This designer clothing doesn't come cheap – W280,000 is the minimum.

KUKJAE EMBROIDERY
Map p50   Handicrafts
☎ 732 0830; Insadong-gil, Insadong; 🕙 10am-8pm; 🚇 line 3 to Anguk, Exit 6
This shop (and other branches nearby) has some of the most exquisite embroidery you will ever see. The owner, Mrs Kim Chang-O, is a legend who has exhibited all over the place, and examples of her designs have been official gifts given by Korean presidents to foreign presidents. That's the embroidery equivalent of winning an Oscar and an Olympic gold medal at the same time.

SEOUL'S ART MARKET

Where did you study art? Hongdae (Hongik University).

Which artists have influenced you most? I would say Max Ernst and Hieronymus Bosch.

Can you describe your artworks in one sentence? They are picking something out of my subconscious and presenting it as a kind of treasure.

What do you think of traditional Korean art? In the Joseon period, painters didn't go to the mountains and paint the real mountains, they painted their idea of a mountain. That was their philosophy of art, art in the head. It's a bit similar idea to me.

How does the gallery system work in Seoul? In the past, galleries would choose artists with talent and exhibit their work, but unfortunately these days more and more galleries are renting space to artists. The artist must pay.

Was your recent exhibition in Insadong successful? Not in regard to sales, but it was interesting that it was mainly foreigners like you who were enquiring about prices and so on.

Who buys modern Korean art? Not many people! I create my works for those who can understand and appreciate them, rather than to sell them. I don't expect many people to be interested in my art.

Have you exhibited abroad? No, it's very difficult to organise. A few galleries will organise exhibitions abroad for Korean artists, but it's much more likely the other way round – Western, Japanese or Chinese artists having an exhibition in Insadong for instance. Modern Chinese art is in fashion at the moment.

Do you know how many of your graduating class are working as artists? I graduated in 1991 and maybe only five or six out of the 40 students in my sculpture class are still doing art seriously.

Is there much art outside Seoul? Seoul is maybe 80%. Every artist prefers to exhibit in Seoul.

What's the best thing about living in Seoul? The city is constantly moving (not necessarily changing) and people are always doing something.

An interview with Min Jung-soo, a female artist who makes carefully constructed but disturbing artworks out of doll parts and other materials.

SSAMZIE Map p50 Handicrafts
Insadong-gil, Insadong; ⏲ 10.30am-9pm; ⓢ line 3 to Anguk, Exit 6

This four-storey complex built around a courtyard is a popular stop for one-off clothing, accessories or household goods. A bag that looks like a shirt or a shirt that looks like a bag – that's the sort of thing you can find here. Impulse shoppers who usually regret their purchases should keep well away.

FILIPINO SUNDAY MARKET
Map p52 Market
Hyehwa Crossroad, Daehangno; ⏲ 9am-5pm Sun; ⓢ line 4 to Hyehwa, Exit 1

Join the jolly Filipino community in Seoul who gather in this lively Little Manila every Sunday to meet, chat and eat Filipino food. Street stalls sell tropical treats such as coconut drinks, cassava cakes, fried bananas on a stick, *adobo* chicken and *longaniza* sausage. Call-back telephone cards are also on sale.

NAKWON MUSICAL INSTRUMENTS ARCADE Map p50 Musical Instruments
☎ 924 0604; Samilro, Insadong; ⏲ 10am-7.30pm Mon-Sat

Spread over the 2nd and 3rd floors of this large arcade is a dazzling maze of shops selling local and imported musical instruments and equipment of all kinds.

MYEONG-DONG, NAMSAN & ITAEWON

Every evening crowds flock to the streets of Myeong-dong to shop for local and imported clothes, shoes, bags, accessories and cosmetics. Cafés, restaurants, department stores and high-rise shopping malls with food courts and cinema multiplexes have made this area megapopular with young people and Japanese visitors, who may be reminded of Tokyo's Shinjuku region.

Itaewon, with an older clientele, has a very different aura. This 1km shopping street caters to American soldiers stationed at the nearby Yongsan base, so most retailers speak a bit of English. Tailor-made suits (W250,000) and shirts are a popular buy as are custom-made shoes. Eel skin, ostrich skin and kangaroo skin products are a speciality. Spectacles (W50,000) and contact lenses are good quality and reasonably priced. Itaewon has cowboy boots, leather jackets, hip-hop clothing, big sizes and stalls with W10,000 clothing racks.

WHAT THE BOOK Map p60   Books

☎ 797 2342; www.whatthebook.com; Sobangseo-gil, Itaewon; ☻ 10am-8pm Mon-Sat, from noon Sun; ❻ line 6 to Itaewon, Exit 3

This large basement bookshop sells new and secondhand English-language books as well as a wide range of American magazines. Browse the titles on the website.

LOTTE DEPARTMENT STORE
Map pp56-7   Department Store

☎ 771 2500; Namdaemunno, Myeong-dong; ☻ 10.30am-8pm; ❻ line 2 to Euljiro 1-ga, Exit 8

Four classy Lotte stores are linked together along this Myeong-dong street – the department store, Lotte Young Plaza, Lotte Avenuel and a duty-free shop – and the complex includes a multiplex cinema, food court, hotel and restaurants. It's impossible not to get lost inside this busy retail bee-hive of brands but it's an experience not to be missed.

MIGLIORE MALL Map pp56-7   Fashion

☎ 2124 0005; Myeong-dongjungang-gil, Myeong-dong; ☻ 11am-11.30pm Tue-Sun; ❻ line 4 to Myeong-dong, Exit 6

Always teeming with young trendsetters, this iconic, high-rise Myeong-dong mall is packed with small fashion shops. There's a food court on the 7th floor and an out-door performance stage by the entrance to boot.

THE BARBER SHOP Map p60   Hairdresser

☎ 795 8876; Sobangseo-gil, Itaewon; haircuts from W5000; ☻ 10am-9pm Mon-Sat, noon-8pm Sun; ❻ line 6 to Itaewon, Exit 3

The laid-back, English-speaking barber here learnt his trade at Vidal Sassoon's in Kingston, London, and his skilful haircuts are an Itaewon bargain.

MARKET BUZZ

You could disappear in Seoul's mind-boggling markets for a week and still not see everything. Whether it's fresh fish, antiques, clothing, accessories, Asian medicines or the latest electronic gadgets, you can find them all in Seoul's wonderful markets.

top picks

SPECIALITY SHOPS

- Dynasty Tailor (p88) Custom-made suits
- Kukjae Embroidery (p84) Exquisite embroidery
- What the Book (left) Secondhand and new books
- ABC Mart (opposite) Shoes, shoes, shoes
- Lush (p89) Natural beauty products
- Huckleberry Farms (p91) Organic food & drinks

SIMO HAIR Map p60   Hairdresser

☎ 792 5610; Sobangseo-gil, Itaewon; haircuts from W10,000; ☻ 10am-9pm; ❻ line 6 to Itaewon, Exit 3

This is a no-fuss, budget unisex hairdressing salon. The staff don't speak much English but they can cut hair the way you want.

GOLDEN EELSKIN Map p60   Leather Goods

☎ 795 3097; Itaewonno, Itaewon; ☻ 10am-8pm; ❻ line 6 to Itaewon, Exit 4

A good place to purchase eel-skin handbags, belts, wallets and purses. Eel-skin goods are an Itaewon speciality that make popular gifts. Owner Mr Kim is quietly persuasive but never hassles anyone.

ALAND Map pp56-7   Market

☎ 318 7654; Myeong-dong; ☻ 11am-10pm; ❻ line 4 to Myeong-dong, Exit 7

Not sure what the concept is here – expensive designer clothing is mixed in among vintage and garage-sale items and decorations that include old broken radios and used paint pots. It's hard to tell what's for sale and what's part of the decor. One fitting room is a battered old cupboard. The music is good and the whole store is so unusual that it's worth a visit.

NAMDAEMUN MARKET Map p87   Market

Myeong-dong, ❻ line 4 to Hoehyeon, Exit 5

You could spend all day in this awesome night-and-day market and not see it at all. Each section has hundreds of stalls. The market specialises in cheaper-range clothing and accessories for all ages and styles, but you can find anything under the sun here – from food and flowers to spectacles and seaweed. The seaweed may be natural or factory-made, and these days can be flavoured with wasabi, kimchi, green tea or even chocolate. Different sections of the market have differ-

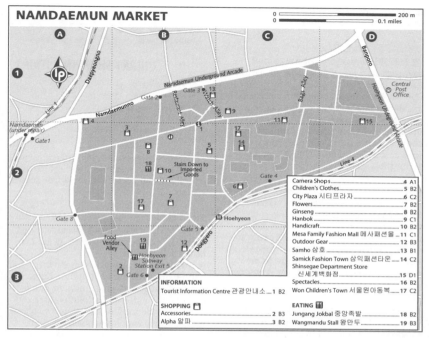

NAMDAEMUN MARKET

0 — 200 m
0 — 0.1 miles

ent opening hours – wholesalers are open all night and many shops open on Sunday.

Alpha (8am-7pm Mon-Sat, noon-6pm Sun) has two floors of toys and two floors of stationery. Samho (hours vary) has a jaw-dropping amount of fashion jewellery spread over two shopping sections, with some of it made on the premises. Mesa Family Fashion Mall (10am-5am), the market's first high-rise mall, has over 1000 shops on 16 floors.

For food, Noodle Alley has a dozen stalls selling *sujebi* (dough and shellfish soup), homemade *kalguksu* noodles and *bibimbap* (mixed rice, meat and vegetables) for around W4000. Restaurant Alley has a huge range of Korean food – all with plastic replicas outside to make choosing easy. A very popular wangmandu stall (8am-8pm) sells these large dumplings freshly made at a bargain price, while a little further on Jungang Jokbal (24hr) sells great-tasting pork hocks (a W15,000 plateful is heaps for two people). It comes with vegetable soup, lettuce wraps, a salad and side dishes.

In complete contrast to the raucous hustle and bustle of the market, wrap yourself in luxury inside Shinsegae Department Store

(310 1234; 10.30am-7.30pm, closed 1st & 3rd Mon). Down in the basement is the opulent supermarket (the cakes are works of art) with one food court, while another is up on the 11th floor together with Starbucks and a garden with seats to relax in after footslogging around the market below.

In the Hoehyeon underground arcade, shops selling secondhand LPs, CDs, cameras, stamps and coins are mixed in with boutiques, money-changers and shops selling bargain spectacles.

SUPREME OPTICAL Map p60 Optician
795 6423; Itaewonno, Itaewon; 9am-8pm, closed 2nd & 4th Tue; line 6 to Itaewon, Exit 4 Eye tests are free, and good-quality spectacles (lenses and frames) cost around W65,000, depending on the frames. The lenses are made on the spot and the spectacles are ready in just 15 minutes.

ABC MART Map pp56-7 Shoes
771 7777; Myeong-dong-gil, Myeong-dong; 11am-11pm; line 4 to Myeong-dong, Exit 8 The biggest and best store in Myeong-dong for casual shoes, this two-storey emporium

has thousands of the latest brand-name shoes for men and women.

DYNASTY TAILOR Map p60 — Tailor
☎ 3785 3035; dynastybruce@gmail.com; off Itaewonno, Itaewon; ⏰ 10am-8pm; ⊕ line 6 to Itaewon, Exit 4

Dynasty has a good reputation, and its suits are all handmade in the traditional way by expert tailors just a few doors down from the shop. Ask to see the workshop to learn about how the suits are made. Pure wool suits cost W250,000 to W300,000 and take about three days to make.

WASHINGTON SHIRT Map p60 — Tailored Shirts
☎ 796 1650; Itaewonno, Itaewon; ⏰ 11am-9pm; ⊕ line 6 to Itaewon, Exit4

Custom-made business-style shirts cost W28,000 to W55,000. Other nearby custom-shirt shops have names like New York, Houston and England. These tailor shops do a neat job, although shirt styles are very sober.

SOGONG Map pp56-7 — Underground Arcade
Myeong-dong; ⊕ line 1 or 2 to City Hall, Exit 6

Stores in this upmarket underground arcade sell ginseng, stationery, antiques, handicrafts, clothing and accessories. The arcade joins up with Myeong-dong Underground Arcade, so you could go subterranean shopping for weeks.

HONGDAE, SINCHON & YEOUIDO

Hongik University (known as Hongdae) is Korea's premier fine-art and design university, and the students sell their art and craft works at the weekend afternoon markets. Walk along Eoulmadang-gil in the evening to visit a string of boutiques selling one-of-a-kind clothes and accessories with a current accent on gypsy, eco and vintage styles. Specialist CD stores in Hongdae are also worth a browse.

Outside the famous Ewha Womans University in Sinchon, a busy, relatively traffic-free neighbourhood of small shops and stalls has been established that sells clothes, bags, shoes, accessories, haircuts and beauty treatments to the fashion-conscious female students. A street of shops near the subway specialises in amazing designer wedding outfits, while Baekkotnarae 5-gil offers a most eclectic range of small trendy shops.

top picks

QUIRKY SHOPPING STRIPS

- Garosu-gil (p72)
- Samcheong-dong-gil (p47)
- Donhwamunno (p43)
- Baekkotnarae 5-gil (opposite)
- Ahyeon-dong Wedding Street (below)

For something completely different, Seoul's biggest and best fish market is south of Yeouido – just follow your nose from Noryangjin subway station.

FREE MARKET Map p63 — Art & Craft Market
☎ 325 8553; cnr Wausan-gil & Eoulmadang 2-gil, Hongdae; ⏰ 1-6pm Sat in summer; ⊕ line 2 to Hongik University, Exit 6

A girl in ripped jeans selling her own hand-painted cigarette lighters; a Korean James Blunt sound-alike crooning into a microphone in front of adoring fans; hand-painted bottle tops, hand-painted suitcases, hand-painted everything; hairpins that look like fruit salad, wallets made of goat leather; a caricaturist, a knitter – all these can be found in this market, where stalls can be hired for W10,000. A similar Hope Market runs here on Sunday afternoons, but it's smaller and has no live music.

AHYEON-DONG WEDDING STREET
Map p64 — Bridal Stores
Sinchon; ⏰ 10am-8pm Mon-Fri; ⊕ line 2 to Ewha Womans University, Exit 4

The one-off designer dresses in the shop windows provide an amazing fashion show with plenty of revealing insights into Korean ideas of glamour. Glide down the aisle in billowing white embroidered lace, shimmer in a tight-fitting lilac gown glittering with thousands of sparkly sequins, or tango at the reception in a red Spanish-themed outfit with a sash. Local designers let their rococo imagination run riot here – if you loved *Project Runway* this street of dreams is for you.

BEAUTIFUL STORE Map p63 — Charity Shop
☎ 332 7778; B1, Merae Plaza, Hongdae; ⏰ 10.30am-6pm Mon-Sat; ⊕ line 2 to Hongik University, Exit 4

One of a pioneering and expanding chain of secondhand shops that raise money for charities in Korea and abroad. Beautiful Store has introduced the joys of op-shopping to Seoul with CDs, shoes and clothes that all sell for W3000. Find it half-way up the stairs of subway Exit 4. Another branch is near Bongeunsa (p71).

LUSH Map p63   Cosmetics
☎ 324 1292; Eoulmadang 2-gil, Hongdae; 🕑 noon-10pm Mon-Thu, 11am-11pm Fri-Sun; 🚇 line 2 to Hongik University, Exit 5
Lush cosmetics chain has been making a splash, setting up all over Seoul as well as around the world. It sells unpackaged but expensive soap cut off in big chunks as if it was cheese, and all the cosmetics are natural and handmade. Many look more like desserts than cosmetics. Some have novelty, if not bizarre, names such as 'Sonic Death Monkey Shower Gel'.

PAPAYA Map p64   Designer Boutique
☎ 392 3641; Sinchon; 🕑 11am-7pm; 🚇 line 2 to Ewha Womans University, Exit 2
Papaya, run by an artist and fashion de-signer, has survived in the fickle fashion industry for over 12 years, with a classical and sophisticated but still up-to-date sense of style. The shop crams an entire museum of artefacts into a tiny space.

BAEKKOTNARAE 5-GIL Map p64   Eclectic
Sinchon; 🕑 hours vary; 🚇 line 2 to Ewha Womans University, Exit 2
From the subway, walk down this narrow street off the main road to Ewha Womans University, and it's surprising what you can find: a Vietnamese noodle restaurant, a tai-lor shop, a bubble tea café, a shop selling handmade jewellery, a chocolatier, a pierc-ing and henna shop, a leather workshop, a tattoo and hair-braiding parlour, and a Goth and punk boutique – and that's all in the first 30 metres!

VOLKSWAGEN Map p63   Fashion
☎ 334 8817; Neumsaem 1-gil, Hongdae; 🕑 noon-11pm; 🚇 line 2 to Hongik University, Exit 5
This casual-wear boutique is bigger than most and has room for all the latest styles, as well as half a Volkswagen car inside. More conventional options than smaller Hongdae boutiques.

top picks

TOP SHOPPING STRIPS
- Insadong-gil (Map p50) Art and crafts
- Itaewonno (Map p60) Foreigner-friendly
- Myeong-dong (Map pp56–7) Fashion
- Namdaemun Market (Map pp56–7) General
- Dongdaemun Market (Map p40) Mainly fashion

NORYANGJIN FISH MARKET
Map p65   Fish Market
☎ 814 2211; 🕑 24hr; 🚇 line 1 to Noryangjin, Exit 1
Every kind of aquatic life form swims around in tanks and bowls in this old-fashioned, cov-ered market. Crabs, rays, tuna and shellfish are on display along with more exotic spe-cies such as sea cucumbers and sea squirts. The orange one is called *meongge* – we don't recommend trying it. Take-away platters of raw fish sell for W10,000, while giant prawns cost W15,000 a kilo. After exiting the subway station, turn right, and cross the railway tracks on the pedestrian bridge. See p107 for an excellent restaurant on the 2nd floor.

EUNHA Map p64   Hairdresser
☎ 362 7777; Ewhayeokdae-gil, Sinchon; cuts W30,000-40,000; 🕑 10am-7.30pm; 🚇 line 2 to Ewha Womans University, Exit 2
Easy to find at the main entrance to Ewha Womans University, styling rather than English is Eunha's strong point, but you can always people-watch rather than talk.

NAPKIN Map p63   Hairdresser
☎ 338 2773; Wausan-gil, Hongdae; men/ladies from W25,000/30,000; 🕑 10.30am-8.30pm Tue-Sun; 🚇 line 2 to Hongik University, Exit 5
A new concept in hairdressing, with a whimsical garden fantasy decor and ideas about 'cross-cultural communication that could lead to interesting conversations'. Staff speak English, and beauty treatments are available.

JAERAESIJANG Map p64   Market
Sinchon; 🚇 line 2 to Sinchon, Exit 8
This indoor market covers a mixed range of goods. It's quiet and out of the way, so there must be bargains around. You can watch rice cakes being made using tradi-tional methods. Upstairs is a *trot* dance club.

PURPLE RECORD Map p63   Music

☎ 336 3023; Wausan-gil, Hongdae; ⏱ 10.30am-11pm; ⓜ line 2 to Hongik University, Exit 5
An always-interesting selection of all music genres can be browsed in this independent CD and LP store. It appeals to local students and anyone with good musical taste.

RECORD FORUM Map p63   Music

☎ 323 9565; Wausan-gil, Hongdae; ⏱ 10am-11pm; ⓜ line 2 to Hongik University, Exit 5
The owner of this tiny shed of a CD store has so far survived the advent of free downloads thanks to his impeccable taste, which covers a wide spectrum of music.

KODAK PHOTO SHOP Map p63   Photography

☎ 334 2109; Saemulgyeol 2-gil, Hongdae; ⏱ 9am-9pm; ⓜ line 2 to Hongik University, Exit 5
With printers being sold for less than the cost of buying printer cartridges, photo shops are a disappearing breed, but this one keeps up to date on the digital front and can deal with all your photographic needs.

GANGNAM & JAMSIL

Apgujeong is a haughty *haute couture* shopping area famous for its designer boutiques, cat-walk clothing and dizzying prices. If a pair of shoes costs W500,000 here, they're probably secondhand. But the most extravagant items are probably the Rolls Royce cars. In Apgujeong or nearby Garosu-gil, young women in miniskirts and Westwood are as wafer-thin as their iPhones, which they chat on while nibbling a green-tea ice cream waffle and sipping an organic Guatemalan latte in an all-white, wellbeing café. Another must-have fashion accessory, tiny dogs with pink ears and maybe a green tail, poke their heads out of their owners' Louis Vuitton handbags. Shops are scattered over a considerable area.

Much less spread out are the shops in the underground COEX Mall (p68), another southside shopping highlight, which contains innumerable shops, including an excellent bookshop, a CD store and a department store. Expect to keep getting lost but don't expect too many bargains. It's a good place to go when it's raining.

BOON THE SHOP Map p68   Designer Clothing

☎ 317 0397; Gangnam; ⏱ 11am-8pm; ⓜ line 3 to Apgujeong, Exit 2

This slimmed-down version of Galleria has stairways and balconies around an atrium courtyard, providing a chic atmosphere as you browse lesser-known brand-name stores. Don't even think about taking a photograph – shopkeepers will think you're trying to copy their designs (styles appear in Apgujeong and a few days later they're out in Dongdaemun).

ANDRE KIM Map p68   Designer Clothing

☎ 540 3001; Dosandaero, Gangnam; clothes W4,000,000-5,000,000; ⏱ 9am-7pm; ⓜ line 3 to Sinsa, Exit 1
Haute couture from Korea's number-one eccentric, celebrity fashion designer doesn't come cheap, especially when it's tailor-made. This shop is full of the ageless Andre Kim's trademark flamboyant and extravagant dresses and gowns amongst the white statuary.

GALLERIA Map p68   Designer Clothing

☎ 344 9414; Apgujeongno, Gangnam; ⏱ 10.30am-8.30pm; ⓜ line 3 to Apgujeong, Exit 1
If you want to play Audrey Hepburn staring wistfully into Tiffany's, don a Helen Kaminski hat, try on a Stella McCartney dress or slip into a pair of Jimmy Choos; the east wing of fashion icon Galleria is the place to be. Dozens of top fashion-designer stores are packed into the two Galleria buildings, the west wing of which is covered in plastic discs that turn psychedelic at night.

BRAND NAME STREET

Map p68   Designer Fashion
Apgujeong, Gangnam; ⓜ line 3 to Apgujeong, Exit 2
Many global fashion icons such as Armani and Cardin have their flagship stores along this street. Rolls Royce and Samsonite have pitched camp here, too. No knock-offs, but prices will punch a hole in your plastic.

DAILY PROJECTS Map p68   Designer Fashion

☎ 3218 4072; Seolleungno, Gangnam; ⏱ 11am-8.30pm; ⓜ line 3 to Apgujeong, Exit 2
Come here for new ideas from young local designers bursting with ideas and talent. You never know what you might come across – sunglasses with eyebrows, belts that tell the time… Who knows? Find out by visiting this ahead-of-the-game fashion store.

SECOND HOTEL Map p68   Designer Goods

☎ 542 2229; Apgujeong, Gangnam; ⏱ 11am-8pm; ⊖ line 3 to Apgujeong, Exit 2
If you like way-out designers, try the Korean-American Suitman's stuff on the 2nd floor of this glass and concrete pyramid. He tries his hand at almost anything.

CHOI JUNG-IN Map p68   Designer Shoes

☎ 512 9637; Gangnam; ⏱ 11am-10pm; ⊖ line 3 to Apgujeong, Exit 2
Handmade designer shoes for women are sold here in a hard-to-find op-shop setting that deliberately has no sign – look for a black flag. The largest size is usually 38½ but shoes can be custom made by the shop's four master craftsmen. High heels are the speciality.

TECHNO MART Map p70   Electronics & General

☎ 3424 3000; ⏱ 10am-8pm, closed 2nd & 4th Tue; ⊖ line 2 to Gangbyeon, Exit 1
Electronic gear takes up seven floors of this high-rise next to Gangbyeon station. It's less overwhelming than Yongsan Electronics Market (p92) but you still have to check prices before you go, as many items have no price stickers. Mobile phones and computers are towards the top of the building. In the entry level basement is a fun food court (p111) and a fashion mall, while a supermarket is another level down. Up on the 10th floor is a cinema multiplex.

RODEO STREET Map p68   Fashion

Apgujeong, Gangnam; ⊖ line 3 to Apgujeong, Exit 2
Rodeo Street has piercing shops, 'now' items, the latest local eco-chic natural look and enough brand-name stores to make a walk along it worthwhile. But don't expect too much – Apgujeong's fashion shops are spread over a wide area, and there are lots of ordinary, everyday stores in between.

CENTRAL CITY MALL Map p68   Mall

☎ 6282 0114; www.centralcityseoul.co.kr; Gangnam; ⏱ 10am-10pm; ⊖ line 3 or 7 to Express Bus Terminal, Exit 7
A popular mall next to the express bus terminal that includes Shinsegae department store (☎ 3479 1234; ⏱ 10.30am-8pm), a food court, a six-cinema multiplex, endless underground shopping and Nolboo Yuhwangorijinheukgui (p110), a great duck restaurant.

HUCKLEBERRY FARMS

Map p68   Organic Produce
☎ 514 3800; Apgujeongno, Gangnam; ⏱ 10am-10pm; ⊖ line 3 to Apgujeong, Exit 2
Over 75% of the items sold in this New Zealand franchise supermarket are organic, and the range must be the best in Seoul. It's choice, bro.

GREATER SEOUL

Although they're out of the way, these markets are easily reached by subway and are well worth seeking out. The Gyeongdong, Janganpyeong and Seoul Folk Flea Markets are all unique and very Korean in their different ways. Yongsan Electronic Market deals in 'now' – TV screens the size of a truck and laptops that weigh less than a sandwich.

JANGANPYEONG ANTIQUES MARKET

Map pp36-7   Antiques
⏱ 10am-4.30pm Mon-Sat; ⊖ line 5 to Dapsimni, Exit 2
It's 'out with the old and in with the new' in Seoul, so ever wondered what happens to all the old stuff? It ends up here, stuffed inside over a hundred small shops housed in four separate arcades of antiques. The shops are so full of old furniture, paintings, pottery and stone statues that customers can barely squeeze inside. There are more Buddhas here than in Thailand. The atmosphere is very quiet compared to the other markets, but if you love to browse through old dusty treasures – from yangban (aristocrat) pipes and horsehair hats to wooden shoes, fish-shaped locks and embroidered status insignia – the arcades are easy to visit.

At the subway exit walk over to the orange-tiled Samhee 6 building behind the car park. A similar arcade on the left is Samhee 5. After visiting them, walk back to Exit 2 and go left along the main road for 10 minutes to reach a brown-tiled arcade, Janganpyeong, with another section behind it. You can't miss them with all the stonework stored permanently outside.

GYEONGDONG MARKET

Map pp36-7   Traditional Medicine
Jegi-dong; ⏱ 8am-6.30pm; ⊖ line 1 to Jegi-dong, Exit 2
You could spend hours exploring the biggest and best Asian medicine market in Korea. All the leaves, herbs, roots, flowers and mushrooms piled up in the shops and

stalls are medicinal. Bark is sold to be made into soup, and *jine* is a long millipede that is boiled to make a soup or else eaten dry – it is said to be good for backaches, and a handful costs W12,000. *Hwang-gi* is a white root that is mixed with rice and is supposed to prevent sweating.

Omija, both dried and undried, are tiny red berries that are soaked in boiling water overnight to produce a delicious 'five flavour' tea. Rose petals and chrysanthemum flowers are also made into tea. The tiny dried nashis are put into alcohol to aid digestion.

Cross the road, turn left at Shinhan Bank and then first right, and on the left is a 2nd-floor arcade with stalls piled high with ginseng and honey products. Underneath

CLOTHING SIZES

Women's clothing

Aus/UK	8	10	12	14	16	18
Europe	36	38	40	42	44	46
Japan	5	7	9	11	13	15
USA	6	8	10	12	14	16

Women's shoes

Aus/USA	5	6	7	8	9	10
Europe	35	36	37	38	39	40
France only	35	36	38	39	40	42
Japan	22	23	24	25	26	27
UK	3½	4½	5½	6½	7½	8½

Men's clothing

Aus	92	96	100	104	108	112
Europe	46	48	50	52	54	56
Japan	S		M	M		L
UK/USA	35	36	37	38	39	40

Men's shirts (collar sizes)

Aus/Japan	38	39	40	41	42	43
Europe	38	39	40	41	42	43
UK/USA	15	15½	16	16½	17	17½

Men's shoes

Aus/UK	7	8	9	10	11	12
Europe	41	42	43	44½	46	47
Japan	26	27	27½	28	29	30
USA	7½	8½	9½	10½	11½	12½

Measurements approximate only; try before you buy

BUG YOUR FRIENDS

Beondegi, a silkworm larvae snack, smells bad and tastes like earth, and is sure to delight your friends. It can be bought in a small tin at supermarkets and convenience stores and taken home as a souvenir gift.

and nearby are hundreds more food-cummedicine stalls, including some selling nuts and dried fruit. A little further on a couple of stalls sell natural medicines such as arrowroot by the cup (all W1000 a cup). They taste pretty bad, but the *maesil* (plum) one is said to improve blood pressure.

YONGSAN ELECTRONICS MARKET
Map pp36-7   Electronics

☎ 701 8200; Yongsan; ☷ 9.30am-7.30pm, partly closed 1st & 3rd Sun; ◉ line 1 Yongsan, Exit 3
If it plugs in you can find it at this geeky universe of high-tech marvels. Computer prices are usually marked but prices on other goods are lacking, so do what the locals do – check out the prices on the web before arriving. Leave the train station plaza via Exit 3, turn right, then right again and walk through the pedestrian overpass to enter the first building of Yongsan Electronics Town on the 3rd floor. Go down a floor to the popular Mac store, and near there another pedestrian overpass goes to the countless shops that line both sides of the main street.

SEOUL FOLK FLEA MARKET
Map pp36-7   Flea Market

☎ 3707 8001; Sinseol-dong; ☷ 10am-6pm; ◉ line 1 or 2 to Sinseol-dong, Exit 6 or 10
Relocated to a new two-storey building that already looks worn, the 1st-floor stalls at the back have a fascinating collection of artworks, collectables and general bric-a-brac. You could root through this lot for hours hunting for hidden treasures – wooden masks and ink drawings, vintage golf clubs, battered trumpets, elephant-shaped teapots, Beatles LPs, valve radio… Follow the signs from the subway station exit, it's only a few minutes' walk.

top picks

What's your recommendation? lonelyplanet.com/seoul

EATING

Eating out every night is a common habit for Seoulites. With thousands of restaurants and street stalls scattered throughout every neighbourhood, there is no problem finding somewhere to eat. Small, unpretentious restaurants serve up local food at very reasonable prices, and restaurants serving Italian and Japanese food are numerous. Western-style fast-food outlets are on every street, as are premium ice-cream parlours, convenience stores and bakeries.

Restaurants in Seoul often specialise in one or two dishes, so Seoulites usually decide what they want to eat and then choose which restaurant to visit. Most Korean-style restaurants offer a table and chairs option, but in some traditional places customers sit on floor cushions at low tables. Few restaurant staff speak English, but most restaurants have some English on the menu or else pictures or plastic replicas of the meals. The Language chapter can help, too.

Sampling the quirky delights of Korean food and drink is one of the joys of visiting Seoul. *The Wonderful World of Korean Food,* published by the Korea Tourism Organisation (KTO), is a free booklet that provides a superbly illustrated introduction to the country's food, snacks and drinks. Download it from www.visitkorea.or.kr. Explore more quirky delights at www.seouleats.com, an extensive expat blog with 'interesting food titbits, restaurant reviews and random tomfoolery'.

Italian food is super popular in Seoul – not just pizza chains but numerous small pasta restaurants that serve reasonably authentic meals, although often with a touch of fusion somewhere. These days pasta and pizza are more common than iconic Korean *bulgogi* (barbecued beef slices with lettuce wrap).

Lotteria is the local version of Western-style fast food, and offers *bulgogi* and kimchi burgers. Many Japanese-style restaurants serve sashimi or inexpensive cutlet, salad and soup sets. Budget Chinese restaurants cook up fried rice and *jajangmyeon* (noodles in a black bean sauce), a Chinese dish never seen outside Korea. Luxury hotels have upmarket and more genuine Chinese food.

Thai, Indian, Vietnamese, Middle Eastern and other ethnic restaurants are clustered in Itaewon, although more and more are opening up elsewhere – for example, French restaurants in Garosu-gil (see Map p68). Fusion restaurants usually provide an American/Italian menu with an Asian twist, such as spaghetti with red-chilli sauce and octopus. The possibilities are endless – anyone for *beondegi* (silkworm larvae) pizza or kimchi Caesar salad?

Drop into any department store or high-rise shopping mall to find a floor of inexpensive restaurants as well as a reasonably priced food court. For dessert, pop into one of the countless ice-cream or yoghurt parlours – Red Mango, Cold Stone Creamery, Baskin Robbins – or a gelati chain. Try the local dessert *patbingsu*, a red-bean, fruit and shaved-ice mixture. Seasonal fruit is for sale from the back of parked vans.

In Seoul, eating out (like everything else) is a group activity, and you don't see many people dining alone. A number of Korean meals, such as *bulgogi, jjimdak* (spicy chicken pieces with noodles) or *hanjeongsik* (a banquet of dishes) are not usually available for just one person.

Fill children up with *jajangmyeon, donkkaseu* (pork cutlet with rice and salad), *juk* (rice porridge), barbecued chicken, convenience-store sandwiches, bakery items, *hotteok* (a kind of pita bread with cinnamon and honey filling) and ice creams.

Some food fads fade fast. A few years ago bubble tea was all the rage, but now it's almost extinct, and the 'wellbeing' wave has swept in, with restaurants proclaiming the health benefits of real fruit juice, low-fat yoghurt and slow-cooked ginseng rice porridge. Seoul has also been struck by waffle and wine manias, but how long they will last is anyone's guess.

On the drinks front a full range of alcoholic and soft drinks is sold by convenience stores, while some cafés offer organic, premium, fair-trade coffee. Teahouses in Insadong still make traditional fruit teas, served hot or cold.

HISTORY

Every spring the Joseon kings headed to Seonnongdan (p76), an altar where they prayed for a good harvest. After the ritual, a special beef and vegetable soup (*seolleongtang*) was served to the assembled peasants. *Seolleongtang* is still popular today.

Budae jjigae (or *Johnsontang*) is a unique dish that originated in the hungry years after the Korean War, when tins of ham, sausages and baked beans from American army bases (such as Yongsan) were bought on the black market and mixed with noodles and vegetable scraps to make a meal. Try it at Nolboo (p108) in Hongdae.

The royal court was based in Seoul for over 500 years. Royal cuisine included *gujeolpan* (snacks wrapped in small pancakes) and *sinseollo* (hotpot). Generally the cooking style is not spicy and requires elaborate preparation and presentation.

ETIQUETTE

The custom in Seoul is that the host pays for everything – if you're invited out by Korean colleagues or friends, it's difficult or impossible to pay the bill or even contribute towards it. Going Dutch is as rare as decent cheese. Arguing about who should have the honour of paying the restaurant bill is a common scene at the cashier's desk.

A traditional Korean meal (breakfast, lunch and dinner) typically consists of meat, seafood or fish, served at the same time as soup, white rice and a collection of dipping sauces and *banchan,* the ubiquitous cold side dishes. Meals are usually eaten communally, so side dishes are placed in the centre of the table and diners eat a bit from one side dish (dunked in a sauce), a bite of the main dish, a little rice, a sip of soup and so on.

At some traditional restaurants, customers sit on cushions on the floor (the *ondol,* an underfloor heating system, is beneath). Before stepping up, always remove your shoes. Sitting with your back to a wall can be more comfortable. Nowadays most restaurants have a table-and-chairs option.

Koreans usually call out to attract a server's attention, so don't be shy to call out *'ajumma!'* or *'ajeosi!'*. Forget all that 'catching the waiter's eye' bunkum, it's OK to just bellow.

Nearly every restaurant in Seoul serves bottled or filtered water free of charge when you first arrive.

SPECIALITIES
Banchan

Korean cuisine is awash with side dishes, served with almost every meal. Kimchi cabbage or radish is the most popular, but there are many others, such as bean sprouts, black beans, dried anchovy, spinach, quail eggs, shellfish, lettuce, acorn jelly and tofu. You can always ask for a refill, and refusing ones you don't like reduces waste.

Barbecues

The many barbecue restaurants have a grill set into the tables on which to cook slices of beef *(bulgogi),* beef ribs *(galbi),* pork *(samgyeopsal),* chicken *(dak),* seafood or vegetables. The server often helps out with the cooking. The inexpensive *samgyeopsal* is bacon and can be fatty. These meals are usually only available in servings of two or more.

Bulgogi, galbi and *samgyeopsal* are served with a bunch of lettuce and sesame leaves. Take a leaf in one hand (or combine two leaves for different flavours) and with your other hand use your chopsticks to load it with meat, side dish flavourings, garlic and sauces. Then roll it up into a little package and eat it in one go. *Tteokgalbi* (or *neobiani*) is a giant marinaded beef patty. Fish such as *samchi* (a superior type of mackerel) are often grilled on a barbecue.

Bibimbap

Bibimbap is a mixture of rice, vegetables and minced beef with an egg on top, which tastes much better than it sounds. Thoroughly mix it all together with a spoon before digging in. It comes with a generous dollop of *gochujang* (red-chilli paste) so remove some to

KOREAN FOOD & CULTURE

If you are what you eat, then Koreans have both a spicy and a bland side to their characters. It's often the hot, spicy food that grabs the headlines, even though there are plenty of menu options with subtle rather than strong flavours, including *gimbap* (sushi) and *mandu* (dumplings), *seolleongtang* (beef broth), *kalguksu* (shellfish soup), *juk* (rice porridge) and *tteok* (rice cakes). But perhaps best-selling Japanese novelist Haruki Murakami was right when he said, 'Pickled crabs represent the essence of Korean culture'. These are small crabs eaten whole, shell and all. Somehow it's the uncompromising, take-it-to-extremes aspects of both Korean food and culture that stay in a visitor's memory, like that *jjimdak* (spicy chicken stew) which nearly blew the roof of your mouth off.

METAL CHOPSTICKS

Although surrounded by nations that use chopsticks made of plastic or wood, Seoulites use stainless steel chopsticks. Why? One explanation is that the Joseon kings, ever vigilant about security, insisted on using silver chopsticks, as silver was thought to tarnish in the presence of toxins. The tradition caught on and was passed down to the *yangban* (aristocrats) and copied by the common people, who substituted cheaper base metal for silver.

make it less spicy. *Bibimbap* is often served with bean sprout soup, but don't mix that in. *Sanchae bibimbap* is made with mountain-grown greens; *dolsot bibimbap* is served in a stone hotpot.

Breakfast

Traditional Korean breakfasts usually consist of soup, rice, kimchi and a few leftovers. More Western-style breakfasts are available in hotels, fast-food outlets, cafés and the ubiquitous bakeries, some of which have a few tables and chairs. Most convenience stores sell the basics – coffee, tea, sandwiches, fruit and pastries. Look out for 'Brunch' signs outside cafés – a recent trend.

Chicken

Samgyetang is a small whole chicken stuffed with glutinous rice, red dates, garlic and ginseng root, and boiled in broth. *Dakgalbi* is pieces of spicy chicken, cabbage, other vegetables and finger-sized pressed rice cakes, which are all grilled at your table. *Jjimdak* is a spiced-up mixture of chicken pieces, transparent noodles, potatoes and other vegetables. Many informal *hof* (pubs) serve inexpensive barbecued or fried chicken to accompany the beer. Street stalls offer chicken kebabs with various sauces.

Fish & Seafood

Seafood (*haemul*) and fish (*saengseon*) are generally served broiled, grilled or in a soup, but *hoe* (raw fish) has many fans in Seoul. Fish are usually served whole with both the head and guts. Visit Noryangjin fish market or the West Sea islands to indulge in raw fish, steamed crab, grilled prawns or barbecued shellfish feasts. *Nakji* (octopus) is usually served in a spicy sauce, but you might want to avoid the raw version of *sannakji* (baby octopus), still wriggling when brought to the table. *Haemultang* is a seafood soup containing so much chilli that even locals have to mop their brows.

Desserts

Desserts are not common in Seoul, but sometimes a piece of fruit, coffee or traditional tea is served at the end of the meal. Ice-cream, yoghurt and waffle parlours are springing up everywhere, not to mention all the cafés and bakeries. From being a dessert desert, Seoul is becoming a dessert-lovers utopia.

Gimbap

Inexpensive sushi is popular for lunch. The Korean style is cold rice rolled in dried seaweed with strips of carrot, radish, egg and

DOS & DON'TS

Dos

- Do pour drinks for others if you notice that their glasses are empty. It is polite to use both hands when pouring.
- Most Koreans use a spoon for the rice and soup, and chopsticks for the side dishes.
- Knives are not supplied, so if you're trying to cut something and your spoon or chopsticks are not up to the job, ask for scissors or a knife.

Don'ts

- Don't start (or finish) your meal before your seniors or elders.
- Don't touch food with your fingers (except when handling leaves for wrapping food).
- Don't pick up bowls and plates from the table to eat from them.
- Don't blow your nose at the table.
- Don't pour your own drinks – allow someone else to do it.
- Don't tip.

ham in the centre. 'Nude' *gimbap* has no dried seaweed wrap. *Samgak gimbap* (triangular sushi) is nowhere near as famous as its circular brother, but is cold rice garnished with marinaded beef, chicken, tuna or kimchi, wrapped in *gim* (dried seaweed). Sold only in convenience stores, it's a delicious and easy-to-eat snack once you've mastered the art of taking it out of the plastic.

Hanjeongsik

Head to Insadong for a banquet for two or more people. It includes fish, meat, soup, *dubu jjigae* (spicy tofu stew), *doenjang jjigae* (soybean-paste stew), rice, noodles, steamed egg, shellfish and lots of cold vegetable side dishes, followed by a cup of tea. It's invariably too much to eat, so *jeongsik,* with slightly fewer main dishes, may be a better option.

Jjigae

These stews are thicker than soups and served sizzling in a stone hotpot with plenty of spices. Popular versions are made with tofu *(dubu jjigae),* soybean paste *(doenjang jjigae)* and kimchi. *Beoseotjeongol* is a less spicy but highly recommended mushroom hotpot. The mushrooms served in Seoul are great.

Juk

Traditional, slow-cooked rice porridge (the rice is cooked with much more water than normal) that is mixed with a wide choice of ingredients has recently become popular as a healthy, well-being food that is not spicy. Joseon kings used to scoff *juk* as an easily digested pre-breakfast snack.

Kimchi

Traditionally, kimchi was made to preserve vegetables and ensure proper nutrition during the harsh winters, but it's now eaten year-round and adds zest, zip and a long list of health benefits to any meal. A cold side dish of the spicy national food is served at nearly every Korean meal whether it's breakfast, lunch or dinner. Generally made with pickled and fermented cabbage seasoned with garlic and red chilli, it can be made from cucumbers, white radish or other vegetables. Kimchi is not always vegetarian as it can have anchovies added. Many local families have a special kimchi refrigerator to keep it at the correct temperature and away from other food. *Mul*

FOR DAREDEVILS

- *Beondegi* (silkworm larvae)
- *Bosintang* (dog-meat soup)
- *Doganitang* (cow-kneecap soup)
- *Sannakji* (raw, squirming baby octopus)
- *Yukhoe* (seasoned raw minced meat)

kimchi is a cold, gazpacho-type minimalist soup and not spicy.

Mandu

An inexpensive and mild favourite with visitors, these small dumplings (*wangmandu* are large ones) are filled with minced meat, seafood, vegetables and herbs. They are often freshly made to a special recipe by restaurant staff during quiet times. Fried, boiled or steamed, they make a tasty snack or addition to a meal. *Manduguk* is *mandu* in soup with seaweed and makes a perfect light lunch.

Noodles

Naengmyeon is chewy buckwheat noodles in an icy, sweetish broth, garnished with shredded vegetables and topped with half a hard-boiled egg – add red-chilli paste or *gyeoja* (mustard) to taste. Popular in summer, it is often eaten after a meat dish like *galbi* as a kind of dessert.

Japchae is a foreigner-friendly Chinese-style dry dish of transparent noodles stir-fried in sesame oil with strips of egg, meat and vegetables. It's sometimes served as a side dish or by royal-cuisine restaurants. *Kalguksu* is thick, hand-cut noodles usually served in a bland clam and vegetable broth. *Ramyeon* is instant noodles often served in a hot chilli soup. Seoulites believe in fighting fire with fire and claim it's a good cure for hangovers.

Pajeon & Bindaetteok

Pajeon are thick, savoury pancakes the size of pizzas, often filled with spring onions and seafood. *Bindaetteok* are just as big and even more filling, made from ground mung beans with various fillings and fried until a crispy, golden brown.

Snacks

Waffles are the current favourite and spreading like wildfire, while *hotteok* (either a doughnut or pitta bread with a cinnamon and honey filling) is a traditional snack. Street stalls also sell *bung-eoppang,* a fish-shaped snack that is crispy on the outside and has red-bean paste inside. *Delimanjoo* are custard-filled minicakes sold in subway stations, but they're facing fierce competition from bakery cake counters.

Tteok (pronounced 'dock') are rice cakes, a bland, unsweetened and healthy alternative to sugary Western cakes, flavoured with dried fruit, nuts and beans.

In Insadong try *kkultarae,* fine threads of honey and cornflour wrapped around a nut sauce, and *daepae saenggang yeot,* a huge slab of toffee shaved off in thin, curly strips and stuck on a stick.

Soups

Soups (*tang* or *guk*) are another Seoul speciality and a highlight of Korean cuisine. 'A meal without soup is like a face without eyes.' They vary from spicy seafood and tofu soups to bland broths such as *galbitang* and *seolleongtang.* *Gamjatang* is a spicy peasant soup with meaty bones and a potato. Hot tip: if a soup is too spicy, tip in some rice.

VEGETARIANS & VEGANS

Seoulites love meat, fish and seafood. Very few locals are vegetarian, although rice and vegetables make up a considerable part of their diet. Seoul's best vegetarian restaurants include Gamrodang (opposite) in Samcheong-dong, Sanchon (p101) and Dimibang (p102) in Insadong, and Pulhyanggi (p110) near Apgujeong. The excellent department-store basement food courts and Indian restaurants always offer some vegetarian meals.

It can be a struggle for vegetarians in ordinary restaurants, but order *bibimbap* or *dolsot bibimbap* without the meat (or egg), *beoseotjeongol* (mushroom hotpot), *doenjang jjigae,* *dubu jjigae* (spicy tofu soup), *jajangmyeon* (noodles and sauce), vegetable *pajeon,* and pumpkin *juk* (rice porridge). If all else fails you can eat a meal of rice and vegetable side dishes, but be warned: quite often these meals have small amounts of meat, seafood or fish added for flavour, so you're likely to be picking bits out. The same is true of kimchi.

PRACTICALITIES
Opening Hours

Most restaurants open every day, usually from 11am until 10pm, but times do vary considerably, so opening hours are given for every restaurant in this chapter. Night owls can always find food at 24-hour fast-food outlets, convenience stores and the odd restaurant.

How Much?

Prices are generally reasonable, especially for Korean food. Convenience stores sell *samgak gimbap* for about W700 and sandwiches for W1700. *Mandu, ramyeon, tteokbokki* (rice cakes in a sweet and spicy sauce) and *gimbap* are also budget fodder at W2000 or less. A meal of street snacks costs less than W5000, while budget Korean diners, food court meals and fast-food outlets charge around W5000. *Bibimbap,* barbecued chicken and *samgyeopsal* is under W10,000 per person, while *jjimdak* and *samgyetang* cost W12,000 to W15,000. *Bulgogi* and *galbi* are both beef and cost W15,000 to W20,000 per person. *Hanjeongsik* (banquets) vary in price depending on what is included and range from W15,000 to W50,000 or more, while royal court cuisine usually costs around W50,000. Typical mains at Western-style restaurants cost W25,000, but expect to pay W35,000 or more at top hotels.

Booking Tables

It is not usually necessary to book tables unless you want your own private room or are in a large group. Telephone numbers of restaurants are given, but few restaurants can find anyone who speaks English, so it's worth asking your hotel receptionist to make the booking for you.

Tipping

Tipping is not a Korean custom and is not expected. Restaurants catering to wealthy businessmen and top-end hotels may add 21% to the bill (10% service charge then 10% VAT).

Self-catering

Small convenience stores, such as Mini Stop, 7-Eleven, Buy the Way, GS25 and Family Mart, are never more than a few hundred me-

PRICE GUIDE	
$$$	mains over W15,000
$$	mains W7000-15,000
$	mains under W7000

tres apart. They open 24 hours a day. Pop into one whenever you want a cheap ice cream, a breakfast snack, a quick and easy lunch, a soft drink or a beer. Bakeries are almost as common. Huckleberry Farms (p91) in Apgujeong sells organic food and drinks.

Department-store basements house supermarkets. Other useful ones include:

Home Plus Express (Map p40; ☎ 737 9994; Gwanghwamun; ⏱ 9am-11pm Mon-Sat; 🚇 line 5 to Gwanghwamun, Exit 7) A downtown supermarket with all the necessities.

Koamart (Map p60; ☎ 797 1703; Beodeunamu-gil, Itaewon; ⏱ 9am-10pm; 🚇 line 6 to Itaewon, Exit 4) A hard-to-find supermarket behind Gecko's Terrace in Itaewon.

GWANGHWAMUN

While Insadong is Seoul's top restaurant patch, more and more Korean restaurants are opening in Samcheong-dong to the north, alongside small snack eateries and specialist cafés selling top-quality coffee and waffles. Downtown Gwanghwamun restaurants specialise in lunch for the many office workers, and can be crowded around noon. Classic budget diners offer fast food Korean-style, while simple *kalguksu*, *bindaetteok* or conveyer-belt sushi meals are other options.

GAMRODANG Map p40 — Temple Food $$$
☎ 3210 3397; Hwagae-gil; courses from W25,000; ⏱ noon-9.30pm; 🚇 line 3 to Anguk, Exit 1
Chef Youn Hie-hong offers a series of small but wonderfully original vegetarian dishes that are bulging with healthy ingredients such as *hamcho*, a salty green herb that grows near the sea, and *deodeok*. Loosely based on Buddhist temple food, the carefully prepared items are full of varied and subtle flavours. Every course is special – the salad with a seven-herb dressing, the fragrant rice wrapped in lotus leaf, the pink cactus juice kimchi, the fried mushrooms in citron juice, the tofu sandwich, and the pink bamboo salt. The children's menu is W12,000. Don't be put off by the tatty exterior.

ANJIP Map p40 — Korean $$$
☎ 3672 7070; off Gyedong-gil; meals W20,000-40,000; ⏱ 11.30am-10pm Mon-Sat; 🚇 line 3 to Anguk, Exit 2
Sit on embroidered cushions in a traditional-style private room and enjoy a typical *hanjeongsik* of over 20 seasonal dishes. With so many plates to bring, the staff are often rushing around. The *bulgogi*, steamed egg, spicy cockles and pumpkin soup are particularly good, and fruit and cinnamon tea finish the feast off nicely.

BOSO Map p40 — Banquet $$$
☎ 3675 5551; Gyedong-gil; set meals W25,000; ⏱ 11.30am-10pm; 🚇 line 3 to Anguk, Exit 2
Gastronomic adventurer? Come to Boso for a more-than-you-can-eat banquet. Tourists don't frequent the place, and the food is uncompromisingly Korean, including raw fish, raw prawns, eel and ray. There's also *galbi*, a whole pumpkin cooked with sticky rice, nuts and a sweet sauce inside, *japchae*, soup, porridge, salad, vegetables, stuffed peppers, octopus, fruit, tea… Oh yes and steamed egg, *dubu jjigae*, mini-*pajeon*, *mul kimchi*… The helpful owner speaks English.

SOLMOEMAEUL Map p40 — Korean $$
☎ 720 0995; Samcheong-dong-gil; meals W10,000-22,000, set courses W20,000 & W26,000; ⏱ noon-10pm; 🚇 line 3 to Anguk, Exit 1
Sit on the floor or on chairs on the narrow balcony to enjoy an excellent multicourse meal for W20,000 that includes *bulgogi*. The *gujeolpan* is a speciality with pink radish wraps, as is the *pajeon* and the sprouty version of *bibimbap*. A bit of a walk from the subway but customers tend to need some exercise after this generous Korean feast.

HOEJEONCHOBAP Map p40 — Sushi $$
회전초밥; ☎ 735 1748; saucers W3300; ⏱ 11.30am-2pm & 4.30-9pm; 🚇 line 5 to Gwanghwamun, Exit 8
Squeeze yourself into this tiny conveyor-belt sushi joint to enjoy Japanese-style raw fish with wasabi. It's on the expensive side – this is downtown, and not a student area.

SANGGAMMAMA TTEOKGALBI Map p40 — Korean $$
☎ 720 7621; Samcheong-dong-gil; meals W9000-20,000; ⏱ 11am-9pm; 🚇 line 2 to Anguk, Exit 1
Order the *ssambap jeongsik* for an enjoyable meal of pork *tteokgalbi* (minced patties), steamed egg, *doenjang jjigae,* hotpot rice, salad wraps and side dishes.

TOSOKCHON SAMGYETANG Map p40 — Korean $$
☎ 737 7446; meals W13,000; ⏱ 10am-10pm; 🚇 line 3 to Gyeongbokgung, Exit 2

JONGNO STREET EATS

Mingle with the evening crowds on both sides of Jongno (Bell St), which runs straight and wide through the heart of Seoul. You can make a dinner of snacks as you stroll past the many food carts.

Near Insadong-gil you can find *ppopgi* (뽑기), a big, round, freshly made candy. Sugar is boiled up in a big spoon, then squashed with a flattener, stamped with a pattern and jammed onto a stick. A common sweet snack is *hotteok*, a small, thick pancake with peanuts and syrup inside. Another delicious one is *kkukwappang* (꾹와빵), made in a hotplate with lots of round holes – it's a mini-*hotteok* but filled with red-bean mush and pumpkin seeds.

Look out for a young guy selling his own homemade sausages, which he claims are 'the second-best in Seoul'. He sells 200 of them every night. One of his BBQ gourmet pork sausages with lashings of salad and sauces in a roll is almost a meal in itself.

Tteokbokki, pressed rice cakes in a spicy red sauce mixed with vegetables, noodles, *eomok* (processed seafood) or almost anything, is a Korean crowd pleaser. But number one for foreigners is probably the BBQ chicken kebabs – only ask for spicy if you want it really spicy! One stall sells a chicken kebab that is a massive 52cm long. Also keep an eye out for small roast potatoes. Or how about roasted chestnuts, *gimbap* (sushi roll), *pajeon* (savoury pancake), dried squid, or the dangerously addictive *dakkoyakki* (Japanese-style octopus balls)?

For dessert you can't beat a slice of pineapple on a stick, or a waffle with honey and ice cream for W1000 (less than US$1). It's not just the taste and the speedy service that bring the customers pouring in night after night: everything is a bargain at the Jongno food carts – some stalls even offer you *sungnyung* (burnt rice tea) for free (referred to as 'service').

Despite the crowds, the *samgyetang* arrives fast and still bubbling. Tip some salt and pepper together into a small saucer and use it as a dip. This 30-year-old icon is housed in a sprawling *hanok* (traditional house), and for many locals – and even ex-presidents – it's the best in Seoul. Black chicken *samgyetang* is W19,000. Walk straight for 100m from Exit 2, turn left at the GS25 convenience store and it's on your left.

JONGNO BINDAETTEOK
Map p40   Korean $$
☎ 737 1857; meals W7000; ⏰ noon-2am; ⊙ line 5 to Gwanghwamun, Exit 8
Don't let the scruffy and dingy decor put you off – the freshly made gourmet *bindaetteok* is crispy and golden and bursting with seafood (*haemul*) or meat (*gogi*). It goes perfectly with a glass or two or three of *makgeolli*.

SAMCHEONG-DONG SUJEBI
Map p40   Sujebi $
☎ 735 2965; Samcheong-dong-gil; meals W6000; ⏰ 11.30am-9pm; ⊙ line 3 to Anguk, Exit 1
A no-frills, no-nonsense restaurant that's famous for its *sujebi*, big dough flakes in a mild soup of sliced vegetables and shellfish. *Dongdongju* (fermented rice wine) goes well with the meal – in fact, for some diners the *sujebi* is just an excuse to enjoy some *dongdongju*.

SEOMMAEUL MILBATJIP Map p40   Korean $
성마을밀밭집; ☎ 723 5922; meals W6000; ⏰ 11am-9pm; ⊙ line 5 to Gwanghwamun, Exit 7
This modern, clean restaurant offers a simple no-fuss meal of *kalguksu* – lots of baby clams in a soup with thick, hand-cut long noodles that represent long life. A minimalist meal with subtle flavours, this makes for a change from the usually spicy Korean fare – a fact appreciated by the restaurant's many fans.

JILSIRU TTEOK CAFÉ Map p40   Tteok $
☎ 741 0258; Donhwamunno; www.kfr.or.kr; tteok/set W1500/5000; ⏰ 9am-9pm; ⊙ line 1, 3 or 5 to Jongno 3-ga, Exit 6
The soft, delicately flavoured hand-made gourmet rice cakes with all sorts of unusual flavours such as citron or coffee. Traditional teas are W6000. Upstairs is a museum (admission W3000; ⏰ 10am-5pm Mon-Sat, noon-5pm Sun) with displays of 50 types of rice cakes with all their different colours, flavourings, shapes and sizes, plus the utensils to make them.

GIMBAPGWAMANDUSAI
Map p40   Gimbap $
☎ 755 5559; meals W2000-4000; ⏰ 6am-midnight; ⊙ line 1 or 2 to City Hall, Exit 2
This simple, neat and absolutely typical budget Korean diner has an English menu and specialises in *gimbap*, including nude *gimbap*, but also serves up big bowls of *bibimbap* as well as noodles, homemade dumplings and *sujebi*.

EATING GWANGHWAMUN

INSADONG & DAEHANGNO

Insadong is home to hordes of traditional-style restaurants displaying giant boards plastered with photographs of their meals, which are generally good old-fashioned Korean food, just like mama used to cook on the rare occasions when she had the time. *Hanjeongsik* restaurants serve a banquet of items with as many as 20 or more Korean dishes including side dishes. Don't try to eat everything. Vegetarian restaurants include one that serves Buddhist temple food, another that specialises in unusual herbs and another with Taiwanese connections. A couple of posh restaurants, one on top of a skyscraper and one in a *hanok*, serve slightly fusion European food and wines. Brits desperate for curry, naan and lassis can head to Namaste (p102) under Jongno Tower.

The Daehangno student district is more famous for theatres than restaurants, but has an excellent new *shabu shabu* (steamboat) restaurant and a classic Korean-style bar serving up the quintessential Korean combo of barbecue chicken and draught beer.

MIN'S CLUB Map p50   Western Fusion $$$

☎ 733 2966; off Insadong-gil, Insadong; sets W60,000-75,000; ⏰ noon-2.30pm & 6-11.30pm; ◉ line 3 to Anguk, Exit 6

Old-world architecture meets new-world cuisine in this classy restaurant housed in a beautifully restored 1930s *hanok* that offers European-Korean meals (more European than Korean). The menu covers classics such as lobster, crab and foie gras, all of which can be matched to the bountiful cellar's 200 wines, many of which are French.

TOP CLOUD RESTAURANT
Map p50   Western $$$

☎ 2230 3000; 33rd fl, Jongno Tower, Insadong; meals W40,000-85,000, buffet W45,000; ⏰ noon-midnight; ◉ line 1, 3 or 5 to Jonggak, Exit 3

European-style fine dining is combined with knockout views in this restaurant perched above downtown Seoul. The atmosphere is subdued but the black-clad staff, the flickering candles and the classy, mainly French food make Top Cloud the place to go for a special treat. Afterwards, relax in the bar (p115) to the sound of live jazz with the city lights spread out under you.

SAMARKAND

Within the vast Dongdaemun market is Samarkand (Map p84; ☎ 2277 4261; off Beorumul-gil, Dongdaemun; starters W2000, mains W10,000; ⏰ 9am-midnight; ◉ line 2, 4 or 5 to Dongdaemun Station, Exit 12), a laid-back, family-run, home-cooking Uzbekistan restaurant. Sitting in the armchairs with Uzbeki pop DVDs on the TV is like eating in someone's living room. The soups (*shurpa* has meat, solid vegetables and chickpeas in a tasty broth) and kebabs (*shashlik* is minced meat served on a huge skewer) are great, and *lepeshka* bread goes well with the meal.

SANCHON Map p50   Vegetarian $$$

☎ 735 0312; off Insadong-gil, Insadong; set lunch/dinner W22,000/39,000; ⏰ 11.30am-10pm; ◉ line 3 to Anguk, Exit 6

The atmosphere created by the Buddhist artworks, music and lanterns makes this a very special restaurant. In addition, the owner, Kim Yun-sik – an ex-monk – is an expert on Korean Buddhist temple food, and the vegetarian marinades, glazes and seasonings are unique. The same meal of 20 small courses is served at both lunch and dinner. The prices may not be very Buddhist, but the food and atmosphere are heavenly. Dancers and drummers perform nightly at 8pm.

GOGUNG Map p50   Bibimap $$

☎ 736 3211; Ssamzie Bldg, Insadong-gil, Insadong; meals from W8000; ⏰ 11am-10pm; ◉ line 3 to Anguk, Exit 6

Hidden away in the basement of the Ssamzie building is this unusually smart and stylish restaurant, with live traditional music on Friday nights at 7pm. It specialises in Jeonju (capital of Jeollabuk province) *bibimbap*, which is fresh and garnished with nuts, but contains raw minced beef. If that puts you off, choose the *dolsot bibimbap*, which is served in a stone hotpot. Both come with side dishes. Another Jeonju speciality is *moju*, a sweet, cinnamon homebrew drink – you should definitely try it. Also on the menu is an 11-dish royal banquet (W35,000).

JIRISAN Map p50   Traditional Korean $$

☎ 723 4696; Insadong 3-gil, Insadong; meals from W10,000; ⏰ noon-10pm; ◉ line 3 to Anguk, Exit 6

A popular, authentic restaurant and a great place to try *dolsotbap* (hotpot rice,

LOST IN TRANSLATION

One Insadong restaurant has 'Mother hand tasty blue director of a bureau' on its menu. You might wonder what sort of cannibalistic meal this is, but it's a translation of '*Eomeoni son mat jeong guk jang*'. It all makes sense (kind of) if you know that *son* can mean 'hand' or 'handmade', that *cheong* (easily confused with *jeong*) is blue and that *jang* can mean either 'soup' or 'office manager'. The meal is actually vegetarian – soybean-paste soup.

In Seoul Grand Park a canteen offers 'Magnetic field a bowl of rice capped', but it's actually *jajang deopbap* (rice and *jajang* sauce topped with a fried egg) in disguise. The mistranslation arises because *jagijang* (similar to *jajang*) means 'magnetic field'.

W10,000). Various ingredients are added to the rice, and you mix it all up in a separate bowl with the sauces and side dishes – a do-it-yourself *bibimbap*. Pour the weak burnt-rice tea from the kettle into the stone pot and put the lid on, then drink it at the end of the meal.

SALE E PEPE Map p52 — Italian Fusion $$
☎ 745 2077; Maronie-gil, Daehangno; mains W15,000; ☻ 11am-2am; ◉ line 4 to Hyehwa, Exit 2
Up on the 2nd floor, the Gaudí-style dome adds a Mediterranean feel to this Italian fusion terraced Daehangno restaurant, which serves wines and *soju* (a Korean liquor similar to vodka) mixed with fresh juice – kiwifruit and pineapple are popular. Every evening the mood is enhanced by live music.

SOSIM Map p50 — Korean $$
☎ 734 4388; Yulgongno, Insadong; meals W7000-20,000; ☻ 11.30am-9.30pm Mon-Sat; ◉ line 3 to Anguk, Exit 6
A small, rustic, home-cooking basement restaurant that serves mainly vegetables, including many types of mushrooms, in varied sauces. Fish is added for non-vegetarians. The W20,000 set course is the best meal, but is overpriced. The helpful owner speaks some English.

DIMIBANG Map p50 — Herbal $$
☎ 720 2417; Insadong 3-gil, Insadong; meals W8000, courses W13,000-35,000; ☻ noon-10pm Mon-Sat; ◉ line 3 to Anguk, Exit 6
This owner has written books about medicinal herbs and the meals and drinks are full of them, especially *hamcho*. The set courses are popular, but *sanyakjuk* (herbal rice porridge) and *yakbap* (medicinal hotpot rice) are both subtly flavoursome. The herbal tea and alcoholic herbal brews are special too.

NAMASTE Map p50 — Indian $$
☎ 2198 3301; World Food Court, Jongno Tower, Insadong; meals W5,000-20,000; ☻ 11am-10pm; ◉ line 1 to Jonggak, Exit 3
This genuine Indian restaurant tempts downtown office workers with its large menu of *banchan*-style thalis, lassis, naan breads and all the usual Indian favourites like tandoori and masala tea. Lunchtimes, with W10,000 thalis on offer, can be hectic.

SEOJEONG RESTAURANT
Map p50 — Korean $$
서정; ☎ 735 8811; off Insadong-gil, Insadong; Hanjeongsik from W10,000; ☻ noon-2pm & 6-10pm; ◉ line 3 to Anguk, Exit 6
Tucked away off the beaten track, this traditional restaurant serves up a budget banquet of 14 dishes in private rooms decked out with scrolls, ceramics and paper-screen doors. Sit on legless chairs or cushions and enjoy *japchae*, *pajeon*, beans, anchovies, chives, pickled walnuts, fish, rice, salad, two soups and plenty of vegetables.

OSEGYEHANG Map p50 — Vegetarian $$
☎ 735 7171; Insadong 4-gil, Insadong; meals W7000-14,000; ☻ noon-3.30pm & 5-9pm; ◉ line 3 to Anguk, Exit 6
A clean, modern vegetarian restaurant run by members of a Taiwanese religious sect. The food combines all sorts of mixtures and flavours, and is proving to be popular. The pumpkin slices garnished with cinnamon and nuts tastes much better than it sounds, and the barbecue-meat-substitute dish is flavoursome. The food is original and worth trying – although noodles in red-bean soup could be a step too far. Non-alcoholic beer and wine is served.

HWANGGEUMJEONG
Map p50 — Korean BBQ $$
☎ 762 7910; Gahoero; meals W10,000; ☻ 10am-10pm; ◉ line 3 to Anguk, Exit 2

Sit inside or outside at this friendly neighbourhood barbecue joint, where diners grill up pork ribs or strips to eat with salad and side dishes. Order rice or *naengmyeon* for a more substantial meal. Just a dozen steps from the subway exit.

BONGCHU JJIMDAK Map p52 Chicken $$

☎ 3676 6981; Maronie-gil, Daehangno; platters for 2 W19,000; ⏱ 11am-midnight; ⊕ line 4 to Hyehwa, Exit 1 or 2

A popular *jjimdak* restaurant with paper lanterns and Zen-style decor. It offers large platters of freshly cooked chicken pieces, potatoes, carrots and onions on top of noodles, and a spicy sauce with the kick of a horse. You need two people for this party food.

ZEN ZEN Map p52 Korean BBQ $$

☎ 3675 1150; Maronie 2-gil, Daehangno; meals from W8000; ⏱ 11am-11pm; ⊕ line 4 to Hyehwa, Exit 2

Eat inside or outside at this large establishment specialising in *samgyeopsal*, often eaten with *naengmyeon*. *Dwaeji galbi* (barbecued pork ribs) is another option. The special marinades and the choose-your-own-salad-wrappings are the special features in this modern Zen steel and glass box, hidden away on the 1st floor.

BEER OAK Map p52 Chicken $$

☎ 747 9982; Daehangno; whole chicken W13,000; ⏱ 3.30pm-1.30am; ⊕ line 4 to Hyehwa, Exit 3

Always popular and noisy, Beer Oak serves delicious barbecue chicken roasted on a spit over a wood fire along with cheap beer (W2500 for a big glass). Order *sogeumgui* for a whole chicken on its own or *modeum-gui* for a whole chicken cut up and served on a platter with pasta, pressed rice cakes, corn and raisins, covered in a sweet chilli sauce.

CHILGAPSAN Map p50 Korean $$

칠갑산; ☎ 730 7754; Sambong-gil; meals W5000-13,000; ⏱ 11.30am-10pm; ⊕ line 1 to Jonggak, Exit 2

This convivial, sit-on-floor-cushions restaurant's specialty is excellent *neobiani* (너비아니), a beef patty the size of a small pizza. Meant for sharing, it comes with a dressed green salad. The barley and rice *bibimbap* is original – you mix in *doenjang jjigae* rather than *gochujang*. Look for a building with a white frontage covered with ivy.

JILSIRU TTEOK CAFÉ Map p50 Tteok $$

☎ 733 5477; Insadong-gil, Insadong; rice cakes W1500, teas W6000; ⏱ 10am-9pm; ⊕ line 3 to Anguk, Exit 6

Enjoy beautiful gourmet rice cakes with unusual flavours at this café-cum-shop owned by a well-known *tteok* cooking teacher. The dry *tteok* go well with a cup of Korean tea. The *tteok* come in all colours, shapes and sizes, and ingredients include black rice, nuts, fruits, mugwort and chocolate.

JUK 1001 IYAGI Map p50 Juk $$

☎ 733 2587; Insadong 6-gil, Insadong; meals W7000; ⏱ 8am-10pm Mon-Sat, 9am-9pm Sun; ⊕ line 3 to Anguk, Exit 6

The unpretentious surroundings reflect this restaurant's food. A large bowl of excellent chicken and ginseng rice porridge is served with four side dishes. There are 19 other options packed with healthy, natural ingredients, ranging from snails, mushrooms and seafood to good old pumpkin. Some choices are vegetarian.

ABOUT SHABU Map p52 Shabu Shabu $$

☎ 747 7730; Maronie 2-gil, Daehangno; meals W7000; ⏱ 10am-9pm; ⊕ line 4 to Hyehwa, Exit 2

This great new restaurant does everything right. There's plenty of excellent fresh food at reasonable prices. Dunk your vegetables into the boiling soup of your choice, and dip in the smoked duck or whatever meat you choose. Later mix in the chewy, gorgeous green noodles for your second course, then drink the soup for your third. Every mouthful tastes different.

BAP & JUK Map p52 Juk $$

☎ 764 8686; Dongsung-gil, Daehangno; meals W7000; ⏱ 10am-9pm; ⊕ line 4 to Hyehwa, Exit 1

A hearty bowl of healthy *haemul juk* (seafood rice porridge) is offered here, a good filler whatever the time of day. Other rice porridges fill out the menu.

WORLD FOOD COURT

Map p50 Western Fusion $$

B1 Jongno Tower, Insadong; meals W4000-10,000; ⏱ 11am-10pm; ⊕ line 1 to Jonggak, Exit 3

Euro-Korean fusion food is the theme here, mainly big platters of it, and the Hite draught beer corner (⏱ 2-9.30pm) serves up beer for only W1800.

SADONGMYEONOK Map p50   Korean $
사동면옥; ☎ 735 7393; Insadong 5-gil, Insadong; meals W6000; ⏰ 9am-10pm; Ⓜ line 3 to Anguk, Exit 6

This bright and breezy eatery is hidden away, but is usually busy and has a long menu. It's famous for *manduguk* – because the dumplings are the largest you'll see (three make a meal). Also famous is the platter of *haemul pajeon* (seafood pancake), known for its size, crispiness and the big chunks of octopus. Use the onion and soy sauce side dish as a dip for both.

TOSOKMAEUL Map p50   Gamjatang $
토속마을; ☎ 735 7018; Insadong; meals W6000; ⏰ 24hr; Ⓜ line 1 to Jonggak, Exit 3

Are you ready for full-on, full-flavoured Korean peasant fodder? *Gamjatang* is served up in this cluttered diner. Pick out the chillies to make it less spicy. The uncompromising side dishes are salty-and-fishy-as-hell shrimps, radish and cabbage kimchi drenched in *gochujang*, raw onions and raw chillies. Thankfully the rice is plain, and there are plenty of paper tissues to deal with runny noses and sweaty brows.

KKULTARAE STALL Map p50   Kkultarae $
Insadong-gil, Insadong; 10 pieces W5000; ⏰ 9.30am-10pm; Ⓜ line 3 to Anguk, Exit 6

Two cheerful, talkative lads put on a show and make *kkultarae* – a delicious bite-sized snack – from cornflour threads, honey and nuts. Choose either almond or peanut.

TOBANG Map p50   Traditinal Korean $
Insadong-gil, Insadong; meals W4000; ⏰ 10am-7pm; Ⓜ line 3 to Anguk, Exit 6

A white sign with two Chinese characters above a doorway leads the way to this small nine-table traditional restaurant, where you sit on floor cushions under paper lanterns. Order the *sundubu jjigae* or *doenjang jjigae* for some Korean home-cooking flavour and excellent side dishes that include bean sprouts, fish, cuttlefish and raw crab in red-pepper sauce, plus a minimalist soup, rice and lettuce wraps. Authentic home cooking for W4000 – no wonder queues build up at lunchtime.

NAKWON ARCADE RICE CAKE SHOPS
Map p50   Tteok $
Around Nakwon Arcade, Insadong; snacks from W3000; Ⓜ line 1, 3 or 5 to Jongno 3-ga, Exit 5

top picks
RESTAURANTS BY CUISINE

- *Bibimbap* – Gogung (p101)
- Fish – Busan Ilbeonji (p107)
- *Kalguksu* – Myeong-dong Gyoja (p107)
- *Mandu* – Sadongmyeonok (left)
- *Patbingsu* – Hyundai Department Store (p111)
- *Samgyetang* – Tosokchon Samgyetang (p99); Baekje Samgyetang (below)
- *Sujebi* – Samcheong-dong Sujebi (p100)
- *Tteokgalbi* – Chilgapsan (p103)

When Japan abolished the Korean monarchy in 1910, the palace *tteok* makers were sacked, so they opened small shops just north of Tapgol Park and sold their *tteok* to the public. Some of the shops are still run by their descendants. White, cupcake *tteok* have a fermented flavour, while others are flavoured with nuts and dried fruits.

CROWN BAKERY Map p50   Bakery $
☎ 735 1933; Insadong-gil, Insadong; snacks W500-3000; ⏰ 7am-10pm; Ⓜ line 3 to Anguk, Exit 6

Many bakeries have turned themselves into cafés by installing a coffee machine and providing a few tables and chairs. Baking is done inside the shop, which also sells the creamy-tasting Korean speciality 'ice candy', a round ice lolly on a round stick (W800).

MYEONG-DONG, NAMSAN & ITAEWON

Myeong-dong is well known for its *kalguksu*, *samgyetang* and *jjimdak* restaurants, as well as all the yoghurt/ice cream/gelati parlours on every corner. Besides Italian-style restaurants, you might spot a Turkish, Vietnamese and Nepalese restaurant. Myeong-dong offers plenty of reasonably priced options, or for a special treat head to Korea House in Namsan for royal cuisine. Fun street eats include 32cm-long ice creams and a spiralling potato on a stick served with salt and cheese.

Itaewon specialises in ethnic restaurants and Sobangseo-gil, the road leading up to the mosque, has a growing Middle Eastern flavour with halal restaurants and kebab kiosks.

These days you can eat your way around the world in Itaewon's ethnic restaurants from A to Z – African, Bulgarian, Chinese, Deutsch, Egyptian, French, Greek, Hong Kong, Indian, Japanese, Korean…

KOREA HOUSE Map pp56-7   Royal Cuisine $$$

☎ 2266 9101; www.koreahouse.or.kr; Namsan; set course W57,200-99,000; ☽ noon-2pm & 5.30-7pm Mon-Sat, 6.30-8pm Sun; ◉ line 3 or 4 to Chungmuro, Exit 3

The chefs (around 17 on any particular day) really care about the royal cuisine they prepare – see below for an interview with the head chef. A dozen courses make up the royal banquet, and portions are dainty and artistic rather than large. The fresh flavours are subtle and quite different from the strong flavours usually associated with Korean food. The *hanok*, the *hanbok*-clad waitresses, the *gayageum* (zither) music and the platters and boxes the food is served in are all part of the experience.

LE SAINT-EX Map p60   French $$$

☎ 795 2465; Itaewon 2-gil, Itaewon; meals W28,000-50,000; ☽ 6pm- midnight; ◉ line 6 to Itaewon, Exit 1

The blackboard menu at this very French bistro with consistently good food and service is always tempting. A heater and even blankets are available for the outside patio. The W17,600 lunch sets are excellent,

and in a sneaky move the irresistible desserts are always on display.

CHEONGSACHORONG Map p60   Banquet $$

☎ 794 1177; Itaewonno, Itaewon; per person jeongsik W12,000, hanjeongsik from W35,000; ☽ 8am-10pm; ◉ line 6 to Itaewon, Exit 2

This well-known restaurant caters to Japanese tour groups but you can join in if you make a reservation (maybe with the aid of hotel reception). The food is a good deal and the *hanjeongsik* includes royal cuisine such as *gujeolpan* and *sinseollo*. Traditional dancing and drumming starts at 7pm daily.

SANTORINI Map p60   Greek $$

☎ 790 3474; Itaewon 2-gil, Itaewon; entrees W7000, mains from W17,000; ☽ 11.40am-10pm; ◉ line 6 to Itaewon, Exit 1

Enjoy genuine Greek food in a homely atmosphere up on the 2nd floor. Mains come with an olive-oil dressed salad, the fish soup is chunky and the meals have quality. Santorini is a survivor in Itaewon's fickle culinary scene.

ITAEWON GALBI Map p60   Korean BBQ $$

☎ 795 1474; Itaewon 2-gil, Itaewon; meals W10,000-30,000; ☽ 10am-11pm; ◉ line 6 to Itaewon, Exit 2

Located on the 2nd floor, this restaurant has been serving up barbecue beef ribs and other Korean staples for ever and a day. Don't forget to try the *dongdongju*.

ROYAL CUISINE

How many chefs work under you in Korea House? Around 25 people work in the kitchen and a royal food expert visits most weeks to advise us on royal cuisine. Preparing royal food is very intricate and time-consuming. We use only the freshest Korean ingredients.

How long does it take to become a royal cuisine chef? I think it takes 10 years to reach a medium level.

What's your favourite royal food? *Gujeolpan* (eight little snacks wrapped in mini pancakes) and *sinseollo* (hotpot). Royal cuisine isn't just the food, it's also the serving dishes. For instance, *gujeolpan* should be served in a wooden container with a lid.

We hear a lot about royal food, but what about royal drinks? Old documents mention that royalty drank *sikhye* (rice-based drink) and *sujeonggwa* (cinnamon and ginger drink). These drinks, like the royal food, were medicinal. Oranges and tangerines might be served to the king if he had a cold.

What do you cook for your family at home? Oh, shredded jellyfish with seasoning, sometimes big clams.

What other non-royal food do you like? *Chueotang* (minced fish soup).

Were you born in Seoul? No, Gunsan, a port city in Jeollabukdo.

What's your favourite restaurant in Seoul? Hanmiri in Gangnam. Do you know it? Is it in your guidebook? [See p109]

An interview with Gwak Joong-seob, head chef at Korea House (above).

ZELEN Map p60   Bulgarian $$

☎ 749 0600; Itaewon 2-gil, Itaewon; meals W9000-24,000; 🕙 11.30am-3pm & 6-11pm Wed-Sun, 6-11pm Tue; ⊕ line 6 to Itaewon, Exit 1

A couple of young Bulgarian guys have done a great job setting up this restaurant. Warm and welcoming, with candles and a mermaid water feature, the Bulgarian food is original and very good. Meat lovers have plenty of options, and there are wines, too. Meals like *kiufte* meatballs are served on a big white platter, while the *giuvedje* stew is smaller but packed with meats. It's best to book if you want to come on the weekend.

THAI ORCHID Map p60   Thai $$

☎ 795 3338; Itaewonno, Itaewon; meals W9000-22,000; 🕙 noon-10.30pm; ⊕ line 6 to Itaewon, Exit 3

This Itaewon institution has been dressed up in a new modern style and moved across the road, but the Thai cooks are still producing the old favourites like seafood in half a pineapple.

ALI BABA Map p60   Egyptian $$

☎ 790 7754; Itaewonno, Itaewon; mains W15,000; 🕙 noon-10pm; ⊕ line 6 to Itaewon, Exit 2

Authentic Egyptian food, coffee, music and surroundings are up here on the 3rd floor. Portions are small so sharing a number of dishes is the way to go. The freshly made pitta bread is particularly delicious. Afterwards, enjoy a *sheesha* (water pipe) – puffing on one of the 15 flavours costs W20,000.

BAEKJE SAMGYETANG

Map pp56-7   Chicken $$

☎ 776 3267; Myeong-dong 2-gil, Myeong-dong; meals W12,000; 🕙 9am-10pm; ⊕ line 4 to Myeong-dong, Exit 6

Famous for its brisk service and reliable *samgyetang*, which includes a thimbleful of *insamju* (ginseng wine). Put salt and pepper into the saucer and dip the pieces of chicken into it. Drink the soup at the end. Black chicken (*ogolgyetang*) is W20,000. The 2nd-floor restaurant has a sign with red Chinese characters.

NUTRITION CENTRE Map pp56-7   Chicken $$

☎ 776 2015; Chungmu 1-ga-gil, Myeong-dong; lunch set W7000-10,000, dinner W12,000; 🕙 11am-10.30pm; ⊕ line 4 to Myeong-dong, Exit 7

A Myeong-dong institution with a fast-food decor that only offers two items: a whole chicken roasted on a spit or *samgyetang* for W10,000. A cheaper chicken set is available at lunch.

GOGUNG Map pp56-7   Bibimbap $$

☎ 776 3211; Myeong-dong; meals W11,000; 🕙 11am-10pm; ⊕ line 4 to Myeong-dong, Exit 10

Authentic Jeonju *bibimbap* is the star attraction here, together with the cheaper *dolsot bibimbap*. Waitresses are dressed in *hanbok*, and upstairs is nicer than downstairs. Order *moju*, a medicinal homebrew that also comes from Jeonju. Another bright, new branch is in Insadong (p101).

SABOTEN Map pp56-7   Korean $$

☎ 756 4510; Myeongryebang-gil, Myeong-dong; meals W10,000; 🕙 9am-10pm; ⊕ line 4 to Myeong-dong, Exit 7

Grab a window seat in this super-clean and bright 1st-floor restaurant, which specialises in nongreasy *donkkaseu* sets. Kimchi, cheese, chicken and seafood are other options, but we recommend sticking with the pork cutlets.

DOLKEMAEUL TOFU HOUSE

Map pp56-7   Tofu $$

☎ 775 3345; off Myeongryebang-gil, Myeong-dong; meals W6000-13,000; 🕙 11am-10pm; ⊕ line 4 to Myeong-dong, Exit 8

The star here is the excellent *sundubu* (uncurdled tofu) cooked in a stone pot and served with hotpot rice, soup, fish and side dishes. Add an egg to the tofu, spoon the rice into a bowl and pour hot water from the kettle into the rice hotpot to make burnt-rice tea that takes away the spiciness.

ANDONG JJIMDAK Map pp56-7   Chicken $$

☎ 310 9174; off Myeong-dong-gil, Myeong-dong; platters for 2 W15,000-17,000; 🕙 11am-midnight; ⊕ line 4 to Myeong-dong, Exit 7

A convivial young crowd comes here for the *jjimdak* experience, a very spicy concoction of chicken, noodles, potatoes and vegetables that comes on a platter meant for sharing. The restaurant is spread over three floors, and seafood and mushroom options have been added to the menu. The signboard has white Chinese characters.

top picks

UNBEATABLE BUFFETS

A great opportunity to sample a wide range of Korean food at one sitting.

- Fresh House (p110)
- Familia Buffet (p109)
- 63 Buffet Pavilion (right)

MYEONG-DONG GYOJA

Map pp56-7   Korean $

☎ 776 5348; Myeongryebang-gil, Myeong-dong; meals W7000; ⏱ 10.30am-9.30pm; ◉ line 4 to Myeong-dong, Exit 8

The special *kalguksu* (noodles in a meat, dumpling and vegetable broth, rather than the usual clam broth) is famous, so it's busy busy, busy. Eating at this Myeong-dong institution is a matter of 'queue, pay, eat, leave!' The soup comes with rice and kimchi.

SIGOL BAPSANG Map p60   Korean $

☎ 793 5390; off Itaewonno, Itaewon; meals W7000; ⏱ 24hr; ◉ line 6 to Itaewon, Exit 2

Enjoy rustic surroundings and countryside food in this eatery that's escaped from Insadong. Order the *sigol bapsang* – 20 mainly vegetarian side dishes served with a spicy soup and rice. You can order a plate of *bulgogi* or fish for W10,000.

SINSUN SEOLNONGTANG

Map pp56-7   Korean $

☎ 777 4531; Myeong-dong-gil, Myeong-dong; meals W6000; ⏱ 24hr; ◉ line 4 to Myeong-dong, Exit 7

The decor is neat and simple, and everyone receives free *boricha* (barley tea). *Mandu*, tofu or ginseng can be added to the beef broth, but purists will want to stick to the traditional version.

COLD STONE CREAMERY

Map pp56-7   Ice Cream $

☎ 3789 0715; Myeong-dong; ice cream plus toppings from W4000; ⏱ 11am-11pm; ◉ line 4 to Myeong-dong, Exit 7

Order your ice cream, toppings and countless mix-ins and they stir it all up on the cold stone counter and serve it in a waffle cone. Low-fat options available.

HONGDAE, SINCHON & YEOUIDO

Hongdae and Sinchon both serve their student population with plenty of well-priced, straightforward restaurants. Barbecue fish, tofu and chicken restaurants offer good eating, and varying degrees of Italian fusion lurk on every street. Yeouido is something of a culinary desert, except for the 63 Building and the seafood restaurants above Noryangjin fish market (p89) just south of the island.

63 BUFFET PAVILION

Map p65   Buffet $$$

☎ 789 5731; 63 Bldg, Yeouido; adult lunch/dinner W52,000/57,000, child 5-13yr lunch/dinner W29,000/33,000; ⏱ noon-3pm & 6-10pm Mon-Sat, 11am-3pm & 5-10pm Sun; ◉ line 5 to Yeouinaru, Exit 4

With too many temptations to count, many cooked on the spot, this buffet is the perfect chance to sample a range of Asian cuisines and flavours. On the other hand, you could just gorge yourself on desserts.

BUSAN ILBEONJI Map p65   Seafood $$

부산일번지; ☎ 813 7799; Noryangjin Fish Market; raw fish platters from W60,000, fish meals W5000-10,000; ⏱ 10.30am-10.30pm; ◉ line 1 to Noryangjin, Exit 1

Generous super-fresh fish and crab meals are a bargain at Mrs Moon's restaurant up on the 2nd floor of the Noryangjin fish market. Match the *hangeul* above to the sign to find it, or maybe just ask someone. *Saengseon-gui* is W5000 and *kkotge* (a crab in a spicy or mild soup) is W10,000 and includes great side dishes such as garnished tofu, sweet red beans, pumpkin, raw fish salad and shredded jellyfish.

CASTLE PRAHA Map p63   Western $$

☎ 334 2181; Solnae 6-gil, Hongdae; meals W16,000-27,000; ⏱ noon-3pm & 5pm-2am; ◉ line 2 to Hongik University, Exit 5

Hidden away down an alley is the most extraordinary facade in Seoul, with an equally bizarre dungeon-cum-cellar interior for the vintage restaurant, the homebrew bar, the bakery and café. Step inside this medieval fantasy for a limited but reasonably priced selection of European food.

EATING HONGDAE, SINCHON & YEOUIDO

BONGHEE SELEONGTANG
Map p64   Korean $$

☎ 313 9181; Myeongmul-geori, Sinchon; meals W6000-25,000; ☻ 24hr; ☻ line 2 to Sinchon, Exit 3
Seolleongtang is a simple no-fuss beef soup with no hint of spiciness that hits the spot for a light lunch when served with rice. Don't be tempted to try *doganitang* (knee-cap soup) unless you like chewing tendon and gristle.

AGIO Map p63   Italian $$

☎ 334 7311; Eoulmadang 2-gil, Hongdae; meals W10,000-20,000; ☻ noon-midnight; ☻ line 2 to Hongik University, Exit 5
Sit outside in the spacious courtyard under shady trees or inside this charming Italian restaurant that serves mainly organic salads and pastas, but specialises in large, thin-crust pizzas, freshly made in a wood-fired oven and served on a wooden platter. Drinkable house wine is W5500.

SHANGHAI Map p64   Chinese $$

☎ 313 3616; by main gate Ewha Womans University, Sinchon; meals W5000-25,000; ☻ 10am-9.30pm; ☻ line 2 to Ewha Womans University, Exit 2
An upmarket-looking restaurant with an open-plan kitchen serving up the usual Korean version of Chinese food. The cheap, comfort food *jajangmyeon* is always a popular choice. *Tangsuyuk* is the Korean version of sweet-and-sour pork, *japchae* is a tasty noodle dish with royal connections, while *mapodubu* is tofu with a Chinese sauce.

BAENGNYEON SAMGYETANG
Map p63   Chicken $$

☎ 325 3399; Yanghwaro, Hongdae; meals W11,000; ☻ 10am-10pm; ☻ line 2 to Hongik University, Exit 5
This well-known, rough-and-ready restaurant serves chicken and ginseng soup. Queues form as summer temperatures soar because locals claim the meal is restorative and this restaurant is the best in the area. Barbecue chicken (*jeongigui dongdak*) is another option.

BSD DUBU HOUSE Map p64   Tofu $$

☎ 362 8897; Myeongmul-geori, Sinchon; meals & sets W7000-15,000; ☻ 11am-midnight; ☻ line 2 to Sinchon, Exit 3
Over 20 varieties of spicy *sundubu* are on offer in this neat and clean basement res-

taurant decorated with collectables, but the traditional beef one is hard to beat. Add a raw egg to the *sundubu*, empty the rice into a bowl and add boiling water to the remaining rice to make burnt-rice tea. Side dishes include freshly fried fish.

NOLBOO Map p63   Korean $$

☎ 3141 7766; Seogyoro, Hongdae; meals W6000-12,000; ☻ 11am-11.30pm; ☻ line 2 to Hongik University, Exit 5
Come to this spacious 2nd-floor restaurant for *budae jjigae* (or *Johnsontang*), which consists of baked beans, macaroni, rice cakes, ham, sausages, tofu, noodles and vegetable scraps, all thrown into a big wok, cooked at your table and served with rice and good side dishes.

CHUNCHEON MYUNGDONG
Map p64   Chicken $$

☎ 313 6788; Sinchon; meals W8500; ☻ 24hr; ☻ line 2 to Sinchon, Exit 3
Rice, chicken and either pork or octopus are cooked up with vegetables on a barbecue hotplate on your table. Order spicy hot or medium sauces. This *dakgalbi* meal originated in the lakeside city of Chuncheon in Gangwon-do.

BAB Map p63   Banquet $$

☎ 334 1866; off Wausan-gil, Hongdae; meals W6000-10,000; ☻ 11am-9pm Mon-Sat; ☻ line 2 to Hongik University, Exit 5
A modern *jeongsik* restaurant with tables and chairs and a choice of *eosanjeok jeongsik* (nicely grilled fish kebabs) or *bulgogi jeongsik* (grilled beef on a hotplate). They arrive along with 10 side dishes, rice and soup.

SAMTONG CHICKEN Map p63   Chicken $$

☎ 326 2892; off Saemulgyeol 1-gil, Hongdae; whole chicken W11,000; ☻ 4pm-5am; ☻ line 2 to Hongik University, Exit 4
This typically convivial beer-and-chicken joint is clean and modern. A tap beer costs W2500 and the chicken comes roasted on a spit or fried. *Jeongiguidongdak* is a whole barbecue chicken served with side dishes of pickled *daikon* (radish) cubes and shredded cabbage topped with mayonnaise.

HWEDRA RAMYEON Map p64   Noodles $$

☎ 337 1506; Saeteo 2-gil, Sinchon; meals W4000-10,000; ☻ 24hr; ☻ line 2 to Sinchon, Exit 1

This tiny, dark, prison cell of an eatery serves up the hottest *ramyeon* in Seoul. The *ajumma* (middle-aged working woman) in charge adds green chillies with a large ladle as if they were spring onions. Said to cure even the worst hangover, you can take up this fear-factor challenge for just W4000.

NANIWA Map p63 Japanese $
나니와; ☎ 333 5337; Saemulgyeol 2-gil, Hongdae; meal sets W6000; 10am-10pm; line 2 to Hongik University, Exit 5
Japanese *donkkaseu* and *udong* (thick white noodle broth) sets are served up fast in this busy restaurant. The fish set with lightly grilled salmon *(yeoneo-gui)* is recommended.

CHUNCHEONJIP Map p64 Chicken $
☎ 323 5597; Myeongmul-geori, Sinchon; meals W3500-8000; 24hr; line 2 to Sinchon, Exit 2
This large and cheerful restaurant with music and paper lanterns never closes. Try its hot and spicy fusion *dakgalbi* with cheese and sweet potatoes or noodles, cooked at your table. Serve yourself side dishes from a buffet – a great idea that reduces waste.

RED MANGO Map p64 Yoghurt $
Sinchon; yoghurt desserts W3500-8000; 11am-11.30pm; line 2 to Sinchon Exit 3
This Korean brand went from three outlets to 150 in just two years. Hand over W5500 for a bowl of unsweetened, low-fat yoghurt with five toppings of your choice, including tinned fruit. Another branch is in Insadong-gil (p50).

HAPPY TABLE Map p64 International $
☎ 363 9991; Myeongmul-geori, Sinchon; meals W5000; 10.30am-9pm; line 2 to Sinchon, Exit 3
Everything in this student eatery is small but cute, from the tables and chairs to the fusion meals such as Shanghai seafood spaghetti, Mexican dishes and chicken salads in an edible basket.

TEOLBOGODOENI Map p64 Fish $
Sinchon; meals W5000; 10am-10pm; line 2 to Sinchon, Exit 2
Order the *samchi baekban* (a fish, rice and soup meal) for a great meal that's also a great deal. Tuck into a fresh fish (huge by Seoul standards) with decent whitish flesh,

dip it into the soy and wasabi sauce, and sip the authentic *doenjang jjigae*. This student hang-out, wallpapered with customer photos, is always full of lively chatter.

RICHEMONT BAKERY Map p63 Bakery $
☎ 332 7778; Seogyoro, Hongdae; snacks W500-5000; 8am-11pm; line 2 to Hongik University, Exit 5
An above-average bakery that keeps creating new goodies (such as giant pretzels) and offers a good-value European breakfast for W4500. It also sells real bread, specialist chocolates and its own ice lollies.

GANGNAM & JAMSIL
Masses of restaurants surround Gangnam subway station, although the turnover is high, while Apgujeong is an upmarket dining hotspot. Some of Seoul's best restaurants are spread over these neighbourhoods, so it's worth making the effort to visit them, especially Hanmiri (royal cuisine; below), Nolboo Yuhwangorijinheukgui (medicinal duck; p110) and Gorilla in the Kitchen (fine-dining health food; p110). Other options include an atmospheric Italian cellar restaurant, a classic *galbi* restaurant, one offering vegetarian sets, a German-style *brauhaus* and a couple of excellent buffets – the choice south of the river is wider than the Han river.

FAMILIA BUFFET
Map p68 Buffet $$$
☎ 3440 8090; Imperial Palace Hotel, Eonjuro, Gangnam; lunch/dinner W55,000/63,000; noon-3pm & 6-10pm; line 7 to Hak-dong, Exit 1
This restaurant in the plush Imperial Palace Hotel provides a superb buffet banquet. Some of the food is freshly prepared by a squad of cooks who work in the dining area, dressed in what looks like ninja outfits. Book for weekends.

HANMIRI Map p68 Royal Cuisine $$$
☎ 569 7165; 2nd fl, Human Starville, Nonhyeonno, Gangnam; set meals W35,000-77,000; noon-3pm & 6-10pm; line 2 to Yeoksam, Exit 6
Be treated like royalty by *hanbok*-clad staff in this oasis of old-fashioned service and decor with embroidery on the walls. The dozen well-presented dishes are a modernised version of royal cuisine, many of them unique, gourmet and foreigner-friendly. The *sinseollo* and the rice cake finale are stand-outs, but nearly everything is good.

NOLBOO YUHWANGORIJINHEUKGUI

Map p68   Duck $$$

☎ 592 5292; Gangnam; one duck W50,000;
🕑 noon-10pm; 🚇 line 3 or 7 to Express Bus
Terminal, Exit 3

This restaurant cooks up a wonderful medicinal duck, packed with glutinous rice, red beans, ginseng, nuts and herbs. The duck is large with little or no fat and the taste is delicious. Try wrapping the meat, sauce and side dishes in the *daikon* slices – a Seoul version of Peking duck. Go up the escalator at Exit 3 and you can see the Nolboo signboard.

GORILLA IN THE KITCHEN

Map p68   Western Fusion $$$

☎ 3442 1688; Gangnam; mains W33,000;
🕑 11am-11pm; 🚇 line 3 to Apgujeong, Exit 2

Owned by Korean actor Bae Yong-jun, this smart, glass restaurant, facing the entrance to Dosan Park, focuses on health food. Chef Han has a handle on fine Euro dining, and most meals come up trumps. Rocket, grapefruit and cheese salad, squid ink, black rice – it's all slightly adventurous, but it works. Tables by the bamboo trees are best.

SAMWON GARDEN Map p68   Korean BBQ $$$

☎ 548 3030; Eonjuro, Gangnam; meals W33,000;
🕑 11.45am-10pm; 🚇 line 3 to Apgujeong, Exit 2

Popular enough to have its own multistorey car park, this *galbi* icon has a beautiful traditional garden and a sizeable waterfall. Samwon has been serving top-class *galbi* in this rural idyll for over 30 years, and plenty of business deals have been hatched in the private dining rooms.

FRESH HOUSE Map p70   Buffet $$$

☎ 416 0606; www.freshhouse.co.kr; Olympic Park, Jamsil; lunch/dinner Mon-Fri W22,000/27,000, lunch & dinner Sat & Sun W32,000; 🕑 11.30am-3pm & 5.30-10pm; 🚇 line 8 to Mongchontoseong, Exit 1

A great spread at a great price has ensured the popularity of this new buffet restaurant at Olympic Park. The cooks are constantly bringing in appetising, mainly Asian food. With the accent on freshness, this buffet is proving to be a hit with meat lovers, sushi lovers, salad lovers, dessert lovers – everyone is catered for. Tip: if *daege* (king crab) is on the buffet, grab a seat as close to it as possible.

PULHYANGGI Map p68   Vegetarian $$$

☎ 545 0415; Eonjuro, Gangnam; lunch sets W18,000, dinner sets W25,000; 🕑 10am-10pm; 🚇 line 3 to Apgujeong, Exit 2

Sit on chairs or floor cushions at this long-running, 2nd-storey restaurant where the popular attraction is the dozen or more items served up in the set meals. The mainly vegetarian sets offer traditional food such as sweet-and-sour mushrooms, sesame soup, acorn jelly, rice cakes and special teas.

MAD FOR GARLIC Map p68   Italian Fusion $$$

☎ 546 8117; Apgujeongno, Gangnam; meals W15,000-28,000; 🕑 11.30am-midnight; 🚇 line 3 to Apgujeong, Exit 2

The bare brick walls, the wine glass and wine bottle decor and the open-plan kitchen make this a top spot for atmosphere and couples. The Italian menu doesn't disappoint, nor does the Dracula Killer starter. Bottles of wine start from W30,000.

O'KIM'S BRAUHAUS Map p70   Western $$

☎ 6002 7006; COEX Exhibition Hall; meals W9000-20,000; 🕑 11.30am-midnight; 🚇 line 2 to Samseong, COEX Exit

More Deutschland than Ireland, this huge but convivial barn of a restaurant/bar has an Oktoberfest atmosphere and live music at 8pm except on Sunday. O'Kim's serves up big platters of steak, ribs, sausages and seafood along with its own brewed-on-the-premises light or dark German-style beer (W4800 a glass). It's near the COEX exhibition halls, not in the mall.

PHO BAY Map p68   Vietnamese Noodles $$

☎ 539 1633; Jinmi-gil, Gangnam; meals W7000-12,000; 🕑 11am-11pm; 🚇 line 2 to Gangnam, Exit 7

A restaurant chain with simple but clean decor that specialises in fresh-tasting Vietnamese rice noodles. The big plus here is that you mix in whatever amount of bean sprouts, chillies, lemon and onion you want.

PYEONGANDOCHAPSSAL SUNDAE

Map p68   Korean $$

☎ 1688 1878; Yeomyeong-gil, Gangnam; meals W6000-12,000; 🕑 24hr; 🚇 line 2 to Gangnam, Exit 7

Squeeze yourself into this popular mouthful of a restaurant to take up the *sundae* challenge. We're not talking fruit sundae, but Korean *sundae*, which is a black noodle

SAMPLING KOREAN CUISINE

Department stores all have a supermarket in the basement where staff offer lots of samples of local foods and drinks. Try various types of tofu, umpteen types of kimchi and greens, *pajeon* (savoury pancakes), sesame soup, BBQ shellfish, ginseng rice porridge, herb-flavoured dumplings, grilled eel, acorn *muk* (jelly) and gingko nuts, as well as unusual drinks such as aloe and cactus flower. So pop into any department store to enjoy a stand-up munch of flavoursome Korean nibbles, all offered with a smile.

sausage. It looks worse than it tastes – the flavour is bland although the skin is chewy. Order *pyeongando jeongsik* for a spicy soup and a plate of *sundae* and pork hocks (W9000).

HYUNDAI DEPARTMENT STORE
Map p68   Korean $$
☎ 547 6800; Apgujeongno, Gangnam; desserts W7000; ☾ 10.30am-8.30pm; ⊙ line 3 to Apgujeong, Exit 6
Take the elevator to the 5th floor and head to Mealtop, which sells excellent *patbingsu*

(red bean and fruit on milky shaved ice), particularly popular in summer.

TECHNO MART FOOD COURT
Map p70   Korean & Western Fusion $$
B1, Techno Mart, north of Jamsil; meals W5000; ☾ 10am-8pm; ⊙ line 2 to Gangbyeon, Exit 1
Stalls compete with each other to pile up as much fusion food as possible on huge platters that are meant for sharing – some W10,000 platters can fill three hungry stomachs. Browse the plastic replicas of the food and see the world's largest bowls of *bibimbap* and giant ice-cream concoctions on shaved ice or fruit (W5000).

COLD STONE CREAMERY
Map p68   Ice Cream $
☎ 2051 5117; Gangnamdaero, Gangnam; ice creams from W5000; ☾ 11am-11.30pm; ⊙ line 2 to Gangnam, Exit 7
This latest food fad to hit Seoul already has over 20 outlets in the city. The point of difference is that staff mix up your choice of mix-ins with your chosen ice cream on a cold slab.

DRINKING

top picks

DRINKING

Competition is strong amongst Seoul's unbelievable number of bars. Most of the expat and gay bars and clubs can be found in Itaewon, which caters to the US troops still stationed in South Korea. Most bars there have English-speaking staff and only get busy around 10pm or later, even on Friday and Saturday. Itaewon is one of the only areas where you see lots of foreigners – it has a different atmosphere to the rest of Seoul.

The other main area that attracts locals and foreigners is Hongdae, a university district where dozens of live music venues and clubs jostle for attention along with bars and restaurants. Clubbing is an all-night activity for crowds of young people, particularly on Friday and Saturday.

Offbeat bars are a Seoul speciality, so there are bars with hammocks, bars with ponds indoors as well as outdoors, bars with fantasy designs, bars serving beer cocktails, bars where customers dance on the tables, and bars that serve *soju* (a vodkalike liquor) in brass kettles. Juicy bars in Itaewon are where scantily clad hostesses sip ultra-expensive juice drinks in tiny dens with signs outside that read 'Sweetheart Club – Drink Food Woman', 'Woman & Cocktails' or the slightly more subtle 'For Gentlemen'.

Seoul also has a tea culture, which includes green, herbal and fruit teas. There's also a recently acquired coffee culture. Starbucks and other chains are everywhere. Goblin-sized teashops in Insadong sell medicinal teas and are so crammed with antiques that you can hardly squeeze inside. One has cute little songbirds flying around inside. The medicinal hot and cold teas are made from roots, leaves, herbs or fruit. A cup of tea costs around W6000 (as much as a cheap meal), but it's a quality product and often served with a rice-cake snack. Green tea predominates in the cafés – it can be difficult to find black tea served with milk.

Some coffee shops roast and grind their own imported coffee beans, which may be organic and fair-trade. Some huge cafés are spread over five floors, each room with a different style; others concentrate on music, with thousands of LPs; book cafés cater to the studious; and waffle and cake cafés cater to the sweet-toothed. There are pavement cafés, art-gallery cafés, underground and rooftop cafés, cafés with footbaths full of fish that nibble your feet, and cafés where you can put on fancy dress. All-white cafés, all-black cafés – every theme imaginable can be found in Seoul, plus a few that can't be imagined until you step inside. The drinks are just as variable – anyone for a pumpkin latte?

SPECIALITIES

Seoul's first beer brewery opened in 1908, and Korean drinkers have knocked back plenty of it ever since. Lager-style local beers *(maekju)* include Cass, Hite and OB. Imported bottled beers are now widely available, and microbreweries have widened the choice still further.

Soju, with an alcohol content of more than 20%, is often likened to vodka in that it's clear, nearly flavourless, has a kick and is cheap to produce. It comes in all sorts of flavours, and Seoul's bar staff mix it with just about anything – including yoghurt. Many bars mix up their own special cocktails.

Makgeolli and *dongdongju* are fermented from rice and have a cloudy appearance. They taste something like fermented lassi. With a much lower alcohol content than *soju,* this peasant drink is served in a brass kettle and drunk from bowls. More sake-like rice wine is often sold by restaurants, as are countless local liquors that are distilled or brewed according to secret recipes – try *insamju* (made from ginseng) or *bukbunja* (made from berries).

In recent years imported wine has caught on in a big way and can be found in Italian restaurants as well as department and convenience stores.

Seoulites consider it unhealthy to drink on an empty stomach, so most bars serve bar snacks *(anju)* such as nuts, dried squid, rice crackers, popcorn or barbecued chicken. Korean-style nightclubs serve large platters of *anju,* but they can cost an arm and a leg, and are a kind of cover charge.

Diners are usually presented with good old H_2O *(mul),* bottled or filtered, when they first arrive in a restaurant. Medicinal tea may be served after the meal. *Nokcha* (green tea) is grown in the southern provinces. Other teas include *boricha* (barley tea), *insamcha* (ginseng tea), *omijacha* (berry tea) and *yujacha* (citron tea). For a country with a tea tradition, Korea has taken to coffee in a big way. Decaf drinkers may be out of luck but it never hurts to ask.

Cans of soft drink include unique Korean ones such as *sikhye*, rice punch with grains of rice inside, and a grape juice that contains whole grapes. Health tonics, available in shops and pharmacies, are made with fibre blends, ginseng and other medicinal herbs, and are supposed to boost your virility, vitamin level and alertness, or cure (or prevent) a hangover.

WHERE TO DRINK

Bars can be found everywhere, but are concentrated in entertainment districts such as Sinchon, Hongdae, Daehangno, Itaewon and north of Gangnam station. Teashops cluster mainly in Insadong, while cafés, like the bakeries and convenience stores, are on every street.

HOW MUCH?

A local beer in an ordinary bar costs from around W2500 to W5000, while a cocktail costs from W5000 to W10,000. A coffee is usually W3000 to W6000, while traditional teas are about W6000.

GWANGHWAMUN

Bars and cafés can be spotted all over Gwanghwamun, but south of Jonggak subway station is the main entertainment area.

BUCK MULLIGAN'S Map p40   Irish Pub
☎ 3783 0004; B2, Seoul Finance Centre; ✆ noon-1am Mon-Fri; Ⓜ line 1 or 2 to City Hall, Exit 4
Live popular music enlivens Buck's at 9pm in this downtown Irish-themed bar with Guinness pie and Jamieson whiskey chicken on the dinner menu (W30,000 to W45,000). The lunch buffet (W25,000) is impressive and global.

SIPJEONDAEBOTANG Map p40   Teashop
☎ 734 5302; Samcheong-dong-gil; teas W4000-5000; ✆ 1am-9pm; Ⓜ line 3 to Anguk, Exit 1
The ladies running this tiny teashop cook up wonderful thick *danpatjuk*, red-bean porridge with ginseng, chestnut and peanuts. The Korean teas are medicinal, authentic and richly flavoured. Established in 1976, nothing has changed since.

INSADONG & DAEHANGNO

Insadong has Seoul's best traditional teashops but is pretty quiet by 10pm, while Daehangno has plenty of student nightlife, including theatres, live jazz, karaoke rooms, DVD rooms and pool halls – and more bars than Seodaemun Prison.

SANTANA Map p52   Bar
☎ 763 9933; Maronie-gil, Daehangno; ✆ 3pm-2am; Ⓜ line 4 to Hyehwa, Exit 2
Lager loathers lurch into this otherwise nondescript bar to indulge in their passion for beers that are on the dark side. Meals are W12,000.

TOP CLOUD BAR Map p50   Bar
☎ 2230 3000; 33rd fl, Jongno Tower, Insadong; drinks from W16,000; ✆ 8.30pm-midnight; Ⓜ line 1 to Jonggak, Exit 3
This candlelit bar with classy staff offers a magical night view of Seoul along with the magic of live jazz music. There's also an equally classy restaurant (p101).

BIER HALLE Map p52   Beer Hall
☎ 744 9996; Maronie-gil, Daehangno; ✆ 3pm-midnight; Ⓜ line 4 to Hyehwa, Exit 2
This cheerful bare-brick, cellar-style bar lures students with its cheap beer – W2800 a glass or W14,800 for a giant 2.7L pitcher – and its Euro menu of sausages and smoked meats (platters W13,000).

CAFÉ JUBILEE CHOCOLATIER
Map p52   Café
☎ 765 7221; Dongsung-gil, Daehangno; chocolates W1500, drinks W6000; ✆ 9.30am-10.30pm; Ⓜ line 4 to Hyehwa, Exit 2
A chocolatier where even the decor is dark chocolate. The 'classic' chocs are not sweet. Be aware that the cold chocolate is nearly all ice.

MINDEULLEYEONGTO Map p52   Café
Minto; ☎ 745 5234; Maronie 2-gil, Daehangno; drinks W7000, meals from W10,000; ✆ 10am-midnight; Ⓜ line 4 to Hyehwa, Exit 2
Perhaps the world's largest café, with masses of different zones and hideaway spots, each with their own decor and furniture. Spread over five floors, the top floor

is candlelit at night. A friendly dog guards the doorway and workers have their own special wave. Walt Disney would have loved it, including the name (which is something to do with dandelions). Mindeulleyeongto 2 is just down the road.

O'SULLOC Map p52   Café
☎ 741 5461; Maronie-gil, Daehangno; drinks W5000; ⏰ 11am-11pm; ⊖ line 4 to Hyehwa, Exit 2
The best green tea comes from Jejudo (Jeju Island), where O'Sulloc's tea plantation is based. This green-tea nirvana serves it up in all sorts of drinkable and edible ways. Design is their strong point – the cakes look too good to be real.

BEAUTIFUL TEA MUSEUM
Map p50   Teashop
☎ 735 6678; Insadong; teas W5000-8000; ⏰ 10am-10pm; ⊖ line 3 to Anguk, Exit 6
This is not a traditional Korean teashop. Instead, it offers the chance to sip teas from around the world in the pleasant covered courtyard of a modern hanok (traditional house), with tea sets on display. Some teas (100g for W80,000) are liquid gold.

DALSAENEUN DALMAN SAENGGAK HANDA Map p50   Teashop
Moon Bird Thinks Only of the Moon; ☎ 723 1504; Insadong 4-gil, Insadong; teas W6500-9000; ⏰ 11am-11pm; ⊖ line 3 to Anguk, Exit 6
This poetically named teashop is packed with plants and rustic artefacts. Bird song, soothing music and trickling water add to the atmosphere. Huddle in a cubicle and savour one of the 15 teas, which include gamnipcha (persimmon-leaf tea). Saeng-gangcha (ginger tea) is peppery but sweet.

DAWON Map p50   Teashop
☎ 730 6305; off Seokjeongol-gil, Insadong; teas W6000; ⏰ 11am-11pm; ⊖ line 3 to Anguk, Exit 6
The perfect place to unwind on a warm summer evening is under the shady fruit trees in this secret courtyard with flickering candles. In winter sit indoors in hanok rooms decorated with scribbles or in the garden pavilion. Small exhibition spaces surround the courtyard. The teas are superb, especially omijacha hwachae (fruit and five-flavour berry punch), a summer drink.

SINYETCHATJIP Map p50   Teashop
New Old Teashop; ☎ 732 6678; Insadong; teas W6000; ⏰ 10am-10pm; ⊖ line 3 to Anguk, Exit 6
Less cluttered than Yetchatjip and with a green courtyard, this atmospheric teashop also offers alcoholic drinks such as wild-strawberry wine and quince wine. The maesilcha (plum tea) is deliciously sweet and sour.

YETCHATJIP Map p50   Teashop
Old Teashop; ☎ 722 5019; Insadong; teas W6000; ⏰ 10am-10pm; ⊖ line 3 to Anguk, Exit 6
Half a dozen little songbirds fly around inside Seoul's most famous teashop. Ethereal music, water features and candles add to the atmosphere – even the unique toilets do their bit. Antique bric-a-brac so clutters this hobbit-sized teashop that it's hard to squeeze past and find somewhere to sit. The nine hot teas and seven cold ones are all special – try the hot mogwacha (quince tea) with a subtle fruity flavour or the tangy, vitamin-filled yujacha (citron tea).

MYEONG-DONG, NAMSAN & ITAEWON

Myeong-dong is known more for its cafés than bars, while Itaewon is the place for gay-friendly bars and expat pubs, usually equipped with pool tables and dart boards. Two notorious drinks served in bars there are the Long Island Iced Tea, a concoction usually made with vodka, gin, Bacardi, tequila and orange juice, and the soju kettle (exactly what the name implies: a kettle full of soju).

ALWAYS HOMME Map p60   Bar
☎ 798 0578; Dokkaebisijang 2-gil, Itaewon; ⏰ 8pm-4am; ⊖ line 6 to Itaewon, Exit 3
Beer is W4000 and cocktails are W5000 at this homely gay bar with a few touches of style about it. The music is not so loud that you can't talk, and the staff are friendly.

BAR BLISS Map p60   Bar
☎ 749 7738; Beodeunamu-gil, Itaewon; ⏰ 7pm-3am; ⊖ line 6 to Itaewon, Exit 4
Away from the main gay strip, bar staff Ted and Lucky keep this a friendly and relaxing bar. A chill-out, relax-on-cushions, shisha-pipe zone is the latest feature, and the eclectic decor includes a reclining Buddha. Any

night someone might start playing a guitar, and the cheese and crackers are tempting.

NASHVILLE SPORTS BAR Map p60   Bar
☎ 798 1592; Itaewonno, Itaewon; ⊙ 11am-2am; ⊙ line 6 to Itaewon, Exit 4

Guinness on tap, big-screen movies, TV sport shows, pool and darts bring in customers to this American sports bar. Upstairs there's a rooftop garden that's popular in summer for a quick drink and BBQ burger.

QUEEN Map p60   Bar
☎ 793 1290; Dokkaebisijang 2-gil, Itaewon; ⊙ 8pm-5am Tue-Sun; ⊙ line 6 to Itaewon, Exit 3

Recently renovated, this modernist gay bar with candles and neon tubes also has sit-and-chat zones and a small dance floor. Try a mojito with fresh mint.

SOHO Map p60   Bar
☎ 797 2280; Dokkaebisijang 2-gil, Itaewon; ⊙ 7pm-5am; ⊙ line 6 to Itaewon, Exit 3

A smart and friendly gay bar (lesbians welcome)with a relaxed vibe. It also features a dance club section for later in the evening.

O'SULLOC Map pp56-7   Café
☎ 774 5460; Myeong-dong-gil, Myeong-dong; cakes & teas W6000; ⊙ 9am-10.30pm; ⊙ line 4 to Myeong-dong, Exit 6

Impeccably presented green-tea drinks and cakes are created here in this smart, green-themed teahouse. All the green tea comes from Jejudo, Korea's southerly, semitropical island, where the best tea is reputed to grow. Green-tea ice cream and homemade green-tea chocolates are recommended, but the green-tea latte tastes like hot milk.

3 ALLEY PUB Map p60   Pub
☎ 749 3336; Itaewon 2-gil, Itaewon; ⊙ noon-1am Sun-Thu, noon-2am Fri & Sat; ⊙ line 6 to Itaewon, Exit 1

Mixing together a friendly pub atmosphere (darts, pool, cheap chicken wings on Tuesdays, a trivia quiz on Wednesdays) with top-notch European-style pub grub (mains W15,000) and nine draught beers is a formula that makes this place an expat magnet, especially with the older crowd.

GECKO'S TERRACE Map p60   Pub
☎ 749 9425; cnr Itaewonno & Bogwangdong-gil, Itaewon; ⊙ 11am-2am; ⊙ line 6 to Itaewon, Exit 4

This comfortable and popular 2nd-floor bar and restaurant has a global menu (meals W11,000), lunch specials and draught beers, plus the obligatory-in-Itaewon darts and pool. The pub supports soccer and ice hockey teams, so it can get rowdy.

REGGAE PUB Map p60   Pub
☎ 749 1533; Itaewonno, Itaewon; ⊙ 3pm-2am Mon-Fri, 2pm-4am Sat & Sun; ⊙ line 6 to Itaewon, Exit 4

Reggae rhythms on the sound system are the main attraction at this Jamaican outpost, but there is pool and darts. Jamaican-style wings, curry and hamburgers are on the menu, and a dance area with disco ball lighting gives the pub a clubby atmosphere as the night progresses on weekends.

SEOUL PUB Map p60   Pub
☎ 793 6666; Itaewonno, Itaewon; ⊙ noon-3am Sun-Thu, noon-6am Fri & Sat; ⊙ line 6 to Itaewon, Exit 4

Recently, the revived Seoul Pub has had a real pub atmosphere – loud and happy – at the weekend, lubricated by plenty of pitchers and the Guinness and Kilkenny on tap. Snacks are W5000, meals W12,000.

HONGDAE, SINCHON & YEOUIDO

Nothing is too weird for Hongdae and Sinchon – anyone fancy a cocktail served in an IV bag? No more spilling your drink as you rave the night away. Evenings often start off at any convenience store (they all sell alcohol) that has a few chairs outside. Some cafés, like some bars, make an effort to stand out from the crowd, with foot baths or a fantasy design, but there are 'normal' ones, too.

360@ Map p63   Bar
☎ 323 2360; Hongik-gil, Hongdae; ⊙ 2pm-5am; ⊙ line 2 to Hongik University, Exit 5

Dip your feet in the pool, sit in a shady garden swing seat or recline on a bed indoors at this eccentric bar, full of places to relax as you listen to their tunes. Large beers are W5000, cocktails W10,000.

FLOWER Map p64   Bar
☎ 322 8708; Sinchon; drinks from W5000, snacks W12,000; ⊙ 5pm-4am; ⊙ line 2 to Sinchon, Exit 2

Step inside this Arabian fantasyland and relax on floor cushions in screened compartments while sucking on a shisha pipe. The extraordinary, extravagantly designed bar has a wraparound balcony and large trees – avoid falling into the river after downing too many drinks. Wine, beer and cocktails range from W5000 to W7000, so how could you not go see?

JANE'S GROOVE Map p63   Bar
☎ 3143 5375; Wausan-gil, Hongdae; drinks from W2000; ☙ 7pm-4am; ◉ line 2 to Hongik University, Exit 5
This chameleonlike bar has computer games, darts and screens, plus dance and chill-out zones. It sometimes morphs into a karaoke, open-mic, fancy-dress or live-music joint (admission up to W15,000). Try a 'Jane's bucket', which is vodka, Red Bull and lemon. Jane's Groove has a cool, relaxed, foreigner-friendly atmosphere.

LABRIS Map p63   Bar
☎ 333 5276; Wausan-gil, Hongdae; ☙ 7pm-2am Mon-Thu, 7pm-5am Fri-Sun; ◉ line 2 to Hongik University, Exit 5
Up on the 8th floor, this newly opened social-cum–dance club is for women only and is lesbian oriented. It attracts locals and foreigners with its three levels of differently coloured, comfortable sofas. DJ nights are Friday to Sunday when the minimum charge for a drink and compulsory *anju* is W17,000.

OG BAR Map p63   Bar
☎ 325 8771; Hongdae; ☙ 5pm-4am; ◉ line 2 to Hongik University, Exit 5
A basic concrete-and-candles bar with cheerful music. It specialises in weird beer cocktails such as sweet-and-sour beer, guava beer and even coffee beer. They taste better than they sound and cost W5000, making this a good spot to start an evening.

PRINCESS Map p63   Café
☎ 335 6703; Hongdae; drinks W7000; ☙ 10am-4am; ◉ line 2 to Hongik University, Exit 5
Candles and chandeliers light the steps down to this winter palace of a café. White curtains around the tables give privacy to your little white princess world. Ballads, a glittery decor and dainty cakes add to the princess effect.

ZIBE Map p63   Café
☎ 3141 1357; Hongdae; drinks W5000-10,000, food W8000-12,000; ☙ 3pm-3am Jun-Aug & Dec-Feb, 5pm-3am Sep-Nov & Mar-May; ◉ line 2 to Hongik University, Exit 5
Pronounced 'Jeebay', the name means 'at home' (a place to relax), but this ramshackle two-storey glasshouse is more like homemade than home. Inhabited by a large footbath and lots of floor-cushion areas with flimsy curtains around them, the music is global.

BEATLES Map p64   Bar
☎ 323 6385; Sinchon; ☙ 7pm-3am; ◉ line 2 to Sinchon, Exit 2
An enviable record collection of over 10,000 LPs fills a wall in this basement log-cabin 'old music' (ie 1960s and '70s) bar where beers cost W4000. The host is laid-back and the atmosphere is quiet and relaxing.

TIN PAN MUSIC BAR Map p63   Music Bar
☎ 322 6949; Hongdae; ☙ 7pm-4am Sun-Thu, to 6am Fri & Sat; ◉ line 2 to Hongik University, Exit 5
Down in the basement, this is a large but welcoming and comfortable bar. Maybe it's the B52s (Baileys, Kahlúa, Bacardi 151 and Cointreau), but there's usually dancing on the tables in the early hours – the railings on the ceiling are to hang on to! The notorious Bacardi 151 is strong enough to be inflammable.

WOODSTOCK Map p64   Music Bar
☎ 334 1310; Sinchon; ☙ 7pm-4am; ◉ line 2 to Sinchon, Exit 2
Years of scribbles have built up all over the walls, tables and chairs in this bar where the big attraction is the loud rock music selected from its huge collection. Beer is W2000 a glass or W10,000 a pitcher.

NAMUGEUNEUL Map p63   Spa Café
☎ 335 3033; Saemulgyeol 2-gil, Hongdae; drinks W5000; ☙ 10am-11pm; ◉ line 2 to Hongik University, Exit 5
The unique experience here is the spa footbath, perfect for relaxing those tired and aching feet. The footbath contains over 50 small 'doctor fish' who just love nibbling at the dead skin on your feet. It's a strange sensation, somewhere between tingling and nipping, but your feet do feel refreshed

after a 15-minute session, which costs only W2000. Look for 'Dr Fish' on the 2nd-floor sign.

GANGNAM & JAMSIL

North of Gangnam subway station on both sides of the road is a popular entertainment district, which includes Irish and German bars. New hot spots are the bars springing up around Dosan Park in Apgujeong and along Garosu-gil.

JUJU TENT BAR Map p68   Bar
☎ 512 3333; Dosandaero, Gangnam; drinks W4000; ⏱ 6pm-6am; ⊕ line 3 to Apgujeong, Exit 6
Particularly popular in summer, this outdoor bar near Apgujeong has a retractable roof and is open all year round. Beer and *soju* are W4000 but the trad food, chicken gizzards, chicken feet, grilled eel, stews and fish, is more expensive (meals W12,000 to W20,000).

ROCK 'N' ROLL BAR Map p68   Bar
☎ 545 4163; Gangnam; ⏱ 8pm-5am; ⊕ line 3 to Apgujeong, Exit 6
A small museum of foreign currencies and personal mementoes adds atmosphere to this long-running three-storey log-cabin bar in pricey Apgujeong, where the cocktails (W9000) are a better deal than the beers (W8000). Meals cost W20,000.

OKTOBERFEST Map p68   Beer Hall
☎ 3481 8881; off Seomyeong-gil, Gangnam; beers W4000; ⏱ 4pm-midnight; ⊕ line 2 to Gangnam, Exit 6
It's much quieter than Oktoberfest at Seoul's first microbrewery but it's still going strong and producing 1000L a day inside this large bare-brick and natural-wood cellar bar. Four freshly produced beers along with German-style meats are served by frock-clad lasses (platters W11,000 to W50,000).

TAKE URBAN Map p68   Café
☎ 519 0001; Bongeunsaro, Gangnam; drinks W2800-5000, food W6000-11,000; ⏱ 8am-midnight; ⊕ line 2 to Gangnam, Exit 7
One of the smart new breed of stylish cafés that are sprouting all over the city. Places like Take Urban add sophistication to Seoul's burgeoning café scene, with indoor and outdoor options, heaps of designer-style fresh bakery items and organic coffee.

DUBLIN Map p68   Irish Pub
☎ 561 3281; Gangnam; meals W18,000; ⏱ 4pm-2am; ⊕ line 2 to Gangnam, Exit 7
Sit outside under the small trees or inside by a window and watch the world go by as you down a draft Guinness or Kilkenny with your toe tapping to Irish music. Bottled beers include Newcastle Brown in this very large dark-wood bar that's almost the size of Dublin.

SEOUL'S HIDDEN BYWAYS

A stretch of traditional homes in Bukchon Hanok Village (p45)

Yetchatjip (p116), one of the many traditional teahouses in Insadon

Blink and you'll miss it – just beyond the glaring glass facades and madding crowds of the capital city, a quieter life is being played out. Seoul's winding alleys and hidden lanes offer a hint of what life was like here before the 20th century barged in on the Hermit Kingdom. Take the crest of a particular hill in Samcheong-dong: the pewter-coloured tile roofs cascade gently toward a city glimmering in the distance. From a silent lane, the flickering sea of lights below seems an abstract vision of the future.

ON THE HUNT

Finding Seoul's hushed passageways is a particular art. Follow the wrong lead and your two-lane road will give way to four lanes, and then to six, an automobile-choked cacophony swelling around you. But choose the right street and you'll come to a lesser road; take it. It will peter out to an alley where the whine of engines is blissfully absent, save for the occasional motorbike winding its way along, carting wares.

Down a passage in Insadong, hairpin turns jut at all angles. A petite teashop lures you with a strong waft of today's brew. You slide into a snug booth and, amid the light scent of the wooden interior and the sweet-spicy bite of your *omijacha* (five-flavour tea), you watch the faint shapes of passers-by through white paper windows as they wind down the tiny alley.

Along another lane on a pale winter's afternoon, a street barber has set up shop against a small stone corner of the back wall of Tapgol Park. Wrinkly septuagenarians gather, vested in crisp *hanbok* (traditional clothing). Several grandpas rasp warmly at someone's joke as they shuffle into line to get a W3000 haircut in a folding chair.

Picturesque Namsangol Hanok Village (p55)

After dark, follow the echoes of equally spirited laughter and it will lure you down a twisting passage in Jongno; round the final corner and you're greeted with the sight of hundreds of after-work revellers dining alfresco at round tables jammed into the improbable neck of a crumbling alleyway. Glasses of *soju* (a vodkalike liqour) clink as slabs of pork sizzle on the table-top grills alongside simmering pots of pungent stew, trails of steam and smoke mingling and rising into the night sky.

Save for the occasional modern flourish, life in these gently winding alleyways is lived out as it might have been a century ago.

HOME, SWEET HANOK

Real *hanok* (traditional homes) are one-story homes crafted entirely from wood, save for the tile roofs, insulated with straw. The windows are made of a thin translucent paper that allows daylight to stream in. They're heated with an ingenious system called *ondol,* with heated smoke sent through underfloor passages. Unlike the ostentatious manor homes of Europe, even an aristocrat's lavish *hanok* was designed

Omija for sale at Gyeongdong Market (p91)

WENDING THROUGH HISTORY

The wages of time have not been kind to Seoul's historic neighbourhoods. But despite Japanese colonialism, the Korean War and post-War bulldozers destroying much of Seoul's historical architecture, several old neighbourhoods remain.

While the buildings of Jongno (Map p40) have been largely rebuilt since the war, its snaking network of alleyways, particularly just northwest of Jongno 3-ga, recall the haphazard layout of old Seoul. Street vendors' steaming carts line many of the passages, and alley grog-shops and little hole-in-the-wall restaurants serve the city's heartiest fare. Tapgol Park (p51) is the heart of Jongno; many of Seoul's older denizens gather here to play checkers or traditional Korean games like *baduk*.

On the northwest side of Gyeongbokgung, the neighbourhood of Hyoja-dong (Map p40) has seen a revival after decades of being closed off to the public due to its proximity to the Cheongwadae (p44), South Korea's presidential residence. Named after the devoted male progeny of a Joseon scholar (*hyoja* means 'filial sons'), the area was once home to those who worked for the royal palace. Now that things have relaxed a bit between North and South, anyone can stroll the streets to visit the tasteful cafés and little shops.

The wide main thoroughfare of Insadong (Map p50), lined with hawkers, artisans and musicians, does not at first lend itself to the feel of a forgotten passageway. But make your way off the beaten path – especially down the small laneways just to the east of the main drag – and you'll find an inviting maze of alleys. Many are lined with mammoth old wooden doorways that seem imposing but open to warm, wood-beamed restaurants and intimate teashops (try Dalsaeneun Dalman Saenggak Handa, p116).

But the best is the Montmartre of Seoul, tucked away in Samcheong-dong (p47). Perched high atop a hill in northern Seoul, nestled between the city's two biggest palaces, the area was considered sacred. This neighbourhood – also known as Gahoe-dong (the place where beauty gathers) – is most striking because of the high concentration of *hanok* (traditional homes) populating its precariously steep alleyways.

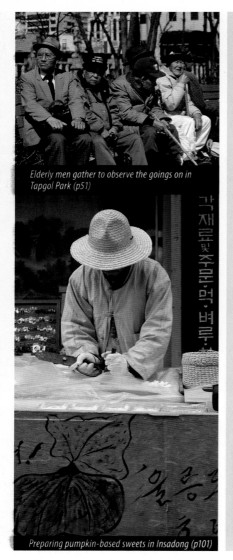

Elderly men gather to observe the goings on in Tapgol Park (p51)

Preparing pumpkin-based sweets in Insadong (p101)

to blend with nature, an aesthetic prevalent through all traditional Korean architecture. All of the rooms look onto an outdoor garden. Life was lived on the floor – eating, working, sleeping and receiving guests – thus all the furniture was low-slung, and people sat and slept on mats rather than chairs and beds.

With South Korea's modernisation, desire to live in *hanok* waned. Their thin walls prevented privacy and made heating difficult. There was no easy space to install indoor toilets. Rooms were small, and living on the floor had its inconveniences. In comparison, Seoul's modern high-rises offered amenities galore. Recently, however, Seoul has seen a revival of interest in traditional homes, with increased efforts to preserve their unique character.

A re-enactment of the gwageo (government-service exam) from the Joseon era (p48)

The roads of Samcheong-dong have not always been restful; in dull moonlight, restless spirits wander these still passages. No surprise -- murder and assassination were part of the fabric of Joseon-era court intrigue.

One of the most famous stories to come out of the area is the sad, sordid tale of King Tanjong. Tanjong assumed the throne in 1452 at barely 12 years of age. His uncle, the calculating Prince Suyang, was thirsty for power and saw an opportunity. Some say he coerced Tanjong into abdicating the throne and forced him to live as a commoner; others say he slaughtered his nephew in cold blood. The massacre that came next is universally acknowledged, as Suyang (now King Sejo) sought to eradicate any remaining officials loyal to his nephew. He arranged for a number of the former king's ministers to be ambushed as they travelled through the area.

No one knows how many lives were lost that day, but the earth was so soaked with blood that great fires had to be lighted to conceal the smell of death. The ashes that fell after the fires had died led to the district being called Jaedong, the 'valley of ashes', just next to Samcheong-dong.

Countless others met a similar fate in the dark of night on the roads that wind their way between the palaces. Though the days of royal reign and the accompanying violence are more than a century in the past, wander the streets of Bukchon in the moonlight and you can still feel a breathless, preternatural stillness.

These days, however, there are newer ghosts in the ranks of the disappeared – they belong to the area's traditional homes themselves, victims of Korea's move into modernity.

Bukchon (p45) is one of the areas in Seoul where you can see hanok close up

Walk through history around Samcheong-dong (p47)

PRESERVATION BLUES

The *hanok* in Samcheong-dong are not the most traditional type, which were quite rambling and featured expansive courtyards. Here, they date largely from the 1930s, after the Japanese colonial government had divided up larger plots of land for smaller houses.

South Korea's efforts to preserve these houses have been met with criticism from activist groups and some private citizens. The city designated the area as full of Local Cultural Assets as early as 1977, and in 2001 rolled out a restoration plan that would provide homeowners with grants and low-interest loans in order to preserve 645,500 sq metres of traditional dwellings. But critics say the plans went awry from there. Due to poor regulation, the government money, they say, was used in many cases to tear down the traditional wooden walls and framework and erect ersatz concrete structures sometimes two storeys high.

In the centre of it all are the residents of these neighbourhoods, and even they fail to agree on the best solution. One set of residents sides with the activists in wanting stricter codes for restoration and greater protection for the last remaining traditional districts. Others make the point that their homes are private property and not a folk village, and they should be allowed to restore their *hanok* along their own terms. These residents say they should also not be denied the ability to make changes to their property and resell it when the real-estate market is hot and every other soul in Seoul is cashing in.

Despite more and more government programs to protect the *hanok*, official statistics show a steady decline in the number of the traditional buildings in the capital. Though there are still 12,000 *hanok* in Seoul today, the number was closer to 800,000 just three decades ago.

But there is a new hope for Seoul's traditional neighbourhoods: the *hanok* is slowly becoming chic. With a national increase in love of all things Korean, even the desire for bigger and better high-rise apartments is being re-evaluated by some locals, who are choosing to build their own traditional dwellings out of natural materials instead. TV shows and films highlight the beauty of these works of art.

While controversial to some traditionalists, these reincarnations of traditional buildings and neighbourhoods are defended by others who say the efforts will help to preserve the special sections of Seoul, giving them new life within the city's fever pitch of change.

OLD HOMES, NEW LIFE

New uses for *hanok* are cropping up everywhere. One of the best ways to experience one is to stay in one of Seoul's cosy *hanok* guesthouses (see boxed text, p149). There is nothing quite like falling into a deep rest in a wood-beamed room, then waking up with the sun to take your tea in a lush, outdoor courtyard.

Other *hanok* have been refashioned into teashops or restaurants, serving everything from traditional fare to wine and cheese. Check out Samcheong-dong (p47) for a diverse culinary collection, as well as Korea House (p105) and Min's Club (p101) for fine fare in a traditional but elegant setting.

Some serve as centres for traditional crafts instruction, including folk painting, needlework and the brewing of traditional Korean drinks, such as chrysanthemum wine and *makgeolli*, a milky, sickly sweet rice wine. Others even serve as dental offices! Patients swear they feel less pain while couched supine in such serene surroundings. Check the Bukchon Culture Centre (p45) for details on all of these activities.

To see *hanok* in a traditional village setting – albeit uninhabited – check out Namsangol Hanok Village (p55) in central Seoul, which features a number of traditional structures from throughout the city restored and moved to a park at the foot of Namsan. For a more interactive excursion, head to the Korean Folk Village (p164) in neighbouring Suwon, where musicians and acrobats entertain you while artisans create pottery, paper and bamboo mats in a setting modelled on a traditional town.

A Korea House banquet (p105)

The farmers' dance at the Korean Folk Village (p164)

Traditional art and crafts are still created at Namsangol Hanok Village (p55)

NIGHTLIFE

top picks

What's your recommendation? lonelyplanet.com/seoul

NIGHTLIFE

Seoulites of all ages love going out and socialising, whether it's with classmates, work colleagues, friends or dates, so entertainment areas are humming every night of the week until late. On Friday and Saturday the revelling continues all night. A common practice is the 'three step' – first choose a neighbourhood to eat and drink, then go to a live-music show or sing in a *noraebang* (karaoke room), and finally hit a dance club and maybe a sauna until the subway system starts up again at 5.30am. Student haunts like Hongdae, Sinchon and Daehangno are swarming with bars, live-music venues, pool halls, *noraebang* and DVD *bang* (a room where you can watch DVDs). The Itaewon expat area has a more foreign party atmosphere on Friday and Saturday nights. On the last Friday of the month, Hongdae's famous Club Day gives admission to 13 dance clubs and live-music venues for W20,000. On these nights Hongdae becomes as crowded as a *Where's Wally?* cartoon.

CLUBBING

Hongdae is home to Seoul's main clubbing scene, but Itaewon and Gangnam have a few choices. Clubs open early but most don't start becoming busy until 10pm and only start buzzing after midnight. Friday and Saturday nights have a real party atmosphere. Clubs have plenty of hard-working DJs, ladies nights and happy hours, while special events often feature foreign DJs. Dress is generally not too strict. Entry costs from W5000 to W10,000 and usually includes a free drink, but may cost more on Friday and Saturday nights or for special events.

BAHIA Map p63

☎ 335 1512; Saemulgyeol 2-gil, Hongdae; admission W5000; ☼ 6pm-midnight Tue-Thu, to 1am Fri-Sun; ◉ line 2 to Hongik University, Exit 5
Seoul's best Latin American dance club, Bahia has a friendly atmosphere and mirrors down one side, so you can check out your moves. Saturday always sizzles, as does Wednesday, which is *bachata* (music originating from the Dominican Republic) night.

CLUB CALIENTE Map p60

☎ 798 1592; above Nashville Sports Bar, Itaewonno, Itaewon; admission W6000; ☼ 6pm-3am Fri-Sun; ◉ line 6 to Itaewon, Exit 4
The varied Latin beats and rhythms laid on by DJ Josh will get you to your feet – especially after a couple of the club's La Rosa *soju* (a vodkalike liqour) mixes. Saturday nights are always packed, and dance lessons are available – ask at the venue for days and times.

CLUB HOOPER Map p63

☎ 011-9122 9569; Wausan-gil, Hongdae; admission W10,000; ☼ 10pm-6am; ◉ line 2 to Hongik University, Exit 5
A hip-hop den in the usual black box with screens, lights, lasers and a smoke machine.

CLUB SAAB Map p63

☎ 324 6929; Wausan-gil, Hongdae; admission W10,000; ☼ 8pm-5am Wed-Mon; ◉ line 2 to Hongik University, Exit 5
Five DJs a night with a hard hip-hop attitude play here, including the popular Schedule 1 and Maniac. It's the nearest thing to gangsta rap in Seoul – you can decide whether it's for show or for real. Beers are W6000.

GRAND OLE OPRY Map p60

☎ 795 9155; Solmaru-gil, Itaewon; admission free; ☼ 6.30pm-1am; ◉ line 6 to Itaewon, Exit 3
This grand ol' country-and-western bar and dance hall, with crates of beer lying around and big Mexican hats on the wall, is still going strong. The barn has plenty of honky-tonk atmosphere, compulsory dancing, staff who chat, cheap drinks and cowboy-music requests, all adding up to a good time for the fans.

JJ MAHONEY'S Map p60

☎ 799 8601; Grand Hyatt Seoul Hotel, Itaewon; admission free; ☼ 6pm-2am; ◉ line 6 to Itaewon, Exit 2
Inside Itaewon's Grand Hyatt Seoul (p152), this classy nightclub has a live band playing every night except Sunday. DJs spin their decks, and special events also liven things up. A beer costs an eye-watering W19,000.

GAY & LESBIAN OPTIONS

Seoul, like the rest of South Korea, is slowly becoming more tolerant of gays and lesbians. The Korea Queer Cultural Festival (p13) has been an annual week-long Seoul fixture since 2000 and includes a parade, parties, live music and films. However, there remains a long way to go before people with alternative sexual preferences are as accepted here as they are in much of the West (see p23).

Utopia (www.utopia-asia.com) features an introduction to Seoul's gay scene. Itaewon is the main area in Seoul, where gay bars and clubs have English-speaking staff and welcome Koreans and foreigners, whether straight or gay. Some of the options:

Always Homme (p116) Chilled-out bar.

Bar Bliss (p116) Friendly, relaxed joint.

Labris (p118) Lesbian-friendly, women-only bar.

Queen (p117) Modern bar with a dance floor.

Soho (p117) Small, relaxed gay and lesbian bar.

Trance (below) Drag princesses hold court at this dance club.

Why Not (p132) Flashy black-box dance arena.

If you get bored you can look at the black-and-white photographs on the wall, but that's assuming you get in – there's a dress code. Take a taxi from the subway.

JOKER RED Map p63
☎ 016-706 7545; www.jokerred.co.kr; Hongdae; admission W5,000; ⏰ 9pm-5am Fri & Sat; Ⓜ line 2 to Hongik University, Exit 5
Up to seven DJs, including Sunshine and Shai, spin the tables at this 'we love techno' club. Its larger and smarter than many others, with enough red lights to justify its name.

KING CLUB Map p60
☎ 794 6869; Sobangseo-gil, Itaewon; admission free; ⏰ 6.30pm-4am Mon-Thu, to 6am Fri-Sun; Ⓜ line 6 to Itaewon, Exit 3
An Itaewon institution that likes to change its spots. Early on the bar girls serve up W5000 drinks to a quiet clientele who play pool and chat, then the GI hip-hop clubbers arrive around 10pm and leave at 1am, when the late, late-night party begins with a more Korean atmosphere. A bottle of Oscar 'champagne' is only W10,000, but you probably won't buy a second.

M2 Map p63
☎ 3143 7573; www.ohoo.net/m2; Hongdae; admission Sun-Thu W10,000, Fri & Sat W20,000; ⏰ 9.30pm-4.30am Sun-Thu, 8.30pm-6.30am Fri & Sat; Ⓜ line 2 to Hongik University, Exit 5
Deep underground is M2, one of the largest and best Hongdae clubs. It has a high ceiling and plenty of lights and visuals.

Top local and international DJs spin mainly progressive house music. Wednesday is ladies night. The only downside at this celeb haunt is that some staff are on the obstinate side.

MACONDO Map p63
☎ 010-3712 4774; www.macondo.co.kr; Hongdae; admission W7000; ⏰ 7.30-11.30pm Mon-Thu, to 5am Fri & Sat; Ⓜ line 2 to Hongik University, Exit 4
Free dancing lessons are a daily attraction at this other long-lasting Latin American dance club where you can show off those salsa, *merengue* and *bachata* moves. It's at the other end of Hongdae from most of the clubs. Drunks aren't welcome.

SK@2 Map p63
☎ 332 9222; Hongdae; admission W10,000; ⏰ 9pm-4am Sun-Thu, to 6am Fri & Sat; Ⓜ line 2 to Hongik University, Exit 5
DJs Hyun Geun and Beat 2 Flow crank up a bit of everything (except ska) on the B1 level. The curtained section with round, red beds is reserved for wealthy whiskey drinkers. Downstairs has house and electronic with a more laser/psychedelic style. Free entry for ladies except Friday and Saturday.

TRANCE Map p60
☎ 797 3410; Dokkaebisijang 2-gil, Itaewon; admission W10,000; ⏰ 10pm-5am; Ⓜ line 6 to Itaewon, Exit 3
Pouting drag princesses Ms Nina and Ms Nang entertain in their own utterly unique style at this small gay club with a DJ and a

stage. The shows don't begin until 2.30am on Friday and Saturday nights. Otherwise this red-and-black dance club serves up mixed dance music.

WHY NOT Map p60

☎ 795 8193; Dokkaebisijang 2-gil, Itaewon; admission W5000 Sun-Fri, W10,000 Sat; ⏲ 8pm-6am; Ⓜ line 6 to Itaewon, Exit 3

This small gay dance arena has been expensively revamped with the latest lights and lasers, splashing green and red stars everywhere. Drag shows start late and DJs crank it up at this 'meet' market until the subway trains start running again at dawn.

LIVE MUSIC

Classy live jazz venues can be found in Daehangno and Apgujeong, as well as in Hongdae and Itaewon. Itaewon has a lively live-music scene, some of it provided by expat bands. But Hongdae is the place for live indie music played in tiny underground venues by Korean student bands with names like Lazy Bone, Vaseline and We Need Surgery. So far only Crying Nut has made it from Hongdae to nationwide celebrity status. Concerts usually run from 7pm to 10.30pm. Gigs are sometimes free and sometimes have a cover charge of up to around W10,000, which usually includes a drink. Find out what's on where from the posters that cover Hongdae, or check out www.koreagigguide.com. Concerts by visiting superstars are often held in Olympic Park or Jamsil sports complex.

ALL THAT JAZZ Map p60

☎ 795 5701; www.allthatjazz.kr; Itaewonno, Itaewon; admission W5000; ⏲ 7pm-1am; Ⓜ line 6 to Itaewon, Exit 1

A fixture on the Seoul jazz scene for over 30 years, top local musicians regularly perform here. The live music starts at 9pm except on Friday (8.30pm) and Saturday and Sunday (both 7pm). Besides beer, you can order frozen cocktails, wines and even dinner. Check the website for the schedule.

CLUB EVANS Map p63

☎ 337 8361; Wausan-gil, Hongdae; admission W7000; ⏲ 7.30-11.30pm Sun-Thu, to 12.30am Fri & Sat; Ⓜ line 2 to Hongik University, Exit 5

Come to Evans (on the 2nd floor) for great jazz and a great atmosphere. Two bands (three on Saturdays) start at around 9pm.

Try to catch harmonica player Jun Je-duk. Drinks are W4000.

CLUB FF Map p63

☎ 011-9025 3407; Hongdae; admission W10,000; ⏲ 7pm-6am; Ⓜ line 2 to Hongik University, Exit 6

A top live venue with up to eight bands playing at the weekend until midnight. Afterwards it becomes a dance club with DJs. Local bands such as Galaxy Express and Pink Elephant play here. The youthful groups let rip with attitude and style.

DGBD Map p63

☎ 322 3792; Hongdae; admission W5000 or W10,000; ⏲ 8-11pm; Ⓜ line 2 to Hongik University, Exit 5

A legendary live-music venue (previously called Drug) where all the top Hongdae bands have played over the years. It's standing-room only, although there are a few chairs and a balcony. The menu is mainly rock but not always, and with the closure of Skunk Hell, punk acts are likely to migrate here.

FEEL Map pp56-7

☎ 778 2401; Samilro, Myeong-dong; admission W7000; ⏲ 8pm-3am; Ⓜ line 4 to Myeong-dong, Exit 10

This place is an unbelievable junkyard and owner Mr Shin is totally eccentric, but he speaks a bit of English and he and his friends cover anything and everything, including Simon and Garfunkel songs played on the accordion.

FREE BIRD Map p63

☎ 335 4576; 2fl, Eoulmadang 2-gil, Hongdae; admission free Mon-Thu, W13,000 Fri-Sun; ⏲ 6pm-midnight; Ⓜ line 2 to Hongik University, Exit 5

More loungelike than it used to be, with a range of live music from death rock to *Sound of Music* outtakes, the long-running Free Bird generally puts on solid shows. A handful of acts play every evening. Wednesday is audition night.

LIVE JAZZ CLUB Map p52

☎ 743 5555; Maronie 2-gil, Daehangno; admission W7,000; ⏲ 5pm-3am; Ⓜ line 4 to Hyehwa, Exit 2

Daehangno is home to the Seoul Jazz Academy, and this large but intimate venue, with black decor subtly blended with blue neon, attracts top Korean jazz stars such as

MUSIC IS MY LIFE

Does your band (Pink Elephant) write their own songs? Yes. All the Hongdae indie bands do their own material. The four band members, we write them together – one does a guitar riff, then another some words, like that.

What do you write about? Young people's lives. Emotions.

Do you write in Korean or English? Both. Our first CD has two English songs and eight Korean ones.

Do you make any money? Not really. In Hongdae we play for nothing, or get paid W50,000 or W100,000. But we play to get known, to improve our music. Outside Hongdae we might get W300,000 for a concert, but Korean people like K-pop rather than rock, so the market is much smaller here than in other countries.

How do you earn money? Our first CD is selling, and I work as bar manager in a live-music club.

Do you have a manager? No. Our fans help us.

Which bands do you admire? Mainly Britpop – The Clash, Strokes, Jam, Libertines, Arctic Monkeys. I travelled to Europe in 2007 and went to the Glastonbury Festival. It was a magical experience for me.

Do you live with your parents? No, I live in Hongdae.

Why Hongdae? Hongdae has culture. It's very creative, it has many colours.

Are your parents happy that you work in a band and not in an office? My brother works in a bank, but I only want to do music. My parents are a little worried about my future.

An interview with Park Ji-won, bass guitarist in up-and-coming Seoul rock band Pink Elephant.

saxophonist Lee Jeong-suk and his quartet. Enjoy two or three sessions every evening in this jazz haven.

OLE STOMPERS ROCK SPOT Map p60
☎ 795 9155; Solmanaru-gil, Itaewon; ⏰ 7pm-2am Sun-Thu, to 4am Fri & Sat; Ⓜ line 6 to Itaewon, Exit 3

This muso-owned Itaewon pub has live music, often a rocking blues expat band, most Fridays and Saturdays around 10pm. Look out for the Battle of the Bands shows, which have big prize money and attract top local talent, both Korean and expat. The signature drink is 'tek and mek' – draft beer with a shot of tequila (W5000).

ONCE IN A BLUE MOON Map p68
☎ 549 5490; Seolleungno, Gangnam; admission free; ⏰ 5pm-2am; Ⓜ line 3 to Apgujeong, Exit 6

An intimate and famous Apgujeong club with live jazz from two groups of performers every night, each performing two sets between 7.30pm and 12.40am. The free admission is offset by charging W15,000 for cocktails and beers, and eating costs lots more.

SOUNDHOLIC Map p63
☎ 3142 4203; Hongdae; admission W10,000-20,000; ⏰ 8-10pm Tue-Fri & Sun, 11pm-1.30am Sat; Ⓜ line 2 to Hongik University, Exit 5

This place is your usual black box of a live-music club. It hosts rock bands, generally loud ones.

TA Map p63
☎ 6085 5150; Hongdae; admission W15,000; ⏰ 7pm-3am Mon-Thu, to 5am Fri-Sun; Ⓜ line 2 to Hongik University, Exit 5

Live acoustic music sets usually run from around 9.30pm until midnight Friday to Sunday. The Turkish-themed decor of floor cushions and bongo drums adds to the relaxing ambiance.

WOODSTOCK Map p60
☎ 749 6034; Itaewonno, Itaewon; admission free; ⏰ 6pm-late; Ⓜ line 6 to Itaewon, Exit 2

Up on the 3rd floor, expat bands blast out rock music every Friday and Saturday, starting around 9pm. Bars named Woodstock are usually deliberately scruffy dens, and this one is no exception.

KARAOKE

Seoul has thousands of *noraebang*, where friends and work colleagues sing along to well-known songs, including plenty with English lyrics. Every Seoulite in every age group seems to sing well. Most *noraebang* open from 2pm to 2am, and prices start at around W12,000 an hour, although luxury ones or large rooms cost more. Want to really impress your Korean business contacts? Belt out a heartfelt version of 'My Way' as loudly as you can and you'll clinch the deal. No alcohol is served, though a few have hostesses who help patrons have a good time by holding their hand and applauding almost enthusiastically after each song, however tone deaf they are. You'll have no trouble finding *noraebang* in pretty much any neighbourhood.

LUXURY NORAEBANG Map p63
☎ 322 3111; Eoulmadang-gil, Hongdae; room per hr W10,000-36,000; ⊙ 24hr; ⊚ line 2 to Hongik University, Exit 5
Sing along with the video songs in a range of mostly palatial rooms in this new breed of *noraebang*, open all night and providing a luxurious setting for acting out those rock-star fantasies. Check out the photos of the room styles before paying. The more expensive rooms can take 10 people.

OPERA HOUSE NORAEBANG Map p52
☎ 766 5198; Maronie 1-gil, Daehangno; small/big rooms per hr W15,000/30,000; ⊙ 2pm-6am; ⊚ line 4 to Hyehwa, Exit 2
Sing as loud as you want in these basement karaoke rooms, which feature red seats, two microphones, a bank of four screens, a tambourine, a disco light and hundreds of English songs.

top picks

The arts are surprisingly well catered for in Seoul. Check out the dance festivals for Western and Korean traditional and modern dance events, which of course leap over any language barrier. Theatre, except for drama festivals, is invariably in the Korean language, but musicals and mime shows (such as *Nanta*) can still be enjoyed by visitors who don't understand any Korean. The very lively theatre scene in Daehangno is worth at least one visit – dive in and who knows what you might find?

Western movies are shown in cinemas in their original language with subtitles at a very reasonable cost, while the many excellent modern Korean movies (see p26) can be watched in DVD *bang* (DVD rooms) with English subtitles.

Concerts of Western and Korean music – traditional, classical and modern – can be heard every day of the week. Whatever you fancy – Mozart or Motown, Billy Joel, Seoul punksters Crying Nut or the latest hot foreign DJ – you can hear it live in Seoul.

THEATRE & DANCE

A handful of theatres present traditional music, dance and drama, often with English commentary on a screen. Shows usually include half a dozen different dance and music styles. The most fun are energetic farmers' *samullori* group dances, where the dancers play a variety of percussion instruments, while the oddest is *pansori,* a solo opera with one singer who sings in a strained voice accompanied by a drummer. Gymnastic stand-up drumming on three drums is a crowd favourite, as is the elegant fan dance. Shamanist and Buddhist dances add a more serious note, and *gayageum* (zither) and flute instrumentals also feature.

Modern Korean musicals such as *Nanta, Jump* and *Ballerina Who Loved B-Boy* can be enjoyed by foreigners, as there are few or no words and they mainly consist of mime, music and dancing. Outdoor theatre has been experimented with recently at Gyeonghuigung (p44) with a musical drama based on the popular TV drama series *Daejanggeum,* the story of a female royal chef set in a Joseon palace. The TV drama has been a hit from Mongolia to Malaysia, and from Jordan to Japan.

Western-style opera, classical music, ballet, modern dance and musicals are regularly staged at the Seoul Arts Centre and the Sejong Centre.

Daehangno is home to a talented, lively and youthful drama scene with over 60 small theatres competing for audiences. At present musicals are all the rage, and sometimes top local film actors or singers star in the shows. Tickets are usually W12,000 to W25,000, but everything is in Korean.

ARKO ART THEATRE Map p52
☎ 760 4640; Marronnier Park, Daehangno; Ⓜ line 4 to Hyehwa, Exit 2
This large red-brick theatre was designed by leading architect Kim Swoo-geun and opened in 1981. The 600-seat and 150-seat venues put on a varied dance-oriented program of events and shows, as well as hosting the annual Seoul Performing Arts Festival and the International Modern Dance Festival.

CHONGDONG THEATRE Map p40
☎ 751 1500; www.chongdong.com; Gwanghwa-mun; shows W30,000-40,000; ⊙ shows 8pm

---

ARTS FESTIVALS

Seoul hosts a cultural festival almost every week (see p12). The Seoul Performing Arts Festival (www.spaf21.com) held every autumn lasts a month and is a mix of top-class local and international acts. A well-established, two-week International Modern Dance Festival (www.modafe.org) is held every spring, based at the Arko Art Theatre (above) in Daehangno. The two-week Seoul Fringe Festival takes over the student area in Hongdae in late August with art, dance, drama and street performances. The National Theatre (opposite) hosts a 10-day Traditional Dance Festival in late August, while the three-week Seoul International Dance Festival (www.sidance.org) in October is based mainly in the Seoul Arts Centre (p138).

TICKET RESERVATIONS

In Daehangno go to the Sarang Ticket Office (Map p52; ☎ 762 4242; Marronnier Park; ⊙ 9.30am-7.30pm Tue-Sat, 9.30am-6pm Sun), which has a list of the shows and a map of where the theatres are. Shows run Tuesday to Sunday. Staff are helpful and there's free internet access.

Tue-Sun Apr-Sep, 4pm Tue-Sun Oct-Mar; ⊙ line 1 or 2 to City Hall, Exit 2
This well-established theatre is centrally located, just around the corner from Deoksugung. Shows last for 1½ hours and usually include lively percussionists, *gayageum* performers, shamanist exorcisms, a *pansori* soloist and a fan dance. English subtitles appear on a screen. Arrive an hour before the show for a percussion class (W15,000). The ticket office opens at 7pm or you can book online.

DONGSOONG ARTS CENTRE Map p52
☎ 741 3391; Dongsung-gil, Daehangno; ⊙ line 4 to Hyehwa, Exit 1
This leading theatre puts on serious modern dramas, sometimes luring famous movie actors to the stage, but all performances are in Korean.

HAKCHON GREEN THEATRE Map p52
☎ 763 8233; www.hakchon.co.kr; off Dongsung-gil, Daehangno; adult/student W28,000/22,000; ⊙ line 4 to Hyehwa, Exit 2
The popular rock musical *Line 1* staged here takes a satirical look at Seoul – the 'Ladies of Gangnam' song and dance routine is a memorable highlight. The nearly three-hour show has English subtitles on a screen on Wednesdays, Fridays and Sundays. After running for 15 years and 4000 performances, at the time of writing there were plans to replace it with a new, updated version – perhaps it will be called *Line 2*.

KOREA HOUSE Map pp56-7
☎ 2266 9101; www.koreahouse.or.kr; Namsan; shows W35,000; ⊙ shows 7pm & 8.50pm Mon-Sat, 8pm Sun; ⊙ line 3 or 4 to Chungmuro, Exit 3
This intimate 150-seat theatre stages one-hour performances after its fine dinners (see p105). Put on by a troupe of top musicians and dancers, the shows have some English commentary on a screen. Tradi-tional items include elegant court dances, *pansori*, a fan dance, a spiritual shamanist dance, *samullori* and *samgomu* – acrobatic female drummers each banging on three drums.

NANTA THEATRE Map p40
☎ 739 8288; Gwanghwamun; tickets W50,000-60,000; ⊙ shows 2pm, 5pm & 8pm Mon-Sat, 3pm & 6pm Sun; ⊙ line 1 or 2 to City Hall, Exit 2
Set in a kitchen, this long-running, high-octane show mixes varied ingredients – magic tricks, circus acts, drumming with kitchen utensils, comedy, dance, martial arts and audience participation – to produce a clever and entertaining musical pantomime that has broken box office records.

NATIONAL THEATRE Map pp56-7
☎ 2274 3507; www.ntok.go.kr; Namsan; ⊙ line 3 Dongguk University, Exit 6
On Namsan, this complex is home to the national drama, national *changgeuk* (Korean opera), national orchestra and national dance companies. Venues include the main hall and outdoor stages where free concerts and movies are put on in summer. The website shows the varied schedule. It's a 15-minute walk from the subway exit or take the yellow bus 2 (W800, every 10 minutes) from the bus stop just behind Exit 6.

SEJONG CENTRE FOR THE PERFORMING ARTS Map p40
☎ 399 1111; www.sejongpac.or.kr; Sejongno, Gwanghwamun; ⊙ line 5 to Gwanghwamun, Exit 1

MY KOREAN ROCK MUSICAL EXPERIENCE

I loved the Korean rock musical that the Sarang Ticket Office recommended, even though I couldn't understand a word of it except for one song in English. The story was about a new rock band trying to make it big. The six members of the band were all distinctive and funny, and they were really accomplished musicians as well as being talented actors. I felt I was actually at a rock gig when they performed their numbers with such gusto and did all the rock-star gestures so convincingly. The theatre was small which meant we were so close to the actors. It was a very enjoyable and fun evening despite not understanding the language.
From an interview with Marie, a traveller from New Zealand.

Centrally located, this leading arts complex puts on major drama, music and art shows – everything from large-scale musicals to fusion *gugak* (traditional Korean music) and gypsy violinists. It has a grand hall, a small theatre and three art galleries. Check out the website for what's on and ticketing options.

SEOUL ARTS CENTRE Map pp36-7
☎ 580 1300; www.sac.or.kr; South Seoul; ⓔ line 3 to Nambu Bus Terminal, Exit 5
This sprawling arts complex has a circular opera house with a roof shaped like a Korean nobleman's hat. It also houses the 700-seat Towol Theatre and the smaller Jayu Theatre. The national ballet and opera companies are based here. Music House consists of a large concert hall and a smaller recital hall and is home to the national choir, the Korea and Seoul symphony orchestras and the Seoul performing arts company.

There are also three art galleries here: Hangaram Design Museum (☎ 580 1490; admission free-W10,000; ⏱ 11am-7pm, closed last Mon of each month), Hangaram Art Museum (☎ 580 1272; admission free-W10,000; ⏱ 11am-7pm, closed last Mon of each month) and Seoul Calligraphy Museum (☎ 580 1282; admission free; ⏱ 11am-7pm). The website has a calendar of the many events, shows and programs.

To reach it, walk straight on from the subway exit and turn left at the end of the bus terminal, or else hop on bus 12 (W800) or grab a taxi (W2000).

SEOUL NORIMADANG Map p70
☎ 410 3168; outside Lotte World, Jamsil; admission free; ⏱ shows 3pm Sat & Sun Apr-Oct; ⓔ line 2 or 8 to Jamsil, Exit 3
This large, covered outdoor arena hosts entertaining traditional music and dance performances on weekend afternoons. Shows include masked satirical plays, dynamic drumming demonstrations and group and individual dancing. The standard is high and local pensioners come along. If you are inside Lotte World, follow the signs to Charlotte Theatre.

YEAKDANG THEATRE Map pp36-7
☎ 580 3300; South Seoul; tickets W8000-10,000; ⓔ line 3 to Nambu Bus Terminal, Exit 5
This theatre, part of the National Center for Korean Traditional Performing Arts (www.ncktpa

.go.kr), puts on an ever-changing program by leading performers every Saturday at 5pm from early January to mid December. The 1½-hour show is a bargain and usually contains seven items including court dances, folk songs, *pansori*, *gayageum*, flute music and drumming. Take a taxi (W2000) or the shuttle bus (W800) from the subway exit, or walk (about 15 minutes).

FILM
Luxurious new multiplex cinemas with large screens and the latest sound equipment are opening all round Seoul. Films are usually shown from around 11am to 11pm. English-language films are shown in cinemas with their original soundtrack and Korean subtitles. Korean-language movies shown in cinemas don't have English subtitles, but you can see them in a DVD *bang* with English subtitles. Cinemas are popular with young people, perhaps because tickets are a modest W7000. Cinemas are all basically the same here.

COEX MALL MEGABOX Map p70
☎ 6002 1200; COEX Mall, Jamsil; tickets W7000; ⏱ 9am-midnight
A mega-popular 17-screen multiplex cinema with over 4000 seats. Queues can build up at busy times.

DVD BANG
A DVD *bang* is the best place to see Korean movies, as they can be shown with English subtitles. See p26 for reviews of some excellent recent Korean films. The hundreds of DVD *bang* are all similar: you watch the film on a big screen sitting on a comfortable sofa in your own private room. Needless to say they are popular with dating couples and some are open all night.

CINE CASTLE DVD Map p52
☎ 741 1580; Maronie 2-gil, Daehangno; tickets W7500; ⏱ 12.30pm-2am; ⓔ line 4 to Hyehwa, Exit 2
Watch a movie in a small *bang* on a big, big screen, lounging back on a reclining seat up on the 4th floor. This one is the budget student version of a DVD *bang*. Take the lift.

SPORTS & ACTIVITIES

top picks

What's your recommendation? lonelyplanet.com/seoul

Seoulites keep fit with a range of activities (besides lifting heavy shopping bags). As with most things, they mix East and West. They're mad keen on 24-hour spas and hiking, taekwondo and golf, and in the freezing winters skiing and ice skating take over. Baseball and soccer have the most armchair fans, but horse racing draws thousands to south Seoul every weekend afternoon.

HEALTH & FITNESS
24-HOUR SPAS

Don't leave Seoul without enjoying a sweat and a soak in one of the many spas, saunas or *jjimjilbang* (luxury spas). Spartan saunas cost only W5000, but upmarket *jjimjilbang* (which have internet and DVD rooms, cafés, and luxury decor), cost from W7000 to W14,000.

Take your shoes off when entering and put them in the locker provided. In the changing room, take off all your clothes, and put on the robe or uniform shorts and T-shirt provided. Then you must wash and clean yourself thoroughly at the communal showers before gently lowering yourself into a hot bath. The heat soaks into weary bodies, soothing tired muscles and minds. Relaxing and turning pink in a hot bath like a steamed dumpling is good therapy, enhanced when you then plunge into a cold bath.

Spas offer a variety of baths (maybe green tea or ginseng) and saunas (mugwort, pine or jade). Soap and shampoo are supplied, as well as toothpaste and toothbrushes, and the ladies section usually has hairdryers, foot massagers, lotions and perfumes. Have your hair cut as well as your shoes shined. Men and women are always separate in the bath area when its time to strip down to your birthday suit, but saunas, napping rooms and other facilities may be mixed.

Most spas are open 24 hours and offer body scrubs, manicures, pedicures and facials. The massages and body scrubs (to remove dead skin) are usually more on the rigorous than relaxing side. Most spas allow patrons to sleep over for the night for an extra W2000 or so – you sleep side by side on thin mattresses in a communal area with a hard pillow.

You pay when you enter, and the more modern spas will give you a locker key that's also an electronic tag to keep track of your spending while in the spa. The basic entry fee usually covers up to 12 hours of unlimited use of all the different baths and saunas.

CHUNJIYUN SPA Map pp56-7
☎ 318-8011; Jungmuro, Myeong-dong; admission W15,000; ⏰ 24hr; ⊘ line 4 to Myeong-dong, Exit 8
Popular with locals and Japanese tourists, this spa is compact and cosy, offering the essentials – a pinewood, jade and clay sauna as well as green tea, ginseng and mugwort hot baths. An extra W82,000 covers a body scrub, oil massage and cucumber facial. With salmon-pink walls and posters of Korean celebs, it can feel as if you've stumbled into a teenage girl's bedroom, but staff are helpful and speak a little English. From the subway exit, take the second alley on the left. It's in the basement of the building with 'Sunshine' written on it in red letters.

DRAGON HILL SPA Map pp36-7
☎ 792-0001; www.dragonhillspa.co.kr; Yongsan; day/night W10,000/12,000; ⏰ 24hr; ⊘ line 1 to Yongsan, Exit 1 or 2
This new luxury spa is spread out over seven floors. In addition to outdoor baths, charcoal saunas, crystal salt rooms and ginseng and cedar baths, there is a golf driving range, cinema and rooftop garden with an Indian Barbeque Village. The outdoor unisex pool is perfect for families.

The spacious interior is a beguiling mix of gaudy Las Vegas bling and Asian chic – there's a sauna shaped like the pyramids but also a bamboo forest lit up with neon green lights. There's always a smattering of foreigners – Russian models, Filipino migrant workers and Western English teachers. The staff speak basic English and many signs are in English.

Exit into Yongsan train station, leave by Exit 1, turn right past IPark Mall and look for the signs. The entrance is through the bamboo grove.

NEW SEOUL MUD Map p60
☎ 747 8802; Itaewonno, Itaewon; sauna W10,000; ⏰ 9am-10.30pm; ⊘ line 6 to Itaewon, Exit 3
Beauty treatments (from W60,000) include foot massages, ginseng baths, special soft

mud packs and skin scrapes as well as body oil, milk, mugwort and steam treatments.

SPA LEI Map p68

☎ 545 4113; www.spalei.co.kr; Gangnam; day/ night rate W12,000/14,000; ☺ 24hr; ◉ line 3 to Sinsa, Exit 5

Sorry fellas, this one is just for the ladies. Spa Lei is a luxurious spa providing excellent services in an immaculate, stylish environment. There are earthy tones of brown, grey and orange using a range of materials including stained wood, marble and rock. Joseon-era furniture, candelabras towering over gilt mirrors and winding vines add an antique touch. The saunas include the much-loved pinewood one, and you can hop from saltwater pool to ginseng, mineral and rose baths. The restaurant and café have patios. Staff are helpful and are used to dealing with foreigners. From Exit 5 go straight and take the second turning on the left. You'll see Spa Lei in the basement to your left.

ACTIVITIES

ADVENTURE SPORTS

White-water rafting tours in the province of Gangwon-do province are run by the USO (p181). Contact Kim Seok-jin at the Adventure Club (www.adventurekorea.com) for caving, rock climbing, white-water rafting, paintball games and other adventurous outdoor activities, including perhaps the ultimate adventure – a trip across the DMZ to North Korea.

BASEBALL

Whack baseballs pitched to you by machine at Baseball Hitting Practice (Map p50; Insadong-gil, Insadong; 11 balls W1000; ☺ 9am-1am) in Insadong or Baseball Hitting Practice (Map p52; Daehangno; 13 balls W500; ☺ 11am-midnight) in Daehangno.

CYCLING

See the entries for Olympic Park (p67) and Ttukseom Seoul Forest Park (p76) for a couple of easy and very enjoyable cycle rides. Cycleways run along both sides of the Han River past sports fields and picnic areas, and there are plenty of bicycle hire stalls (per hr W3000; ☺ 9am-8.30pm Mar-Nov). Bring your own padlock, and you must leave a driving licence or other ID. The riverside cycleway can be crowded on weekends.

Yeouido to the World Cup Stadium

Take subway line 5 to Yeouinaru station and leave by Exit 2. Walk down the steps to the bicycle rental stall (per hr W3000; ☺ 9am-8.30pm Mar-Nov). Cycle left along the river before taking a detour to the green-domed National Assembly (p66). From the National Assembly, cycle on for about 1km to Yanghwa Bridge, which you use to cross over the river. Walk up the steps on the far side of the bridge, pushing your bike up the little bike track beside the steps.

Stop half-way across the river to look around Seonyudo (Map p64), a very pretty island with lily-covered ponds, plant nurseries and plenty of plantings. The fast-food café–bar Naru (meals W2500-7000; ☺ 11am-11pm) has wonderful river views.

On the other side of the river, wheel your bicycle down the steps and turn right. After 10 minutes you should reach Hangang Windsurfing (☎ 337 6663; per hr W20,000; ☺ 9am-6pm Feb-Nov). Carry on under the orange Seongsan bridge, ride over a small bridge across a stream and turn right (no sign) and then left (at the sign) and you will soon reach the World Cup Stadium (p75).

For a 6km (30-minute) detour, cycle around what is now an attractive green hill (but used to be a mountain of garbage). Cross the major road to Nanjicheon Park (Map pp36–7; ☺ 6am-7pm) and just keep going.

Return to Yeouido retracing the same route. Without the detour the 7km cycle ride takes about three hours including time spent looking around.

GOLF

Private golf courses are usually for members only, but there are driving ranges in top-end hotels and elsewhere. At Olympic Coliseum Golf (Map p68; ☎ 514 7979; Seolleungno, Gangnam; ☺ 5am-10pm; ◉ line 3 to Apgujeong, Exit 2) customers can hit golf balls, use the gym and relax in the spa, all for W30,000 (70 minutes).

ICE SKATING

Lotte World's indoor ice-skating rink (p69) is open all year. In winter skate under the stars at the magical, inexpensive ice-skating rink that appears on Seoul Plaza (Map p40), outside City Hall. Swimming pools along the Han River freeze over and become skating rinks, as does the pool at the Grand Hyatt Seoul (p152), which can only be reached by taxi.

POOL, FOUR BALL & THREE BALL

Seoul is full of pool halls – look for the cues-and-coloured-balls signs. The halls usually have both pool tables (pool is called 'pocket-ball' here) and tables for four ball and three ball. The cost can be as low as W6000 per hour but it might be more.

Four ball is played in Belgium and the Netherlands but is most popular in South Korea. There are no pockets – players must hit cannons (or caroms). Two red balls and two white ones are used. The players (any number) hit the white balls in turn.

Players try to reach a score of zero. It's a handicap system, so beginners start with a score of three points. When you improve you start with five points, then eight, then 10 and so on. When your score reaches zero, to finish you must do a more difficult shot – hit the side-cushion three times while hitting both red balls without hitting the other white ball. A player scores minus one if they're successful and their white ball hits both the red balls without touching the other white ball, and can take another turn. Players score nothing for hitting just one red, and plus one for hitting the other white ball or missing everything.

With three ball you must hit both balls and a cushion.

Some of the many options:

Hidinck Pool (Map p52; Maronie-gil, Daehangno; per hr W12,000; ☺ noon–5am; ◉ line 4, Exit 2) Named after a Korean hero, the coach of Korea's 2002 World Cup soccer team, this is an expensive but very pleasant pool parlour, up on the 4th floor. It's mainly *dangujang* (four ball) but there is pocketball (pool), too.

Lotte World Pool Hall (Map p70; B3 fl, Lotte World, Jamsil; pool/three ball/four ball per hr W6800/9600/10,800; ☺ 10am–10pm; ◉ line 2 or 8 to Jamsil, Exit 3)

SKIING

The cold winters and mountainous terrain make Korea an ideal country for winter sports. Prices are reasonable and ski resorts offer a range of accommodation from youth hostels and basic *minbak* (private homes with rooms for rent) to condominiums and luxury hotels. The ski season runs from December to February. Ski clothes and equipment and English-speaking instructors can be hired. The dozen or so ski resorts have offices in Seoul and offer all-inclusive one-day package

tours from W80,000. The USO (p181) organises weekend ski trips.

Five ski resorts in Gyeonggi province are close to Seoul, but they can be very crowded, so it's best to go on a weekday, get up early and ski in the morning. Bear's Town (Map p161) has 10 slopes and is popular with foreigners, but serious skiers should consider going further afield to Korea's best ski resort at Yongpyong (www.yongpyong.co.kr) in Gangwon-do, which has a longer season and is determined to stage the Winter Olympics one day.

SWIMMING

Recently upgraded outdoor swimming pools open in July and August in the parks dotted along the Han River. These include Yeouido Hangang Swimming Pool (Map p65) and Ttukseom Swimming Pool (Map p70), both of which are close to subway stations. The indoor swimming pool in Olympic Park (Map p70) is sometimes open to the public.

The Hamilton Hotel (p153) in Itaewon has a popular outdoor pool open to nonguests, and most top-end hotels have indoor pools. Caribbean Bay (p167) is Seoul's best water park. Eulwangni Beach (p169), on the western side of Yeongjongdo, is Seoul's nearest beach.

TAEKWONDO

This traditional Korean martial art developed out of *taekyon*, which can be traced back to ancient tomb murals in the Goryeo dynasty. Taekwondo is now an Olympic sport and is increasingly popular with martial arts fans all over the world. All Korean army personnel receive taekwondo training and five million people worldwide have reached certificate standard. A Taekwondo Experience Programme (☎ 563 3339; www.kukkiwon.or.kr) is held at Gyeonghuigung (p44).

TENPIN BOWLING

Tenpin bowling is available throughout the city for around W3000 a game plus W1000 for shoe hire. Seoulites take the sport, like everything else, seriously.

LCI Bowling (Map pp56–7; ☎ 771 2345; Myeong-dong; per game W3200, shoe hire W1000; ☺ 10.30am–1am; ◉ line 4 to Myeong-dong, Exit 3)

Lotte World Bowling (Map p70; B3 fl, Lotte World, Jamsil; adult/child W3600/3200, shoe hire W1400; ☺ 10am–midnight; ◉ line 2 or 8 to Jamsil, Exit 3)

SPECTATOR SPORT

The day may come when soccer eclipses baseball as the national pastime, but for now, baseball rules (unless Korea is playing Japan at soccer). The home league draws plenty of fans, and major-league baseball in North America has a handful of Korean players, eagerly followed back in their home country.

BASEBALL

Watch South Korea's best players slug it out at Jamsil Baseball Stadium (Map p70; admission W15,000-25,000). There are three Seoul teams in the eight-team Korean League and two of them – the Doosan Bears and the LG Twins – play at Jamsil, so games are held there nearly every evening during the March to October season, except for the summer break. Matches are well-attended and have a good family atmosphere. They usually start at 6.30pm.

SOCCER

Soccer (as it's called here) got a huge boost from the efforts of the spirited South Korean 2002 FIFA World Cup team, which reached the semifinals. (The World Cup was co-hosted by South Korea and Japan that year.) The home league has 13 teams and Seoul FC plays its home K-league matches (tickets W7000 to W20,000) between March and November at 3pm or 7pm in the World Cup Stadium (p75). The crowds are much bigger and there's more atmosphere when the national team is playing at the giant stadium and the Red Devil supporters are cheering on their team.

BASKETBALL

Seoul has two teams, Samsung Thunders and SK Knights, in the 10-team Korean Basketball League (www.kbl.or.kr). Matches are played from November to March at Jamsil Gymnasium (Map p70), with play-offs continuing until May. Two foreign players (usually Americans) are allowed in each team.

HORSE RACING

SEOUL RACECOURSE Map pp36-7

☎ 509 2309; www.kra.co.kr; South Seoul; admission W800; ⊗ races 11.20am-6pm Sat & Sun; ⊕ line 4 to Seoul Racecourse Park, Exit 2
Enjoy a day at the races in luxurious grandstands, which hold 77,000 avid punters. Huge screens on the track show the odds, the races and close-ups of the horses. Short races around the sandy track take place every half-hour and bets are limited to W100,000. Foreigners can use their own smart and comfortable suite – just walk left into the new Lucky Ville grandstand, take the elevator to the 4th floor and turn right. English-speaking staff are on hand, but betting is easy enough. Despite the big crowds (legal gambling opportunities are very restricted in Seoul) everything is well-organised. The only problem is picking the winners.

The Equine Museum (☎ 509 1283; admission free; ⊗ 9.30am-6pm) has modern displays of historical items relating to horses, some of which are surprisingly beautiful.

Races are held every weekend except for New Year, Chuseok, late December (too cold) and late July and early August (too hot) – check the calendar on the website. Night races (first race at 3pm) are held in summer. From the subway, the racecourse is a 10-minute walk under a covered walkway. Or, to arrive in style, look over to the right of the subway station and you can usually see a horse and carriage for hire.

SSIREUM

Ssireum is Korean-style wrestling, more like Mongolian wrestling than Japanese sumo. Wrestlers start off kneeling, then grab their opponent's piece of cloth – *satba* (tied around the waist and thighs) – and try to throw each other to the ground. Major *ssireum* competitions are held at Jangchung Gymnasium (Map pp56–7; ☎ 2237 6800; ⊕ line 3 to Dongguk University, Exit 5) during the Lunar New Year and Chuseok holidays.

TAEKWONDO

KUKKIWON Map p68

☎ 563 3339; www.kukkiwon.or.kr; Gangnam; ⊗ office 9am-5pm Mon-Fri; ⊕ line 2 to Gangnam, Exit 8
The Kukkiwon *dojang* (hall) hosts a regular schedule of taekwondo displays, training courses and tournaments. Visit on Wednesday from 10am to noon to see a training session by the world's best taekwondo demonstration team. Expect to see graceful movements, graceful pine-board breaking and acrobatic high kicking that defies gravity. The museum (admission free; ⊗ 9-11.30am & 1-5pm Mon-Fri) has photos, cups, medals and uniforms relating to the sport. English is spoken if you telephone.

SLEEPING

top picks

- **Imperial Palace Hotel** (p155)
- **Westin Chosun** (p152)
- **W Seoul Walkerhill** (p158)
- **Ibis Myeong-dong** (p153)
- **Metro Hotel** (p153)
- **Hotel Sunbee** (p150)
- **Noble Hotel** (p150)
- **Hotel D'Oro** (p153)
- **Seoul Guesthouse** (p149)
- **Beewon Guesthouse** (p151)

SLEEPING

Seoul is bursting with accommodation, from five-star suites to five-bed dorms – including backpacker guesthouses, budget motels under W50,000, homestays and a stack of midrange and top-end hotels and serviced apartments. Accommodation is invariably charged per room, with little or no discount for singles, although homestays and guesthouses can be a little more generous. Backpacker guesthouse dorms offer the cheapest option for singles. Hotel rooms with Western-style beds are common, but for the same price you can often opt for a *ondol* room, a Korean-style room where you sleep on a *yo* (padded quilt) on the *ondol* (heated) floor. These rooms are ideal for groups. Plenty of accommodation in all price ranges can be found in very central areas such as Gwanghwamun, Insadong and Myeong-dong. Only a handful of top-end hotels are not near a subway station. Guests in these places must rely on hotel shuttle buses, and the city's reasonably priced taxis.

Prices don't normally change with the seasons although midrange and top-end accommodation may offer special deals at quiet times and some relate prices to occupancy. All accommodation options listed offer air-con, a private bathroom and fast internet access unless otherwise indicated.

ACCOMMODATION STYLES

Backpacker Guesthouses

Seoul has a growing number of small, friendly backpacker guesthouses that cater specifically to budget-conscious foreigners. They appeal to older travellers as well as youthful ones. Rooms – dorms and doubles – tend to be small and budget-looking, but are nearly always en suite. A big plus is that the young staff speak English and can give advice about getting the most out of your stay in Seoul. Communal facilities usually include a satellite TV and DVD lounge, a kitchen, a free breakfast, free use of a washing machine, and broadband internet computers.

Motels & Love Motels

Motels (older ones are called *yeogwan* but these are almost extinct in Seoul) are small, family-run budget hotels, and there are thousands of them scattered throughout Seoul. Don't be put off by cluttered lobbies and the proprietor napping in a cubicle at the entrance. The rooms are always on the small size but they are packed with facilities – en suite, TV, DVD or video, telephone, fridge, drinking water, air-con and heating, even toothbrushes, skin lotions and hairdryers. Some have computers. Nearly all the rooms have beds, but some are Korean-style rooms with a *yo* on the floor, which can cater for groups of three or more. The downside of the motels is that staff rarely speak any English and, for sociable types, they have no communal facilities.

Sometimes looking like fairyland castles, love motels cater for daytime, pay-by-the-hour couples, but they also accept conventional overnight guests. They're easy to spot by the plastic curtains shielding the parked cars from prying eyes. Dimly lit corridors are another giveaway. A big drawback of some love motels is that they require a late check-in, around 9pm. But they can be a good option, especially if you fancy a two-person whirlpool bath, a round bed, satin sheets, purple velour and a boudoir decor with stars painted on the ceiling. While some love motels have extravagant-looking rooms, most have smart, regular rooms, and are used by both local and international tourists as they are reasonably priced, clean and modern.

New or renovated motels are always the best and charge no more or only a little more than the older, unrenovated ones.

Hotels & Serviced Apartments

Seoul has no shortage of midrange and luxury hotels, and a dozen serviced apartments have sprung up to provide competition, offering more home conveniences such as kitchen and laundry facilities. Broadband internet access is always available, as is air-con and heating. Luxury rooms can be plain, but the gym/sauna/spa/pool facilities and the restaurants (Chinese, Japanese, Korean and Western) are usually excellent. A number of Seoul's midrange hotels are old-fashioned, with clunky TVs and carpets that need cleaning or dumping, so it's best to avoid the unrenovated ones.

Hotels and apartments with character and style are rare, but Seoul's top hotels rate with the best anywhere in terms of facilities and services. Their weak point is that some reception staff lack English-language skills, know little about the city and don't seem to have been near a charm school. Ironically, the best-informed and most helpful reception staff generally work in backpacker guesthouses. Always ask for a room with a view, which doesn't generally cost any extra.

Homestays

Some Korean families in Seoul offer home-stays to foreign visitors, who can then experience Korean food, customs and family life at close quarters. Most Korean families join the scheme to meet and make friends with foreigners and to practise their English. Some families offer pick-ups and dinner, and rates are greatly reduced if you stay long-term. And you could make life-long friends. Book online a month before your arrival date.

Go Homestay (www.gohomestay.com) Global site with some Seoul homestays.

Homestay Korea (www.homestaykorea.com) Placement fee of US$30, but the site has been going for a decade.

Labostay (www.labostay.or.kr) Long-established.

Lex (www.lex.or.kr) Short, no-cost stays but there is a placement fee.

LONGER-TERM RENTALS

Renting an apartment can be tricky because of the traditional payment system. *Jeonse* is when you loan W30 million to W500 million to the landlord and get it all back at the end of the rental period. Another system is *wolse,* when you pay a smaller returnable deposit of W3 million to W10 million (usually referred to as 'key money') plus a monthly rental fee. Yet another system is to pay all the rent upfront before you move in. However, some accommodation in Seoul is available to foreigners on the Western system with a small returnable deposit and a monthly rent. Other options include the increasing numbers of serviced apartments. Browse real-estate websites for what's on offer – www.nicerent.com or www.nearsubway.com. Real estate is measured in *pyeong* (1 *pyeong* is 3.3 sq m).

Apartment sharing is another option, although spare rooms can be hard to find – check out www.englishspectrum.com, www.seoul.go.kr or try the newspaper websites

(p181). A few Seoul listings are on Craig's List at http://seoul.craigslist.co.kr.

Backpacker guesthouses and motels offer reduced rates for long-termers. Staying in a Korean student hostel is the cheapest option, but rooms are tiny, may not have a window, and facilities are shared. Click onto www.namsanguesthouse.com for details and photos of a typical one – cubicle-sized rooms have cable TV, fast internet access and air-con, and shared kitchen, laundry, toilet and shower facilities. The cost is from W10,000 a day or W200,000 a month. Doing as the locals do and sleeping in a 24-hour sauna is a possible but rather desperate option, as is putting your head down in a 24-hour McDonald's.

ROOM RATES

Luxury hotels at present add 10% to their rates to cover service charges, and we've included this in the prices quoted. Unfortunately, at the time of writing this surcharge was possibly going to 21% if the government stops excluding foreign visitors at luxury hotels from paying VAT. Top-end and many midrange hotels try to fleece travellers with high rack rates (often over W300,000), but a rough guide to real prices is around W120,000 for midrange and around W220,00 for top end. Hotels are coy about their discount rates, which can vary with the season, the occupancy rate and whether it's a weekday or the weekend. Some hotels offer special packages at slack times or special deals if you book through their website or a hotel discounter. But others (often old-fashioned midrange hotels) put rack rates on their websites and charge a more reasonable rate to walk-in guests.

Plenty of small but smart new hotels charge well under W100,000 for just a comfortable room; the ones that charge higher than this offer more facilities – restaurants, bars, business centres, gyms and the like – rather than better rooms. The quality of the rooms depends more on how recently they've been renovated than the price.

Over a dozen serviced apartments range from good-value modern studios that can be

PRICE GUIDE

$$$	double over W150,000
$$	double W46,000-150,000
$	double up to W46,000

discounted to W60,000 per night up to large and luxurious apartments at W220,000.

For something completely different, staying in a *hanok* (traditional house) guesthouse (single rooms cost W35,000 to W40,000, doubles W50,000 to W70,000) in Bukchon is a unique experience – see the boxed text, opposite. The historical, homestay atmosphere more than makes up for any inconveniences.

The price of homestays with Korean families in typical Seoul apartments varies depending on how you book it (see p147). The average cost for bed and breakfast is around US$30 or $40 a night for a single person and US$50 or $60 for a couple.

Motels provide excellent-value rooms for around W40,000, which lack only space, while guesthouses provide less impressive rooms but a priceless friendly ambience with communal facilities and lots of free services at a similar price. Guesthouses also have dorm beds ranging from W15,000 to W19,000, ideal for single travellers.

GWANGHWAMUN

The downtown area has a surprising variety of accommodation to suit all budgets and tastes. You can stay in a beautiful *hanok* guesthouse with a charming and restful garden in the quiet and traditional Bukchon district or in a facility-filled budget motel, an ultramodern upmarket motel or a love motel. Bargain backpacker guesthouses can also be found here. Midrange and top-end hotels cluster around City Hall, although they tend to be of average quality, relying on their location to bring in customers. Other downtown accommodation is listed in the Insadong (p150) and Myeongdong (p151) neighbourhoods.

KOREANA HOTEL Map p40   Hotel $$$
☎ 2171 7000; www.koreanahotel.com; r from W236,000; ⊕ line 1 or 2 to City Hall, Exit 3
A sleek exterior, a marble lobby and welcoming staff are a promising start, but the rooms only just make the grade. The executive queen rooms are a better bet and include the usual executive-floor extras. A handful of restaurants offer global grazing (the Japanese one is the pick of the bunch) but Koreana's three big advantages are location, location, location.

BEST WESTERN NEW SEOUL HOTEL
Map p40   Hotel $$
☎ 735 8800; www.bestwesternnewseoul.com; Taepyungro; r from W144,000; ⊕ line 1 or 2 to City Hall, Exit 4
Rooms have been given a much needed and much more up-to-date style, but for some reason they have been decked out in very dark colours, almost like a cave. Perhaps the styling guru hopes that guests will find the gloom soothing. Bathrooms are still a tight fit, but the updated facilities and the bulls-eye location more than make up for that.

NEW KUKJE HOTEL Map p40   Hotel $$
☎ 732 0161; r from W108,000; ⊕ line 1 or 2 to City Hall, Exit 4
New Kukje is anything but new, and the rooms are as tired-looking and old-fashioned as the lobby. The hotel is popular with Japanese tour groups, who presumably receive discounts, and there's a certain staying-at-gran's ambience. Steam in the sauna or sample a buffet spread, but the only reason to stay here is its location – within spitting distance of City Hall's backside.

EULJIRO CO-OP RESIDENCE
Map p40   Serviced Apartments $$
☎ 2269 4600; http://rent.co-op.co.kr; studios W84,700; ⊕ line 2, 4 or 5 to Dongdaemun Stadium, Exit 12
These smart, white studio apartments aren't downtown but they provide a chic little nest high above the 24-hour hurly-burly of Dongdaemun Market (p83). Everything is bright, modern, stylish and mini-sized – not much elbow room. Otherwise these studios are perfect and all your needs are catered for. An Uzbekistan restaurant is a few minutes' walk away.

BUKCHON HANOK EXPERIENCE

Traditional *hanok* are one-storey wooden buildings with tiled roofs, built around a small courtyard or garden. Most original structures were built in the 1930s for *yangban* (aristocrats) who were usually employed in government service. Rooms are small and used to have paper windows and interior doors. Underfloor heating systems (*ondol*) keeps them snug in winter. Staying in one is a unique and memorable experience.

Anguk Guesthouse (Map p40; ☎ 736 8304; www.anguk-guesthouse.com; Hakdang-gil, Gwanghwamun; s/d/tw W40,000/50,000/70,000; ⑥ line 3 to Anguk, Exit 1) Soak up the historical atmosphere in this *hanok* with gorgeous varnished wood that nevertheless has all mod cons – rooms have their own en suite as well as a computer. Beds rather than *yo* mattresses are supplied. The kitchen can be used to make a DIY breakfast. Owner Mr Kim speaks English and is usually around from 10am to 5pm. Down a quiet alley, the five guest rooms are spread around a courtyard. It's a five-minute walk from Insadong-gil.

Bukchon Guesthouse (Map p40; ☎ 743 8530; www.bukchon72.com; Gyedong-gil, Gwanghwamun; s/d/tw/tr W35,000/50,000/60,000/70,000; ⑥ line 3 to Anguk, Exit 3) Another beautiful *hanok*, but like *hanbok* (traditional dress), it's not super comfortable. Rooms are small and bathrooms are shared, but the historical ambience is priceless. Guesthouse-style communal facilities are available, as are dyeing and sewing lessons (W25,000). Staff usually depart at 6pm, so warn them if you may arrive later than that.

Hanok Tea Guesthouse (Map p40; ☎ 3675 9877; www.teaguesthouse.com; Gyedong-gil, Gwanghwamun; s/d & tw/f W40,000/70,000/150,000; ⑥ line 3 to Anguk, Exit 3) An enchanting *hanok* in a fairyland garden setting that has a very traditional-style room where the free breakfast is served. The shared bathrooms are high quality, with bidets and walk-in showers. The rooms have ultra-modern computers/TVs; the modern facilities are successfully blended with the picturesque and historical building.

Seoul Guesthouse (Map p40; ☎ 745 0057; off Gyedong-gil, Gwanghwamun; www.seoul110.com; s/d/f W35,000/50,000/100,000; ⑥ line 3 to Anguk, Exit 3) This wooden *hanok* has the best garden, and the English-speaking owners (who have two lovely big dogs) are helpful hosts. They were the first to open their *hanok* to tourists. It's a delightful place to stay, but remember that *hanok* rooms are small, bathrooms are cramped (but modern), and you sleep on a *yo* (padded quilt) mattress on an *ondol*-heated floor. Except in the more expensive rooms, the computers, TV lounge, washing machine and kitchen facilities are all shared. You can have a whole *hanok* to yourself for W200,000.

HOTEL LEES Map p40   Hotel $$
☎ 762 4343; d & tw/tr/ste W60,000/70,000/80,000; ⑥ line 1 to Jongno 5-ga, Exit 1;
Off the beaten track and surrounded by small restaurants and neighbourhood ma-and-pa stores, Lees is a hotel with motel prices. The clean, fresh rooms have a few stylish features such as window shutters, and at these prices why not go for the larger suites? The subterranean bar/breakfast room has live music every evening, and the receptionists are friendlier than most. A five-minute walk from the subway exit, go straight and then turn right opposite the entrance to Gwangjang Market, where time has stood still for half a century.

GWANGHWA MOTEL Map p40   Motel $
강화모텔; ☎ 738 0751; r W40,000-45,000; ⑥ line 5 to Gwanghwamun, Exit 7
The helpful owner speaks a little English and she takes great pride in her motel. The rooms and bathrooms are immaculate, and larger than most in this price range. They're all a bit different, with different facilities, so look at a few before settling in. Ultramodern TVs and ornate, faux-Regency furniture combined with the central downtown location make this an excellent budget option. There's a supermarket next door.

GUESTHOUSE KOREA Map p40   Guesthouse $
☎ 3675 2205; www.guesthouseinkorea.com; Sumun 2-gil; dm/s/d & tw W17,000/29,000/39,000; ⑥ line 3 to Anguk, Exit 4
The large communal living room is furnished with comfy armchairs, free computers, a breakfast area and, yes, even a bar. Newcomers to Seoul and solo travellers can mix in and mingle easily even when there's no party raging. The rooms and dorms have air-con and modern en suites, while the nondorms also have a TV and fridge. Fussy types might say the guesthouse is messy, but it's a friendly place to park your pack.

INN DAEWON Map p40 · Guesthouse $

☎ 725 0380; dm/d & tw W19,000/35,000, s $25,000-29,000; ⓑ line 3 to Gyeongbokgung, Exit 4

As lovable as a scruffy dog, this long-running inn has the cheapest *hanok*-style accommodation, built around a covered courtyard. Everything is cramped, and guests sleep on floor mattresses, except in the dorm. Toilets and showers are shared, and the steep stairs up to the dorm could be tricky after a night of clubbing in Hong-dae. The usual guesthouse freebies are offered, but Daewon's greatest asset is the owner, Mr Kim, and his wife (they live next door), who are brimful of kindness.

INSADONG & DAEHANGNO

Insadong is not a place for party animals, but it is the cultural and gastronomic heart and soul of Seoul, and the most pleasant place to stay in the city. Many people never tire of wandering up and down the main street and its attendant alleyways, full of craft shops, art galleries, teashops and restaurants. You could stay here a month and still not discover everything. Accommodation varies from a handful of backpacker guesthouses to budget Korean-style motels, and more upmarket rooms right up to a luxury serviced residence. Daehangno has guesthouses and motels but Insadong is more convenient, within walking distance of the palaces, Myeong-dong, Namdaemun Market and even Dongdaemun Market.

FRASER SUITES
Map p50 · Serviced Apartments $$$

☎ 6262 8888; http://seoul-central.fraser hospitality.com; Hwaenamu-gil, Insadong; 1/2/3-bedroom apt W330,000/440,000/550,000; ⓑ line 3 to Anguk, Exit 5; 🏊

The apartments are modern, light and airy, with large windows and a splendid inner atrium. They are fully equipped and staff try hard to make Fraser a home away from home – so kick back, fill the large fridge with drinks, throw your dirty clothes in the washer/drier, and veg out with a free DVD. In the morning take a dip in the pool before diving into the dining room for a free breakfast. Golf, yoga, babysitters and a grocery shuttle bus are available. Discounts for long-term stays.

HOTEL SUNBEE Map p50 · Hotel $$

☎ 730 3451; Insadong 6-gil, Insadong; d/tw/ondol W84,000/96,000/121,000; ⓑ line 3 to Anguk, Exit 6

Looking for a luxury room in the heart of Insadong at a modest cost? Look no further than Sunbee. Spacious, airy rooms in this hidden-away honey have whirlpool baths, toilets separate from the bathroom, big-screen TVs, computers and a dash of style. What Sunbee lacks is any restaurant, café, sauna or communal facility. Breakfast is toast and orange juice in your room – or else a bakery is a short walk away. There's no bar, but you can order drinks in your room. Room designs and bath sizes vary so check out a few before moving in.

HOTEL CROWN Map p50 · Hotel $$

☎ 3676 8000; www.hotelcrown.com; Insadong; r from W80,000; ⓑ line 3 to Anguk, Exit 4

The pleasant, reasonably priced rooms in this once-plush hotel are light-coloured with mock-Regency furniture. The atmosphere is charming or old-fashioned, depending on your point of view. Bathrooms may be a tad small, but there's a two-desk business centre and a restaurant/bar/coffee shop. The Crown is past (okay, well past) its regal heyday, so what's the big plus besides the price? It's in Insadong.

HOTEL TOMGI Map p50 · Love Motel $$

☎ 742 6660; Insadong; r W50,000-110,000; ⓑ line 1, 3 or 5 to Jongno 3-ga, Exit 4

This upmarket love motel has photos of all its smart rooms in the lobby – one has a ping-pong table! All the rooms have computers, DVDs and modern TVs, and some have Korean coupledom's latest must-have – a double whirlpool bath. Tomgi is centrally located, only 20 steps from the subway exit. Downside? You may only be able to book in after 8pm (9pm at the weekend). Prices are only this low because of the day users.

NOBLE HOTEL Map p50 · Hotel $$

☎ 742 4025; www.noblehotel.co.kr; off Yulgongno, Insadong; r W50,000-60,000; ⓑ line 3 to Anguk, Exit 4

Looking for just a nice room? In a good location? Want a computer in it? And a giant LCD TV? And a whirlpool bath? And free drinks? Free body lotions? All at a cheap price? Look no further than Mr Yoon's budget-traveller palace. With sparkling marble floors and a touch-card security system, it's ahead of some top-end hotels.

SAERIM HOTEL Map p50   Hotel $$
☎ 739 3377; Eorumgol-gil, Insadong; r W50,000;
Ⓜ line 3 to Anguk, Exit 6;
Slimline TVs as large as the double beds feature in this excellent-value, quiet and clean hotel in the heart of Insadong. Facility-filled rooms are as good as they get in Seoul at this price, and everything works. The new wallpaper designs are quite flash. Some rooms have computers at no extra cost.

HOLIDAY IN KOREA HOSTEL
Map p50   Guesthouse $
☎ 3672 3113; www.holidayinkorea.com;
Gureumjae 3-gil, Insadong; dm/s/d & tw W17,000/39,000/44,000; Ⓜ line 3 to Anguk, Exit 4
With 30 rooms, this is the largest backpacker guesthouse in Seoul. It's got a PC *bang* (internet room) with seven computers, and DVDs are shown on a big screen in the communal area. A vending machine sells beer, and there's even an elevator. The motel-style rooms are plain but have all you need.

BANANA BACKPACKERS
Map p50   Guesthouse $
☎ 3672 1973; www.bananabackpackers.com;
Gureumjae 3-gil, Insadong; dm/s/d/t W18,000/30,000/40,000/60,000; Ⓜ line 3 to Anguk, Exit 4;
Banana, with multicoloured and mural-covered walls, has a real backpacker atmosphere about it. The laid-back youthful staff are pretty much…you know…whatever. The usual washing machine, computer and breakfast freebies are here, and the rooms and dorms are reasonable for a budget place, with clean, tiled en suites. Purpose-built, Banana deserves its popularity. The *ondol* keeps it snug in winter.

BEEWON GUESTHOUSE
Map p50   Guesthouse $
☎ 765 0607; www.beewonguesthouse.com; off Donhwamunno, Insadong; dm W19,000-22,000, d & ondol/tr W40,000/58,000; Ⓜ line 3 to Anguk, Exit 4
Combining facility-filled motel-style rooms with free, guesthouse-style communal facilities, the owner and staff keep this guesthouse clean and tidy. Beewon is generally quiet and friendly, and appeals to an older clientele. This is not a place to party – the neighbours complain! Receptionist Jun is a star and Beewon is a cut above average.

top picks
SMART HOTELS

These new modern hotels offer just a decent room, but prices are much lower than at traditional midrange hotels.

- **Noble Hotel** (opposite) Near Insadong
- **Hotel Sunbee** (opposite) Insadong
- **Hotel D'Oro** (p153) Itaewon
- **Hotel Benhur** (p154) Yeouido
- **Hotel Highland** (p157) Gangnam

Look for an orange-tiled building, hidden behind the incongruous GS gas station that faces Changdeokgung (p39).

MOTEL SARANGBANG Map p50   Motel $
☎ 733 3033; Insadong 2-gil, Insadong; r W40,000;
Ⓜ line 3 to Anguk, Exit 6;
The light and spacious (for a motel) rooms in this above-average motel make this a great budget option. Check out a few rooms to find one that suits – some have computers, some have sleep-on-the -floor mattresses, and room 201 has a whirlpool bath at no extra cost. Perfectly located, round the corner from a breakfast bakery and a chopstick's throw from heaps of traditional Korean restaurants.

JONGNOWON Map p50   Guesthouse $
☎ 763 4249; www.jongnowon.com; Gureumjae 3-gil, Insadong; dm/s/d & tw W17,000/28,000/35,000; Ⓜ line 3 to Anguk, Exit 4
This Korean-style motel has turned itself into an international guesthouse with a big 'Welcome' banner out the front. Staff are used to dealing with foreigners, although no one speaks much English. En suite rooms are bright, there's a matchbox-sized galley kitchen, and a printer and fax machine are crammed in next to the computer. The tiny patio is popular with smokers.

MYEONG-DONG, NAMSAN & ITAEWON
The nearly traffic-free streets of Myeong-dong, just a stone's throw from City Hall, heave with young people every evening. The neighbourhood is a shopping, dining and

entertainment mecca for locals and foreigners alike. The star accommodation options are the top-end Westin Chosun (arguably Seoul's best hotel), the new Ibis and Prince hotels – modern and cheerful with no hint of the old-fashioned dowdiness that haunts so many midrange hotels in Seoul – and the cheaper Metro, which is as near to a boutique hotel as can be found in Seoul. The two backpacker guesthouses do a good job, too.

Itaewon, south of Namsan, is another dining, shopping and entertainment area, especially popular with American soldiers, expat English teachers and other newcomers from the Middle East and Africa. The mix of stalls, shops, pubs, gay bars, nightclubs and ethnic restaurants gives Itaewon a lively, slightly seedy atmosphere. The amount of foreigners makes it hardly feel like Seoul at all – more like some English-speaking suburb that's floated down the Han river from, say, Atlanta and been anchored here. Accommodation is famously crummy in Itaewon, so don't expect much and you won't be disappointed. The only decent place is the brand new D'Oro Hotel, unless you can afford to perch yourself up the hill in the Grand Hyatt.

SEOUL PLAZA HOTEL Map pp56-7 Hotel $$$
☎ 310 7710; www.seoulplaza.co.kr; Myeong-dong; s/d from W300,000/370,000; ◉ line 1 or 2 to City Hall, Exit 6; 🏊
The Plaza's rack rates are ridiculous, especially when you consider that single rooms are very tight for space, have old TVs and other imperfections (the elevators are bigger than the bathrooms). You can graze around the globe in the Plaza's many restaurants, but only consider this hotel at a hefty discount, despite the posse of welcoming staff and central location.

GRAND HYATT SEOUL Map p60 Hotel $$$
☎ 797 1234; www.seoul.grand.hyatt.com; Itaewon; r from W275,000; ◉ line 6 to Itaewon, Exit 2; 🏊
The hilltop Hyatt makes the most of the stunning views. The drawback is that the subway doesn't go up the hill – you'll need a taxi. A duo plays classical music in the lobby and the hotel oozes class. The older green-themed rooms verge on being dull, but the newly renovated ones are much fresher and brighter, with decent TVs and blinds replacing net curtains. Keep fit by

swimming indoors or outside, whacking a tennis ball, at yoga or aerobics classes, or by hitting the dance floor at at JJ Mahoney's (p130). In winter ice-skate on the pool. Prices depend on the occupancy rate.

LOTTE HOTEL Map pp56-7 Hotel $$$
☎ 771 1000; www.lottehotelseoul.com; Myeong-dong; r from W250,000; ◉ line 2 to Euljiro 1-ga, Exit 8; 🏊
The public areas here are palatial, with a lobby long enough for Usain Bolt training runs. Ask for a recently renovated room if you want modern style with everything up to date. Other rooms, even in the new block, can be businesslike and surprisingly plain. In an enviable location and surrounded by Lotte's own wonderland of upmarket brand-filled fashion shops, the huge hotel is very Korean – there's a ladies-only floor with a book-lined lounge. Renowned French chef Pierre Gagnaire's new restaurant is on the 35th floor.

WESTIN CHOSUN Map pp56-7 Hotel $$$
☎ 317 0404; www.westin.com/seoul; Myeong-dong; r from W250,000; ◉ line 2 to Euljiro 1-ga, Exit 4; 🏊
What makes the Chosun arguably Seoul's best hotel? Is it the almost faultless rooms, each equipped with a rent-free mobile phone and a flat-screen TV? The immaculate work of its dedicated cleaners? The state-of-the-art business centre and pool? Super fast check-ins? The small details – umbrellas in every room, the choice of 10 types of pillows, a folder full of restaurant recommendations? The downtown location? The Chosun is not Seoul's most spectacular hotel, but the relaxing atmosphere and the conscientious staff keep it a cut above the rest.

HOTEL PRINCE Map pp56-7 Hotel $$
☎ 752 7111; www.hotelprinceseoul.co.kr; Toegyero, Myeong-dong; d/tw/ondol W130,000/155,000/200,000; ◉ line 4 to Myeong-dong, Exit 2
A hop and a skip from the subway station in brand-name conscious Myeong-dong, this new hotel has no whiff of old-fashioned features. Rooms are smallish but sparkling, with some bright primary colours to alleviate the all-white regime. Online booking discounts can make the Prince an excellent deal as it tries to grab market share from established hotels.

HAMILTON HOTEL Map p60   Hotel $$

☎ 794 0171; www.hamilton.co.kr; Itaewonno, Itaewon; s/d & tw W100,000/132,000; ⊕ line 6 to Itaewon, Exit 1; 🏊

The Hamilton's best features are the rather basic 24-hour sauna and the rooftop pool (open July and August). The subway and Partytown are on its doorstep, and discount rates for a double can sink below W100,000. That's the good news. Rooms are nothing flash and are more old-fashioned than quaint, with net curtains and army surplus blankets. And how do they manage to find such off-hand and unhelpful receptionists?

ITAEWON HOTEL Map p60   Hotel $$

☎ 792 3111; www.itaewonhotel.com; Itaewonno, Itaewon; d & tw from W130,000; ⊕ line 6 to Itaewon, Exit 2

Ideally located on the main Itaewon strip, 200m from the subway, rooms have large windows and are decked out in neutral tones, but look tired. Everything is only just up to standard, even once you're past the depressing lobby. The atmosphere is underwhelming, as if everyone is waiting for something to happen. Rooms are often discounted to below W100,000.

PACIFIC HOTEL Map pp56-7   Hotel $$

☎ 777 7811; www.thepacifichotel.co.kr; Myeong-dong; d/tw W120,000/140,000; ⊕ line 4 to Myeong-dong, Exit 3

This traditional midrange hotel is keeping up to date, so modern art has been hung on the walls of rooms that otherwise exude old-fashioned elegance. The Pacific is a grandma in hotpants, trying hard to stay with it. Light neutral colours, greenery and a natural-wood effect are the design style. Bathrooms are a tad cramped. Ask for a Namsan view and a discount.

IBIS MYEONG-DONG Map pp56-7   Hotel $$

☎ 6361 8888; www.ambatel.com/myeongdong; Myeong-dong; d/t/ondol & ste W119,000/129,000/ 159,000; ⊕ line 2 to Euljiro 1-ga, Exit 6

Myeong-dong's newest business hotel is a clone, but it does everything right, from the neutral tones and booth showers to the buffet meals and pleasant staff. Everything is practical rather than luxurious (no minibar!), but that's how the prices stay low. Thoughtful quirks include a fire extinguisher in every room and free use of shoes

and clothing for a workout in the minigym. Some rooms suit the disabled. Exact prices depend on the occupancy rate.

HOTEL CROWN Map p60   Hotel $$

☎ 797 4111; www.hotelcrown.com; Banporo, Itaewon; r regular/deluxe W100,000/145,000; ⊕ line 6 to Itaewon, Exit 4

Away from the main Itaewon strip, the lobby and well-worn, quiet rooms are decorated in an ornate mock-Regency style. Windows are triple glazed but rooms could use some freshening up. The more expensive ones are hardly worth the extra cost. Except for the lively Club Volume on Friday and Saturday nights, the Crown is just marking time, waiting for the renovators or undertakers.

ASTORIA HOTEL Map pp56-7   Hotel $$

☎ 2268 7111; astoria1959@naver.com; Toegyero, Myeong-dong; d/tw & ondol W90,000/109,000; ⊕ line 3 or 4 to Chungmuro, Exit 4

White and pine decor make for pleasant rooms. They're reasonably sized, but a faded look is creeping in. Ask for a room with a Namsan view and keep your eyes on that. Moderate prices at this one-time luxury hotel – it does have a *noraebang* (karaoke room) and a Korean-style whiskey bar – compensate the lack of refurbishment.

METRO HOTEL Map pp56-7   Hotel $$

☎ 752 1112; www.metrohotel.co.kr; Myeong-dong; s/d/tw W74,000/88,000/111,000; ⊕ line 2 to Euljiro 1-ga, Exit 6

Concealed in the north of fashionable Myeong-dong is this modern 75-room hideaway that is almost a boutique hotel. Splashes of style abound, beginning with the flashy, metallic-style lobby and its laptops. Room size and design vary – try to nab one of the larger ones with big windows. Prices cover a Western breakfast.

HOTEL D'ORO Map p60   Hotel $$

☎ 749 6525; fax 749 0033; Itaewonno, Itaewon; d standard/deluxe W66,000/88,000, ste/royal ste W110,000/132,000; ⊕ line 6 to Itaewon, Exit 2

At last, a decent hotel on the main Itaewon strip! Everything is new and smart, with some style and attitude, verging on the hip. It offers sparkling modern equipment and furnishing, and six free soft drinks rather than an expensive minibar. The hotel is an upmarket motel (no restaurant), but ethnic restaurants and expat bars abound in Itae-won. Why not splash out on a room with a whirlpool bath?

SEOUL MOTEL Map p60   Motel $

☎ 795 2266, fax 797 0300; Itaewonno, Itaewon; d/tw W45,000/80,000; ⓢ line 6 to Itaewon, Exit 4
Twin rooms are overpriced but the modern, fully equipped double rooms are better than the other shabby *yeogwan* in Itaewon, and provide a den to return to after prowling the local nightlife. The receptionist speaks English, but single women may feel uncomfortable here.

SEOUL BACKPACKERS
Map pp56-7   Guesthouse $

☎ 3672 1972; www.seoulbackpackers.com; My-eong-dong; s/d/f W35,000/45,000/65,000; ⓢ line 4 to Hoehyeon, Exit 4
The big plus here is that everything is sparkling new and well decorated, but there are no dorms. The 19 motel-style en suite rooms have TVs, but everything's a bit cramped. No communal areas means there's none of the usual guesthouse sociability. Small windows look over a down-at-heel area. From the subway exit take the first alley on the left and then walk down the second alley.

NAMSAN GUESTHOUSE
Map pp56-7   Guesthouse $

☎ 752 6363; www.namsanguesthouse.com; My-eong-dong; d & tw/ondol W45,000/50,000; ⓢ line 4 to Myeong-dong, Exit 2
The friendly, guitar-playing manager Mr Kim tries hard to please his guests with the usual freebies plus free bicycles and even cheap mobile-phone hire. When the weather's fine the outdoor garden patio is a big plus, especially for smokers. No dorms here but a group could negotiate to share an *ondol* room.

HONGDAE, SINCHON & YEOUIDO

The Hongdae/Sinchon area is not flush with accommodation, although Sinchon has a galaxy of love motels near the subway station and a small guesthouse has opened a short walk from Hongik subway station. The homely Kims' Guesthouse is off the beaten track, but worth searching out. Yeouido has business

hotels but few attractions or facilities to tempt tourists to stay there.

HOTEL BENHUR Map p65   Hotel $$

☎ 783 2233; Yangmalsan 4-gil, Yeouido; d/tw & tr W80,000/120,000; ⓢ line 5 to Yeouinaru, Exit 1;
One of the new-style business hotels, Ben-hur is more practical than luxurious, with the money spent on the rooms rather than the lobby. The rooms have jazzy equipment and fittings, such as computers, flat-screen TVs and DVD players, and whirlpool tubs and a steam sauna cabinet shower in the bathrooms. A minibuffet breakfast is thrown in, too. The nearest you can get to a chariot race is to hire bicycles over the road in Hangang Park.

LEE & NO GUESTHOUSE
Map p63   Guesthouse $$

☎ 336 4878; www.lnguesthouse.com; Hongdae; dm/s/d & tw W20,000/40,000/50,000; ⓢ line 2 to Hongik University, Exit 2
Down a quiet cul-de-sac in arty-party Hongdae is this four-room guesthouse run by laid-back ex-backpacker Mr Lee and his wife. Bathrooms are shared but there's a patio and a bigger-than-usual free breakfast (perhaps explaining the higher-than-usual prices). From Exit 2, take the second left, then cross over the road to Hana Bank and walk straight for 5 minutes. Turn right at Grazie Espresso, and it's on your left.

KIMS' GUESTHOUSE Map p64   Guesthouse $

☎ 337 9894; www.kimsguesthouse.com; Huiujeong 4-gil, Near Sinchon; dm/s/d W15,000/28,000/38,000; ⓢ line 2 or 6 Hapjeong, Exit 8
Run by a brother and sister who live next door, this is a genuine home-away-from-home guesthouse. A pleasant modern sub-urban house with a balcony and a patio in a quiet residential area not far from Hong-dae and the Han river, Kims' has all the usual communal guesthouse facilities. The only drawback is the shared bathrooms. It's a challenge to find, so download the map from the website.

GANGNAM & JAMSIL

With a wide choice of midrange and top-end hotels, south of the river in Gangnam is the best area to stay in Seoul. The neighbourhood is seething with fashion stores, restaurants, cafés and bars catering to the upscale residents who live in Gangnam's expensive apartments and the workers who pour out of the high-rise offices every evening. Apgujeong is Seoul's most upmarket area and Garosu-gil the most chic street. The cluster of hotels and serviced apartments on Bongeunsaro is around 800m from a subway station, but only a short taxi ride from the COEX convention centre and mall. South of the river is a business and retail region rather than a sightseeing area, but Lotte World, COEX and Olympic Park are major attractions, and historical sites include a Buddhist temple and royal tombs. The subway or deluxe taxis can whisk passengers to the downtown palaces (or anywhere else) quickly and easily.

The Imperial Palace is unbeatable for luxury surroundings, but the COEX Inter-Continental and the business-class Ibis are the closest to the COEX Exhibition Centre. The serviced apartments are nothing fancy, but offer more conveniences than a hotel room, while Highland is the pick of the budget hotels and Jelly is as hip as it sounds. Seoul is full of quirks – nowhere more so than the youth hostel perched halfway up a midrange hotel in Olympic Park.

LOTTE WORLD HOTEL Map p70   Hotel $$$
☎ 419 7000; www.lottehotelworld.com; Jamsil; r/ste from W375,000/432,000; Ⓜ line 2 or 8 to Jamsil, Exit 4; 🛄
Part of Lotte World (p69), this luxury hotel is typical of Lotte's version of 'euro palatial'. Natural wood and pastel shades make the rooms less flamboyant than the public areas. Babysitters are W10,000 an hour (book ahead). Two floors have corridors and rooms gaily decorated with colourful cartoon characters as well as PlayStations, but squeals from junior come at a cost – W540,000 before any discount (30% or 40%).

COEX INTER-CONTINENTAL HOTEL
Map p70   Hotel $$$
☎ 3452 2500; http://seoul.intercontinental.com; Jamsil; r from W344,000; Ⓜ line 2 to Samseong, COEX Exit; 🛄
In an enviable position next door to the COEX Mall and Convention Centre, this luxury hotel has a modernist functional design with spotless rooms and great service. There's a wide choice of pillows, bedding is all-white, the decor is wood effect and the showers are glass-cased. Top features include the spa and the restaurants – the new Asian Live food court offers five Asian

cuisines, and up in the Sky Lounge the Pacific Rim chefs are as good as the view.

RITZ CARLTON Map p68   Hotel $$$
☎ 3451 8000; www.ritzcarlton.com; Bongeunsaro, Gangnam; r from W340,000; Ⓜ line 2 to Gangnam, Exit 7; 🛄
This hotel wraps guests in soothing luxury with high levels of service, plenty of facilities and a European atmosphere stretching from the furniture to the food. Some rooms have huge balconies (a soccer team could sunbathe there), but all have some warm colours to contrast with the pervasive white. Traditional but not old-fashioned. Discount prices start around W200,000.

IMPERIAL PALACE HOTEL
Map p68   Hotel $$$
☎ 3440 800; www.imperialpalace.co.kr; Eonjuro, Gangnam; r from W330,000; Ⓜ line 7 to Hak-dong, Exit 1; 🛄
A name like this raises expectations, but they are all met at Seoul's most luxurious hotel. The antiques and wood panelling create a stately, genuinely European ambience, and from the magnificent lobby to the well-appointed rooms and immaculate spa, opulence and no-expense-spared are the twin themes. A buffet of delights is doled out at Familia (p109).

JW MARRIOTT HOTEL Map p68   Hotel $$$
☎ 6282 6262; www.marriott.com; Gangnam; r from W290,000; Ⓜ line 3 or 7 to Express Bus Terminal, Exit 7; 🛄
Built in 2000, rooms and bathrooms are spacious compared with other top Seoul hotels, and still look fresh and new after an early renovation. The Marriott is a feel-good hotel that's classy and comfortable, with top facilities everywhere. Sitting above two subway lines, it's conveniently located in the heart of Gangnam. A mall, department store and a great duck restaurant (p110) are a few footsteps from the lobby. Expect weekend discounts.

NOVOTEL AMBASSADOR Map p68   Hotel $$$
☎ 567 1101; www.ambatel.com/gangnam; Bongeunsaro, Gangnam; r/exec fl W260,000/299,000; Ⓜ line 2 to Gangnam, Exit 7; 🛄
The Ambassador's impressive open-plan lobby looks out on a waterfall. The service, food and gym are all impressive, but it's best to avoid any unrenovated rooms. The

executive floor rooms have warmer colours and are more stylish, with pleasant meeting rooms and free soft drinks and cakes. The bar has live music nightly except Monday. The website's virtual tour is more virtual than real.

RIVIERA HOTEL Map p70 Hotel $$$
☎ 541 3111; www.hotelriviera.co.kr; Yeong-dongdaero, Jamsil; r from W210,000; ◉ line 7 to Cheongdam, Exit 13

This large luxury hotel is an inconvenient walk from the subway but just a short taxi ride from the COEX Convention Centre. Although located in the upmarket Apgujeong/Cheongdam neighbourhood, the traffic-ravaged immediate surroundings aren't classy. Ask for a room in the new wing, and hit the Sky Bar early to grab seats with a river view.

BEST WESTERN PREMIER GANGNAM
Map p68 Hotel $$$
☎ 6474 2000; www.bestwesterngangnam.com; Bongeunsaro, Gangnam; s/d & tw/ste W156,000/176,000/280,000; ◉ line 2 to Gangnam, Exit 7

Arty features brighten up this business hotel that still looks new and modern. Big windows provide great views from the higher rooms, but the suites don't impress – you need binoculars to watch the small LCD TV. Still, this is above average for a Best Western hotel (as the name suggests).

ELLUI Map p70 Hotel $$$
☎ 514 3535; Jamsil; d & tw from W176,000; ◉ line 7 to Cheongdam, Exit 14

Dashes of style, such as a glass-view elevator, an outside waterfall and leaf motif mosaics on the lobby floor, make the small Ellui a pleasant and relaxing hotel. But the location is traffic-dominated and the hotel needs a touch-up here and there. Ask for a room with a river view (no extra cost).

HOTEL BLUE PEARL Map p70 Hotel $$
☎ 3015 7777; Jamsil; d & ondol/deluxe tw/superior W130,000/180,000/320,000; ◉ line 7 to Cheongdam, Exit 14

Everything has a modern feel (the hotel opened in 2002) with an almost Zen-like simplicity. A corner room like Room 601 has great views, but rooms on the other side away from the road are quieter. Rooms have blinds and computers, and breakfast is included. Taking taxis is a safer and easier

option than crossing the road to and from the subway station.

M CHEREVILLE Map p68 Serviced Apartments $$
☎ 3480 6000; www.mchereville.com; Seomyeong-gil, Gangnam; studio/1-bedroom apt/2-bedroom apt W125,000/155,000/170,000; ◉ line 2 to Gangnam, Exit 6;

Opened in 2003, with a lively entertainment district on its doorstep, M Chereville offers more home comforts than a hotel room. Chuck dirty socks into the washer/dryer, shove dirty crocks into the dishwasher and soothe tired muscles in the steam sauna showers. All that's needed is artwork on the walls, an extra elevator and quite a bit of touching up to keep the decor and furnishings up to scratch (don't be misled by the website photos).

YOUNGDONG HOTEL Map p68 Hotel $$
☎ 542 0112; www.youngdonghotel.co.kr; Dosan-daero, Gangnam; s/d/tw/ste W110,000/120,000/140,000/220,000; ◉ line 3 to Sinsa, Exit 1

This hotel makes an effort but is full of quirks. You can borrow a laptop computer free of charge from reception, but corridors are dark and there's no bar. The laundry room is the most well-equipped in Seoul with a settee, a TV set and even a music centre – great if you plan to do heaps of laundry. Some rooms have microwaves and toasters. Trendy Garosu-gil (p72) is just across the street.

DORMY IN SEOUL
Map p68 Serviced Apartments $$
☎ 6474 1515; www.dormy.co.kr; Bongeunsaro, Gangnam; studios from W121,000; ◉ line 2 to Gangnam, Exit 7

These light, modern studio apartments have all the conveniences of home. Toilets are cramped but there is a walk-in shower. Don't expect anything special and you won't be disappointed. The price is reasonable and includes a buffet breakfast.

POPGREEN HOTEL Map p68 Hotel $$
☎ 544 6623; www.popgreenhotel.com; Apgujeongno, Gangnam; r/ste incl breakfast W115,440/177,600; ◉ line 3 to Apgujeong, Exit 2

Light, modern and reasonably sized rooms and bathrooms are on offer at Popgreen, with touches of style here and there. Rooms vary so check out more than one – suites are just bigger rooms. The hotel is very near the subway station and even nearer to a Baskin Robbins ice-cream parlour.

HUMAN STARVILLE
Map p68   Serviced Apartments $$
☎ 553 0050; www.humanstarville.co.kr; Non-hyeonno, Gangnam; standard/deluxe studios incl breakfast W110,000/135,000; Ⓢ line 2 to Yeoksam, Exit 6

Nothing fancy here, and some areas look positively spartan – the renovation money has been spent on big LCD TVs, a computer and a dishwasher in every studio apartment rather than decorative finishing touches. Higher-up studios are quieter and have better views. Prices given are for the renovated studios.

IBIS Map p70   Hotel $$
☎ 3011 8888; www.ambatel.com/gangnam; Jamsil; r W110,000; Ⓢ line 2 & Bundang Line to Seolleung, Exit 1

This neat business hotel is hidden behind the Posco Centre, a 10-minute walk from the COEX Exhibition Centre. The restaurant, bar, sauna and exercise room are nothing special, but there's nothing wrong with them either. Rooms are a tad on the small side, but all have walk-in showers and everything is smart and gleaming. Ibis keeps the price down (no silly rack rates) and makes everything simple and modern.

HOTEL DYNASTY Map p68   Hotel $$
☎ 540 3041; www.hoteldynasty.co.kr; Bongeun-saro, Gangnam; d/ste W84,000/120,000; Ⓢ line 2 to Gangnam, Exit 7

The lobby is gloomy despite the chandeliers and the hotel lacks life and atmosphere. The rooms are just about okay at this price, but avoid the suites. Standing inside the lacklustre lobby you can't help but feel that Hotel Dynasty might soon be following the Joseon dynasty into oblivion. Only for those hankering after a fin-de-siècle experience at a modest price.

JELLY HOTEL Map p68   Love Motel $$
☎ 553 4737; www.jellyhotel.com; Gangnam; r W70,000-280,000; Ⓢ line 2 to Gangnam, Exit 8

The corridors are as dark as a coalmine (safeguarding guests' anonymity), but the more expensive rooms of this upscale love motel are spacious, exotic and classy. Jelly is as hip as the name wants you to think, although the receptionist could be friendlier.

Every room is different and you can check them out on the lobby screen – Persian or princess style? The most spectacular and expensive room has a full-sized pool table, a heart-shaped spa, two huge TV screens, his and hers computers, a gilt mirror, black armchairs… Elvis would have loved it.

HOTEL HIGHLAND Map p68   Hotel $$
☎ 541 1250; Dosandaero, Gangnam; r W66,000; Ⓢ line 3 to Sinsa, Exit 1

The low price is due to the Highland being more of an upmarket Korean-style motel than a hotel. The rooms are white, clean and modern, with shutters and a touch-card entry system. If you're after just a room, it's hard to find better in Gangnam at this price.

TIFFANY HOTEL Map p70   Hotel $$
☎ 545 0015; www.tiffanyhotel.com; Yeongdong-daero, Jamsil; r W65,000; Ⓢ line 7 to Cheongdam, Exit 14

Near the subway and an Incheon airport bus stop, this simple, no-frills hotel has a helpful receptionist and a restaurant/bar/coffee shop, but lacks the type of class its name suggests. With 50 quite large, light rooms (the shower heads are huge), it's a definite step up from a motel, although the elevator is shoddy. Being out of the way helps keep prices down.

OLYMPIC PARKTEL YOUTH HOSTEL
Map p70   Guesthouse $
☎ 421 2111; www.kyha.or.kr; Olympic Park, Jamsil; dm W22,000; Ⓢ line 8 to Mongchonto-seong, Exit 1

If you're a youth hostel member you can stay in this midrange hotel at a youth hostel rate. Inside Olympic Park, it's a long, long way from downtown, but the dorms have big windows with superb views. TV, air-con, heating and a fridge are part of the package, as are two double bunks and two pull-out beds in each room. The drawbacks are the receptionists and the tiny, windowless cubicles for en suite toilets and showers.

GREATER SEOUL

The accommodation here includes a couple of reasonably central near-budget options near Itaewon, just a short subway or taxi ride from downtown. Seoul's most stylish hotel is rather isolated on the banks of the Han River, but taxis and shuttle buses link it to the rest of the city. The only way-out-of-Seoul hotel listed is on Yeongjongdo, the island home of Incheon International Airport, useful in case of a crack-of-dawn flight.

W SEOUL WALKERHILL
Map pp36-7   Hotel $$$
☎ 465 2222; www.wseoul.com; r from W390,000; ⊙ line 5 to Gwangnaru, Exit 2; ☒
The extraordinary lobby, with a resident DJ from 9pm and the longest bar in Seoul (18m!), sets the tone for this designer hotel. Rooms look like design-magazine photos – very modernist, with floor-to-ceiling windows. The W is full of surprises, including a polka-dot exterior, a stunning pool view and a whatever/whenever policy that allows pets (about W35,000 a night plus a W140,000 clean-up bill). All that's needed is more guests and getting the subway station moved closer. Special deals are advertised at W250,000.

NEW AIRPORT HOTEL Map p169   Hotel $$
☎ 032-752 2066; Airport Town Sq, Yeongjongdo; r regular/deluxe W85,000/105,000
Smart new regular rooms have internet access while deluxe rooms have a computer, and the price includes free transport

to nearby Incheon International Airport. A weekend surcharge of W10,000 applies. There's a bunch of similar hotels nearby.

HOTEL RAINBOW Map pp36-7   Hotel $$
☎ 792 9993; near Yongsan; s/tw/ondol/tr W55,000/63,000/65,000/73,000; ⊙ line 1 to Namyeong, Exit 1
Hidden away in a busy area of eateries and stores, just two stops south of City Hall, this small, homely hotel has rooms a notch better than the motels. Rainbow is a no-fuss, no frills place that leaves plenty of cash in your pocket. At the subway station exit turn right and then first right.

KAYA HOTEL Map pp36-7   Hotel $$
☎ 798 5101; www.kayahotel.net; Yongsan; d/tw W53,000/63,000; ⊙ line 1 to Namyeong, Exit 1
Near the US army's Yongsan base and convenient for USO tours (p181), this 50-room hotel with a business centre cubicle and a comfortable restaurant is used to dealing with foreigners. Rooms are light and pleasant enough, but it's only the bargain prices that attract customers – the web pictures are hardly more realistic than a North Korean propaganda mural. Downtown is 10 minutes away by subway or taxi.

DAY TRIPS

Seoul is not Korea. Public transport is great, so there is no excuse not to stretch your horizons beyond the city and experience other aspects of the Korean puzzle. Mix your time in the capital with days exploring beyond its reaches. Visitors are spoilt for choice when it comes to day trips.

Take a tour north to (or over) the border to feel the pain of national division at the Demilitarized Zone (DMZ) and be confronted by the nightmare reality of life in the North. Head south to Suwon and explore a World Heritage fortress and its palace. Visit the Korean Folk Village to learn about life in Korea when it was truly the Hermit Kingdom – Confucian shrines, *hanok* (traditional homes), public markets and floggings. Experience a traditional community in a West Sea fishing village, not to mention a dose of sanity away from the concrete and cars. For a bit of fun, spend a day at South Korea's answer to Disneyland. Above all hit the mountain-hiking trails to mingle with a whole new subculture and a new green perspective on the Korean Peninsula.

There's no need to hire a car as frequent subway trains, buses and ferries can whisk you wherever you want to go quickly, cheaply and efficiently. Take advantage of everything on offer beyond the urban frontier. Some of these day trips have sleeping options if you want to stretch them out into longer excursions.

CROSSING OVER TO THE 'DARK SIDE'

Don't leave Seoul without taking a day tour to one of the weirdest and scariest spots on the planet – the DMZ (right), the border between North and South Korea. Two armies have glared at each other across the DMZ for over 50 years, ever since the end of the Korean War in 1953. You can step across the frontier inside the blue UN buildings that straddle the border, but go any further and you'll die in a hail of bullets.

But you don't have to stop at the border in Panmunjeom. It may be possible to cross over the border in a coach tour and see a city, Kaesong (p163), in a country that very few Westerners have visited.

STEPPING BACK INTO THE PAST

Another relic of war is the World Heritage Hwaseong (p166), a very impressive reconstructed 17th-century fortress in Suwon. The reconstructed palace within has tales of its own to tell.

A different way to experience the past is to venture inside the Korean Folk Village (p164), just outside Suwon. Hundreds of traditional houses have been re-erected here to re-create the atmosphere of rural life in a bygone age when peasants and slaves toiled for their Confucian *yangban* (aristocrat) masters. It's a great day out and very educational.

ESCAPING FROM THE CITY

Join thousands of locals and enjoy a day in the forest-covered mountains that are so conveniently close to Seoul at Dobongsan (p164) in the beautiful Bukhansan National Park. If your energy flags, take a shot of the hiker's friend, pine-needle *soju* (a vodkalike liquor), to power you to Dobongsan's granite-tipped peak and its spectacular views.

Another escape from urban stress is on the West Sea Isles (p168), where visitors can relax and feast on fresh crabs and shellfish from the surrounding mud flats. These small islands, home to fisherfolk, are surprisingly unspoilt and laid-back despite being within easy reach of Seoul.

FUN, FUN, FUN

The perfect day trip for children is the sprawling Everland (p167), with the Disneyland-with-a-Korean-twist Festival World and the excellent Caribbean Bay water park next door.

THE DMZ & PANMUNJEOM

Situated just 55km north of Seoul, the truce village of Panmunjeom and the Joint Security Area (JSA) is the only place inside the Demilitarized Zone where visitors are permitted. Established on the ceasefire line at the end of the Korean War in 1953, negotiations

between North and South took place in the blue UN buildings. Only an armistice was signed at the end of the war, not a full peace treaty. Access to Panmunjeom is only for tour groups and you must carry your passport and follow a strict dress code – no offensive T-shirts, ripped shorts, flip-flops or miniskirts.

In the past a gun battle and gruesome axe murders have taken place in the JSA, but the last serious incident was back in 1984. These are described by US and ROK (Republic of Korea) soldiers stationed in Panmunjeom who accompany all the tour groups.

The 4km-wide DMZ scars the land from coast to coast and divides the Korean Peninsula into two antagonistic countries. It's probably the most heavily fortified border in the world – high fences topped with barbed wire, watchtowers, an antitank wall and obstacles. Thousands of landmines line both sides of the DMZ. The Berlin Wall seems like a child's toy compared to this sucker. Seeing the military build-up on both sides, a visit here is a sobering experience.

Surprisingly there are two villages inside the DMZ near Panmunjeom: Daeseong on the South side of the Military Demarcation Line, Kijong on the North side. All of Kijong's buildings used to be empty, but this ghost town may slowly be coming to life. A 160m tower looms over it, from which flies a huge North Korean flag that weighs 300kg. The flag on the South Korean side is smaller. One wonders if the starving North Korean citizens care as much about the size of flags as the country's rulers do.

The tour includes visiting one of the small, blue UN buildings that straddle the border and look like temporary classrooms. Inside are simple tables and chairs. Walk to the far

DMZ NATIONAL PARK?

The Demilitarized Zone (DMZ) cuts across the Korean Peninsula like a knife. The 4km-wide and 240km-long buffer zone is lined on both sides by tank traps, electric fences and landmines. Most of the DMZ has been sealed off to all human beings for more than 50 years, and ironically, this has made it an eco paradise, encouraging wildlife such as Manchurian cranes, whooper cranes and white herons, as well as rare plants. Environmentalists hope that when the two Koreas eventually cease hostilities, the DMZ will be preserved as an official nature reserve and memorial to the nation's period of division.

TRANSPORT: THE DMZ & PANMUNJEOM

Distance from Seoul 55km

Travel time All-day tour

Direction North

Bus Tour bus

end and step into North Korean territory – a strange feeling. North Korean soldiers used to peer in the windows, but recently they have kept watch from a distance. On the South Korean side soldiers in sunglasses strike a taekwondo pose – partly to intimidate the North Koreans and partly to provide a photo opportunity for the tourists. Welcome to showtime, DMZ-style.

The Monastery Visitors Centre sells DMZ baseball caps, T-shirts and other souvenirs. Nearby is the world's most dangerous golf course, with just one 192yd, par three hole surrounded by barbed wire and landmines. The bunkers here are made of concrete rather than sand.

After lunch the highlight is walking along 265m of the 73m-deep Third Tunnel of Aggression (☎ 031 940 8341; admission free; ☸ 9am-5pm Tue-Sun). The third such tunnel found under the DMZ, it was dug by the North Koreans so that their army could quickly march through and launch a surprise attack on Seoul. Coal was smeared on the walls and when it was discovered in 1978, the North Korean authorities claimed it was a coal mine!

Information

USO DMZ Tour (day tours US$44; ☸ depart 7.30am, return 3.30pm, twice weekly) The best tour available, so book as early as you can with the USO's Seoul office (p181).

Other DMZ Tours (half/full day W40,000/70,000) Numerous Korean companies run DMZ tours, but check that a guide speaks English and that Panmunjeom is included.

Eating

Bring along a packed lunch or have *bibimbap* (rice, meat and vegetables) or *bulgogi* (wrapped BBQ beef slices) at the restaurant where the tour buses stop for an early lunch.

USO Diner (☎ 795 3028; meals US$2-5; ☸ 7am-2pm Mon-Fri) Inside the USO building is a US-style diner decked out in red, white and blue with a jukebox.

KAESONG

A one-day coach tour across the DMZ from Seoul to Kaesong, a city in North Korea, is long enough to learn a surprising amount about the secretive North. Part *1984*, part third-world refugee camp, part nationalist cult – in the final analysis the bizarre nation doesn't fit into any category.

Crossing the border into the North takes time, but usually presents no problem, although the North's customs officers check every camera (only digital allowed). The crossing itself is an anticlimax – everything looks normal. No tanks or fortifications in view, only empty, green countryside.

Across the border the tour buses skirt the Kaesong Industrial Complex, funded and built by South Korea. Over 12,000 North Korean workers and 800 South Korean workers are employed there.

Arriving in Kaesong city (population said to be anywhere between 145,00 and 330,000) is a shock. All the buildings look like photos of Seoul taken in 1950. Every building looks in need of repainting and repair. Even the newer apartment blocks look old. They're surrounded by patches of dirt – no concrete paths and not one flower or tree.

No city buses operate in town, except for South Korean buses taking workers to the industrial complex. There are no gas stations and no traffic lights; traffic police in white uniforms stand around at intersections, although they have virtually no traffic to direct except pedestrians and cyclists.

Everyone on Kaesong's streets is soberly dressed in work-style clothes. People usually walk or cycle in single file. It's all just that bit *too* orderly. Coming directly from the animated, lively streets of Seoul highlights the differences across the border: no groups of picnickers, no pavement cafés, no open-air restaurants or bars, no street food. The entire city is eerily quiet – no vehicles, no raucous pedestrians, no music blaring from shops.

The North Korean guides don't speak English but they talk in a friendly way with the South Koreans on the tour. They all wear a little pin photo of Kim Jong-il, and if a banned topic (eg questions about salary) is mentioned, they just say (in Korean) 'We wish our great leader a long life and we wish for unification.'

At every tourist site there is a cordoned-off area which visitors must remain within. Photos can't be taken while on the bus, and are restricted when off the bus.

TRANSPORT: KAESONG

Distance from Seoul 76km

Travel time All-day tour

Direction North

Bus Tour bus

Tours visit Sonjukyo, an ancient stone bridge, where in 1392, Lee Bang-won, son of the first Joseon king, assassinated Jung Mong-ju, the last loyal follower of the previous Goryeo dynasty, which had its capital in Kaesong. Nearby are giant turtle statues called Pyochungbi – males should touch the female turtle's nose and females the male one in order to have good luck (though it's hard to differentiate the statues' genders). Seonggyungwan (the top Goryeo-dynasty Confucian college) houses a small, old-fashioned museum, which includes reproductions of royal Goryeo-era tomb paintings. A couple of shops at the museum sell food products, propaganda postcards and craft items.

The countryside is no better off than the city. Many of the hillsides are wasteland, covered in low bush. The trees have been cut down, but there are no crops or replanted forests taking their place. The small fields of rice, corn and other crops are mostly straggly. Farmers have virtually no equipment – just a bullock cart or a museum-piece tractor if they're lucky. Bizarrely, every dirt road to a few houses is guarded by a soldier, who stands stiffly to attention as the tour buses pass by.

The 37m Pakyon waterfall, 25km north of Kaesong, has none of the clutter of souvenir shops, food stalls and restaurants found at every major temple and national park in South Korea.

Information

Please note: tours to Kaesong and Geumgang-san were suspended in 2008. It was assumed this was temporary, but at the time of writing there was no information regarding when or if the tours would resume. Check with the tour organisers for the latest information.

Hyundai Asan (Map p40; ☎ 3669 3897; 12th fl, Hyundai Bldg, Yulgangno; ◉ line 3 to Anguk, Exit 3) runs a day trip (W188,000, W10,000 extra at weekends and holidays; departs Seoul 6am, returns 5pm) to Kaesong. An application form, a colour ID photo and a photocopy of your passport must be submitted at least 10 days before your planned visit to North Korea.

Book direct, or join one of the monthly tours by the Adventure Club (www.adventurekorea.com) run by Kim Seok-jin. These cost more (W260,000) but the tour guide speaks English.

Hyundai Asan also runs two-night trips into North Korea's Geumgangsan, a scenic area with jagged mountain peaks, waterfalls and lakes – see www.mtkumgang.com.

Pick up tour buses near the Hyundai building (Map p40) or the Sejong Performing Arts Centre (Map p40).

Eating & Drinking

Tourist refreshment stalls and shops sell North Korean ice creams and snacks. Lunch in the huge Tongilkwan tourist restaurant is about the only sign of normality on the trip – lots of small, mainly vegetable side dishes are served with rice and soup.

North Korean beer, folk liquors and soft drinks can be bought at tourist refreshment stands and shops. Taedonggang lager (made with British brewery equipment) is only US$1 for a big bottle, while a small bottle of water is US$2. (Ironically, only US dollars are accepted here. You can buy US cash at the South Korean side of the border.) Buy the beer quickly as it may run out.

KOREAN FOLK VILLAGE

The more than 150 thatched and tiled Korean traditional houses and buildings in this village (031 286 0000; www.koreanfolk.co.kr; adult/child/teenager W12,000/8000/9000; 9am-6.30pm Apr-Sep, to 5.30pm Oct-Mar) take all day to explore thoroughly.

Go back to the time when long-haired aristocrats in horse-hair hats ruled their wives,

TRANSPORT: KOREAN FOLK VILLAGE

Distance from Seoul 45km

Travel time Three hours return

Direction South

Subway & bus Take subway line 1 to Suwon station (W1600, one hour). Exit the station and on your left is the tourist information centre. From here catch the free shuttle bus to the Korean Folk Village. The bus takes 30 minutes and leaves at 10.30am, 11.30am, 12.30pm, 1.30pm and 2.30pm, returning at 2pm, 3.30pm, 4.30pm and 5pm. If these times are inconvenient, take local bus 37 (W1000).

concubines and slaves with a rod of iron. Soak up the special atmosphere of a Buddhist temple, experience the austerity of a Confucian shrine and relax in a jovial traditional market. See storehouses, a bullock pulling a cart, household furnishings and agricultural tools. The magistrate's house has examples of punishments, which included breaking the offender's legs, branding and severe floggings – usually 60 to 100 strokes. Life was short, brutish and nasty in the good old days.

In a quaint rural atmosphere, artisans in *hanbok* (traditional clothing) create pots, make paper and weave bamboo, while other workers tend vegetable plots and chickens. Snacks, teas and handicrafts are for sale.

If you have the stamina, a string of other attractions – folk museums, exhibitions, an amusement park and a haunted house – cost a little extra.

Information

Tourist information centre (031 228 4672; outside Suwon train station; 9am-6pm) Has free internet access.

Eating

Traditional Korean meals (W5000 to W9000) such as mushroom stew, barbecues, *bibimbap*, oyster *pajeon* (savoury pancakes) and ginseng chicken are served in rustic restaurants or the folksy food court at the far end of the village.

Entertainment

Traditional musicians, dancers and acrobats put on half-hour displays, including tightrope walking, a wedding ceremony and a farmers' dance, twice daily, starting around 11pm and 3pm.

DOBONGSAN HIKE

Bukhansan National Park straddles the northern border of Seoul. It's home to forests, rivers, Buddhist temples and rocky granite peaks over 700m. Dobongsan, which offers splendid – if hazy – views, is one of those peaks.

Hiking is a popular activity in Seoul, so it's best to avoid weekends and the hordes of well-equipped hikers that they bring. (Seoulites are the world's best-dressed hikers – check out those red waistcoats, black ninja outfits and Darth Vader sun visors.) This national park receives over four million visitors annually, but there's very little litter lying around. The

DOBONGSAN HIKE

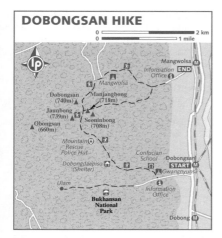

Dobongsan hike is the most popular, partly because it's within walking distance of the subway station.

From the station walk along the long lines of hiking equipment shops. Prices of outdoor gear are marked, and are a better deal than you'll find in Namdaemun Market. Fuel up with foil-wrapped *gimbap* (sushi), boiled eggs and yellow 'hikers' bread as well as water, *soju* and *makgeolli* (fermented rice wine). Restaurants line the hiking trail outside the national park at both ends of the climb, but most hikers take a picnic and eat it while enjoying the fantastic views from the mountain peaks.

It's a 15-minute walk to the information office (☎ 909 0497; ⏰ 7.30am-6pm), which has a basic hiking map in English. The path left goes to Uiam, but walk straight on for the 3km, 1¼-hour hike up to Jaunbong (자운봉, 739m). Almost immediately on the right is Gwangnyunsa, a typical Buddhist temple and monastery, many of which are scattered around the green hillsides. Further on is a Confucian school but only one building remains and that is usually locked.

Continue along the river and the crowds start to thin out as you ascend past another temple on the left. It's uphill all the way to Dobongdaepiso (shelter), a two-storey stone structure housing a rustic coffee shop and large, multiperson wooden bunk beds that cost nothing to sleep on. The shelter is a 40-minute hike from the information office.

Follow the signs to Jaunbong, which is still 1km away. The rock-strewn footpath is generally easy to follow, and there tend to be other hikers around if you have any difficulty. Fifteen minutes further on is the mountain rescue

police hut (☎ 954 5600). Just above it, turn left at the sign to Jaunbong. Keep on plodding upwards for half an hour and then stop at the big rock. This is where the real adventure begins as you go left for a short, sharp climb up the rock face to the top of Jaunbong, with its exhilarating, top-of-the-world 360° views.

Back down at the big rock (no sign), go down the gully and then up along the top of the ridgeline. This section is not for the faint-hearted – you have to use ropes and railings to go up and over and down the big rocks. The Podaeneugsan (ridge) section of the hike takes 70 minutes, but longer at weekends and holidays due to the crowds of eager beaver hikers, all in a hurry.

At the sign, turn right to Mangwolsa (망월 사) for the 15-minute descent to this isolated and beautiful temple. The two-storey main hall has wonderful lattice doors carved with animal and flower designs, and there are decorative, golden screens behind the main Buddha statue. The lower funeral hall has faded, unusual folk-art paintings on the outside, together with Zen sayings written in Chinese characters and English.

From here it's a 40-minute walk along a boulder-filled stream past the site of Um Hong-gil's house to the Mangwolsa information office. The legendary Korean mountaineer Um Hong-gil (born in 1960) was brought up and trained here for his record-breaking climbs of 16 Himalayan peaks over 8000m between 1989 and 2007.

At the first restaurant bear right, and at the *jokbal* (pork hocks) restaurant bear left, and you reach Mangwolsa subway station (on the left) 30 minutes after leaving the Mangwolsa information office.

For an easier hike, head to Uiam from Dobongsan subway station, or just hike up to Jaunbong and back (1½ hours up, one hour back). An even easier option is to hike up to Mangwolsa and back from the Mangwolsa subway station.

TRANSPORT: DOBONGSAN HIKE

Distance from Seoul 20km

Travel time 50 minutes one way

Direction North

Subway & bus Take subway line 1 or 7 to Dobongsan station (not Dobong, the stop before it); leave from Mangwolsa station for the return journey

HWASEONG & HAENGGUNG

Hwaseong (Brilliant Fortress, aka Suwon Fortress) is a World Heritage fortress in Suwon city (population over one million). The majestic fortress wall snakes 5.7km around the city centre and 95% has been faithfully restored. It was originally constructed between 1794 and 1796 during the reign of King Jeongjo, a monarch who was much loved due to his filial piety and concern for ordinary people.

The fortress itself is a symbol of filial piety – King Jeongjo had it built when he moved the original Suwon city there because the original site was on the most auspicious spot for his father's tomb. The fortress was also a product of the 'New Learning', meaning novel methods, such as pulleys, were used in its construction, as well as new materials such as bricks.

The fortress wall is made of earth and faced with large stone blocks, while additional features are built of grey bricks. Hiking all the way around the walls takes two hours and includes ever-changing views of the city.

Walk from Paldalmun to the beginning of the fortress wall. It's best to visit the palace,

Haenggung, first, so turn right and walk for five minutes to the palace plaza.

Haenggung (☎ 031 251 4435; http://hs.suwon.ne.kr; adult/child/teenager W1500/700/1000; 9.30am-5pm) was a temporary palace built by King Jeongjo, who stayed here on his visits to his father's grave. Jeongjo's father, Prince Sado (1735–62), the victim of court intrigues, was suffocated in a rice chest on the orders of his father.

Courtyard follows courtyard inside the large, walled palace. One hall depicts the 60th birthday party of King Jeongjo's mother, while another features a popular TV drama, *Daejanggeum*, which was partly filmed here. On the weekends you can dress up in old costumes, and make pots and paper flowers (all W2000). Beyond the furnished royal apartments are the rooms where the eunuchs lived and worked. On the right is Hwaryeongjeon, where King Jeongjo's portrait is enshrined.

On the new plaza is the Information Centre & Museum (☎ 031 228 4410; admission free; 9am-6pm), spread over three floors. The DVD show has an English-language button.

From the palace, walk through the car park and up the hill at the rear of the renovated palace to the dragon bus (☎ 031 251 4435; adult/child/teenager W1500/700/1100; 10am-6pm). This bus winds around in and out of the fortress wall to the archery field in the northwest corner of the fortress.

At the dragon bus stop, walk left for five minutes to reach the Hwaseong wall (☎ 031 251 4435; adult/child/teenager W1000/500/700; 9am-6pm). Walk up alongside the wall, keeping an ear out for cuckoos in the spring. Near the command post, Seojangdae, is a large bell you can toll (W1000), and Seonodae, a tower that was used by crossbow archers. Walk outside the wall for at least part of the way, as the fortress looks much more impressive the way an enemy would see it .

On the wall's north side is Hwahongmun, a watergate over a stream. Further along is the archery centre. For W2000 you can have a go at this traditional sport (one for which Koreans often win Olympic medals).

Nearby is Dongbukgongsimdon, another watchtower but with a unique design – a high, tapering structure with rounded corners, a stone base and a brick tower. The entire fortress was innovative back in the 18th century. Further on are the Bongdon beacon towers, which were used to send messages around the country.

HWASEONG & HAENGGUNG

0 ————— 500 m
0 ————— 0.3 miles

Suwoncheon

Dongbukgongsimdon
Dongjangdae
Archery Field &
Yeonmudaejeontongchatjip
Janganmun
Changnyongmun
Seobukgongsimdon
Yeonpo Galbi
Hwahongmun
Hwaseomun

Haenggungjeongwon

Palace Plaza
Bongdon Beacon Towers
Haenggung
Dragon Bus Stop
Information Centre & Museum

Paldalsan (143m)

Seojangdae
Tourist Information Booth
Paldalmun
Ticket Booth
Hyowon Bell
Seonam
Ttaeng Mart
Jidong Market
Paldalsa
Yeongdong Market

Hotel Central

To Suwon Train Station (2km)

Information

Tourist information centre (☎ 031 228 4672; outside Suwon station, on the left; ☺ 9am-6pm)

Eating

The subway station concourse has fast-food outlets, a food court and more options in the GS supermarket.

Haenggungjeongwon (행궁정원; ☎ 031 244 2021; palace plaza; galbitang W8000, galbi W11,000-39,000; ☺ 10am-10pm) A popular lunch is *galbitang* – meaty bones in a meaty broth served with rice and side dishes (it's the best in the world). Opposite Haenggung's information centre, the restaurant is easy to spot – three storeys high with large balconies. For a drink try the refreshing *cheongha* – Japanese *sake*-style rice wine. Free self-serve coffee.

Yeonpo Galbi (연포갈비; ☎ 031 255 1337; galbitang W7000, galbi W15,000-35,000; ☺ 11.30am-10pm) Down the steps from Hwahongmun, this famous restaurant serves up its special Suwon version of *galbitang* – chunks of meat and a big rib in a seasoned broth with noodles and leeks. *Galbi jeongsik* is another lunch option.

Drinking

Yeonmudaejeontongchatjip (☎ 031 257 0099; teas W6000; ☺ 10am-10pm) Rest your feet and sip local teas in this antique-style teashop above the archery centre.

Sleeping

Hotel Central (☎ 031 246 0011; www.hotelcentral.co.kr; Haenggung-gil; d/tw W65,000/70,000) Rooms vary (ask for a hillside view) but are generally light and well-maintained and the price includes a minibuffet breakfast. The lobby has homely features, and you can keep in touch with home via the business centre.

Shopping

At the end of the walk around the wall, the Jidong and Yeongdong Markets make for a fascinating wander with lower prices than Seoul.

Ttaeng Mart (땡마트; ☎ 031 255 5180; btwn Yeongdong Market & Paldalmun; ☺ 9am-10pm) A bargain-hunter's dream shop with prices you won't believe.

EVERLAND

This world-class amusement park (☎ 031 320 5000; www.everland.com), less than an hour southeast of Seoul by bus, has four separate parts.

Festival World (day pass adult/under 13yr W35,000/26,000; ☺ 9.30am-10pm autumn-spring, to 11pm summer) follows the classic Disneyland formula and encompasses a large area filled with fantasy buildings, thrill rides, fairground attractions, zoo animals (lots of monkeys), impressive seasonal gardens, budget restaurants, live music and an 'Aesop's Village'. Don't miss the wooden rollercoaster. A novelty feature is the 15-minute African Safari bus ride through wildlife zones, which offers close-up views of tigers, lions, ligers and hyenas in one area; giraffes, zebras and elephants in the next; and bears in another. The safari is a popular attraction, so be prepared to queue for an hour. The parades and festivals are always something special, and when it's lit up at night, the park takes on a magical atmosphere.

Caribbean Bay (adult/child Jul & Aug W65,000/50,000, Sep-Jun W30,000/23,000; ☺ 10am-5pm autumn-spring, 9am-8.30pm summer) is a superb water park, designed so cleverly that a visit here is just like being at the beach. The outdoor section is open from 1 June to mid-September and features a huge wave pool that produces a mini-tsunami every few minutes. Comfortable sun lounges and huts provide places to sunbathe and relax. A body-surfing pool, diving pool, speedy and gentle tube rides and a super-scary water-bobsleigh ride are other features, along with regular swimming pools. The indoor section has a small wave pool, a few other pools, a spa and sauna. Despite the high price, the place is packed in summer.

The Speedway Circuit (admission free; ☉ varies) is the only one in Seoul and sometimes has races at the weekend.

The Hee Won Garden & Hoam Art Museum (☎ 031 320 1801; www.hoammuseum.org; adult/child W4000/3000; ☉ 10am-6pm Tue-Sun) is a special place. The wonderful Korean-style gardens act like a Buddhist temple gateway to induce a calm frame of mind so that visitors can fully appreciate the art treasures inside the museum. The emphasis is on spotlighting select historical artworks rather than packing in as many exhibits as possible. Each one of the paintings, screens, celadon and other exhibits reveals stunning skill and craftsmanship. A free shuttle bus runs from the main entrance to Festival World on the hour (from 10am to 4pm except at noon).

Eating

Festival World and Caribbean Bay both have plenty of budget Korean and fusion food options (under W10,000), as well as fast food (W5000).

ISLAND HOPPING IN THE WEST SEA

Sandy beaches and mollusc-packed mudflats, sea views, rural scenery, vineyards, fresh air, and fresh fish and seafood restaurants – the West Sea Isles are a whole different planet to the cars, concrete and rush-rush-rush of

---

Seoul. Discover islands inhabited by elderly fisher folk and eat super-fresh prawns on this hop-on, hop-off tour of the islands to the west of Incheon city.

The International Airport Course Tour Bus (adult/child W6000/3000; ☉ tours depart 9.45am-4.45pm) runs six times daily around Yeongjongdo from outside Incheon subway station. You can hop on and hop off the tour bus whenever you want. The first bus leaves at 9.45am. Check that the last bus is running. If you miss the last tour bus of the day, you can take an ordinary bus back to Seoul.

The first island after the ferry crossing is Yeongjongdo, which used to be two islands and has seen many changes since it was connected to the mainland by two bridges. A town has sprung up to service the airport and a seawater spa and a 72-hole golf course have been built. Rough-and-ready seafood restaurants are strung along the west coast, along with motels and a resort.

For a less-developed island, jump off the tour bus at the Geojampo stop, the gateway to Muuido. Walk 2km past the seafood restaurants and onto the causeway to Jamjindo. At low tide the mudflats look as desolate as a WWI battlefield. The ferry ride to Muuido (W3000 return, half-hourly until 7pm, 6pm in winter) takes only five minutes.

Stepping onto Keunmuri wharf on Muuido, more seafood restaurants greet you, along with the island bus and minibus taxi. Walk up the wooden stairs to go hiking in the thickly wooded hills. To visit Hanagae Beach, the island's best, take the bus (W1000) or negotiate a taxi price. This beach has plenty of golden sand, a handful of seafood restaurants and 100 very basic beach huts under the pine trees or on the beach. The chalet-style house on the beach was a film set for the Korean TV drama Stairway to Heaven. Just beyond it is the start of a 2.5km hike through dense woods to the top of Horyonggoksan (244m).

Another option from Keunmuri wharf is to walk for a few minutes to Keunmuri, a delightfully traditional fishing village despite the Family Mart. Crab pots and fishing nets lie around while red peppers dry in the sun.

Work off a meal with a 1km walk over the hill to Silmi Beach. The beach is nothing to write home about, but there's a freshwater swimming pool and campsites and huts under the pine trees. At low tide you can walk to Silmido, an uninhabited island where the Korean movie of that name was filmed. Poking about in the mud for shellfish is a popular activity.

TRANSPORT: ISLAND HOPPING IN THE WEST SEA

Distance from Seoul 50km

Travel time 90 minutes to Yeongjongdo wharf

Direction West

Subway Take subway line 1 to Incheon station (W1700, 70 minutes from City Hall station). From here you can jump on the tour bus or take a ferry.

ISLAND HOPPING IN THE WEST SEA

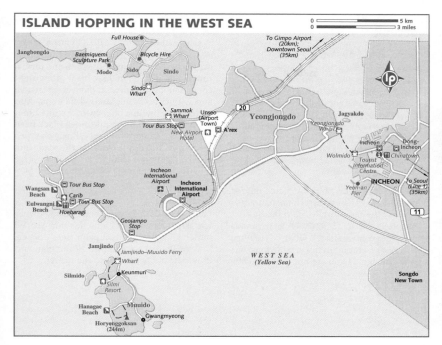

Make your way back to Yeongjongdo and pick up the tour bus to visit Eulwangni Beach, or catch a local bus if that saves time. Eulwangni is the most popular beach because even when the tide goes out, there's more sand than mud. Motels and a resort have been built here, as well as restaurants and stores.

From Eulwangni, it's a 20-minute walk along the road to Wangsan Beach, which has less development on the beachfront – just some fishing boats, a few restaurant shacks and watersport equipment for hire during the summer season.

In the summer peak, holidaymakers let off fireworks and there's lots of activities, but out of season, not a lot goes on. For most Koreans the main attraction is the raw fish restaurants, not the beach.

The tour bus route runs from here past Sammok Wharf and across the bridge to the mainland, stopping outside Incheon subway station. Cross the road and walk up the street facing the station and you are soon in Incheon's Chinatown. Chinese restaurants and shops crowd the streets and even the lampposts are red with gold dragons climbing up them. Shops sell Chinese medicines, liquors, slippers and gaudy brocade clothes, and a

Chinese bakery sells 'empty' bread that looks like a soccer ball.

Information

Tourist information centre (☎ 032 1330; ☻ 9am-6pm) Outside Incheon subway station.

Eating

The hundreds of seafood restaurants on the islands offer much the same fare, which you can see swimming around in aquarium tanks outside. *Wangsaeu* (fresh jumbo prawns) cost around W20,000 for 500gm – ask for *gui* (grilled). A big bowl of mixed barbecued shellfish (*jogaegui*) costs around W30,000. Order *bap* (rice) or *pajeon* to make a meal of it. The price of raw fish (*gwangeo* or *ureok*), *kkotge* (crabs) or *nakji* (octopus) depends on the weight. *Kalguksu* (around W5000) is clams with noodles and a vegetable garnish in broth.

Jungganghoesikdang (중앙회식당; Keunmuri, Muuido; meals to share W30,000; ☻ varies) Buy a heap of shellfish – giant, big and small – which is enough for three or four people and includes scallops, mussels and trumpet shells. Cook it up at a

DETOUR

Sindo, Sido & Modo

Hankering for a DIY tour? Hop off Yeongjongdo's tour bus at the Sammok Wharf stop, walk 10 minutes and catch the car ferry (adult W5000, hourly, 7am to 6pm) to these three undeveloped islands which are linked by bridges. Explore by bus or bicycle to enjoy a close-up view of planet rural Korea. There are a few restaurants, shops and *minbak* (homestay accommodation). You might never want to leave, but if you do, head back to Yeongjongdo to catch the tour bus back to Incheon.

barbecue set in your table, but watch out for popping shells! The nondescript restaurant is just before the right turn to Silmi Beach.

Hoebaragi (회 바라기; ☎ 032 746 3611; Eulwangni Beach, Yeongjongdo; meals to share W30,000; ☼ 11am-1am) The largest restaurant in this seaside town has a large red sign. If you are not into *hoe* (raw fish), try BBQ prawns, crab or shellfish. (Why not ask for a mixture of all three?)

Gonghwachun (☎ 032 765 0571; Chinatown, Incheon; meals W3000-50,000; ☼ 11am-10pm) The set meals are the best deal at this quite posh and formal restaurant. A W25,000 set meal offers eight courses, not large portions but well-presented and with contrasting seafood flavours. Also included is the invented-in-Incheon-Chinatown *jajangmyeon* (noodles with black bean sauce). The scallops in a spicy, finely chopped sauce are a stand-out. Walk up the road from Incheon station – Gonghwachun is the large four-storey restaurant facing you.

Sleeping

Carib (☎ 751 5455; Eulwangni Beach, Yeongjongdo; s/d W40,000/80,000) You can't miss this ship-shaped motel with plastic, neon palm trees outside. Rooms like 501 have a fantastic circular window view of the beach and the sunset.

Seoul's wonderful subway trains are fast, inexpensive and comprehensive, but avoid rush hours. Public buses are not foreigner-friendly, but the many taxis all have meters and are cheap and easy to use, although drivers can't speak much English. Flights, tours and rail tickets can be booked online at www.lonely planet.com/travel_services.

AIR

South Korea used to have only two domestic carriers – Korean Air (☎ 1588 2001; www.koreanair.com) and Asiana Airlines (☎ 1588 8000; www.flyasiana.com), but recently low-cost airlines such as Jeju Air (☎ 1599 5000; www.jejuair.net, in Korean) have appeared on the scene. The newcomers have struggled to compete with the two main carriers, who have set up low-cost affiliate companies, Jin Air (☎ 3660 6000; www.jinair.com, in Korean), launched in July 2008 by Korean Air, and Air Busan (☎ 1588 8009; www.flyairbu san.com), launched by Asiana in October 2008.

Domestic flights are reasonably priced and run to the country's major cities, as well as Jejudo, Korea's southern holiday and honeymoon island. Fares are cheaper from Monday to Thursday, when you are also more likely to obtain a seat. Flights on public holidays are more expensive and are often booked out. Fares are discounted for students and children. For-

eigners should carry their passports for ID purposes on all domestic flights. The longest flight (Seoul to Jejudo) takes just over an hour.

Airlines

The following major airlines have offices in Seoul:

Air Canada (AC; ☎ 3788 0100)

Air China (CA; ☎ 774 6886)

Air France (AF; ☎ 3788 0440)

Asiana Airlines (OZ; ☎ 1588 8000)

Cathay Pacific Airways (CX; ☎ 311 2800)

Japan Airlines (JL; ☎ 757 1711)

KLM Royal Dutch Airlines (KL; ☎ 2011 5500)

Korean Air (KE; ☎ 1588 2001)

Lufthansa Airlines (LH; ☎ 3420 0400)

Malaysia Airlines (MH; ☎ 777 7761)

Northwest Airlines (NW; ☎ 732 1700)

Singapore Airlines (SQ; ☎ 755 1226)

United Airlines (UA; ☎ 751 0300)

Airports

Virtually all international passengers arrive at Incheon International Airport, situated

---

CLIMATE CHANGE & TRAVEL

Climate change is a serious threat to the ecosystems that humans rely upon, and air travel is the fastest-growing contributor to the problem. Lonely Planet regards travel, overall, as a global benefit, but believes we all have a responsibility to limit our personal impact on global warming.

Flying & Climate Change

Pretty much every form of motor transport generates CO_2 (the main cause of human-induced climate change) but planes are far and away the worst offenders, not just because of the sheer distances they allow us to travel, but because they release greenhouse gases high into the atmosphere. The statistics are frightening: two people taking a return flight between Europe and the US will contribute as much to climate change as an average household's gas and electricity consumption over a whole year.

Carbon Offset Schemes

Climatecare.org and other websites use 'carbon calculators' that allow jetsetters to offset the greenhouse gases they are responsible for with contributions to energy-saving projects and other climate-friendly initiatives in the developing world – including projects in India, Honduras, Kazakhstan and Uganda.

Lonely Planet, together with Rough Guides and other concerned partners in the travel industry, supports the carbon offset scheme run by climatecare.org. Lonely Planet offsets all of its staff and author travel.

For more information check out our website: www.lonelyplanet.com.

on an island in the West Sea that is linked to the mainland by a road and rail bridge. Gimpo International Airport, despite its name, is the domestic airport and only has two international flight destinations: Tokyo and Shanghai.

GIMPO INTERNATIONAL AIRPORT

This airport (Map pp36–7; ☎ 660 2114; http://gimpo.airport .co.kr; West Seoul) has a large domestic terminal and a much smaller international terminal.

The domestic terminal handles all Seoul's domestic flights except for a handful of flights to and from Busan and Jejudo, which arrive and depart from Incheon International Airport. The 1st floor is for arrivals, the 2nd floor is for checking in, and the 3rd floor is for departures. Flights, none lasting more than an hour, go to Jejudo, Busan and seven other cities. The usual shops and restaurants are inside the terminal.

The international terminal only handles flights to Haneda (Tokyo, eight daily) and Shanghai (four daily). Taking this route avoids the hassle of getting out to Incheon and Narita airports, which are some distance from their respective capital cities.

INCHEON INTERNATIONAL AIRPORT

This spacious, world-class airport (Map p169; ☎ 032 1577 2600; www.airport.kr), 52km west of

THINGS CHANGE...

The information in this chapter is particularly vulnerable to change. Check directly with the airline or a travel agent to make sure you understand how a fare (and ticket you may buy) works and be aware of the security requirements for international travel. Shop carefully. The details given in this chapter should be regarded as pointers and are not a substitute for your own careful, up-to-date research.

Seoul, opened in March 2001, and relegated Gimpo International Airport to handling mainly domestic flights.

The 1st floor (arrivals) has foreign currency exchange counters, Global ATMs and a tourist information centre (☎ 02 1330; ☼ 7am-10pm). Gate A is for the handful of domestic flights to Jejudo, Busan and Daegu.

The 2nd floor has airline offices, mobile-phone rental desks and a post office (☼ 9am-6pm Mon-Fri).

The 3rd floor is for departures and has shops, convenience stores and bakeries. Exchange any won before leaving the country. To obtain a tax refund on goods you bought at a shop that participates in one of the tax refund schemes (see p83), show the goods and receipts to one of the customs officers behind the check-in counters. Also on this

GETTING INTO TOWN

Gimpo International Airport
Subway line 5 runs from Gimpo International Airport (W1300, 35 minutes to downtown), as do limousine buses (W3000) and taxis (regular W25,000, deluxe W35,000). Between the Gimpo and Incheon airports, take a limousine bus (standard W5000, deluxe W6500) or A'rex train (W3200). Both run frequently and take half an hour.

Incheon International Airport
Located on the island Yeongjongdo in the West Sea, fleets of buses, trains and taxis go back and forth from the airport to all parts of Seoul and to other cities. Special airport limousine buses run every 10 to 30 minutes from around 5.30am to 10pm and the trip to downtown Seoul takes around 80 minutes depending on traffic conditions. City limousine buses cost W9000 and run along a dozen routes, while KAL deluxe limousine buses (www.kallimousine.com) run along four routes, cost W14,000 and drop passengers off at 20 top hotels around Seoul. If your accommodation is near one of these top hotels you can hop onto one of these.

Limousine buses also run every 10 minutes to Gimpo airport along a special airport road, which takes about 30 minutes and costs W5000 on the City limousine buses or W6500 on the KAL ones. The new A'rex train (airport railroad; www.arex.or.kr) is cheaper (W3200) and takes 30 minutes too. The A'rex train should go all the way to Seoul station some time in 2010.

When catching a bus back to the airport, remember that the airport buses have their own special, signed stops.

Regular taxis charge around W45,000 for the 70-minute journey to downtown Seoul and a deluxe or jumbo taxi costs around W75,000, but the prices can rise if traffic is jammed – meters run on a time basis when the taxis are not moving. A road toll (W7100) is added to the meter price. From midnight to 4am regular taxis charge 20% extra.

floor is the left-luggage storeroom (W3000-9000; 7am-10pm).

Transit Tours (☎ 032 741 3139; http://transit.freedom .co.kr; 3rd fl or Gate 3, 1st fl; 6.30am-9pm) organises guided tours for transit passengers that run to a nearby Buddhist temple, a shopping mall, a luxurious seawater spa, around the airport island, Yeongjongdo, and further afield to Sindo, Wolmido, Sukmodo, Icheon and around Seoul and Incheon. Tours cost between US$5 and US$100 and last from one hour to all day. A round of golf costs US$230. Some tours have minimum numbers.

Restaurants are up on the 4th floor, while down in the basement are more informal eating places, a pharmacy and a medical centre (☎ 743 3119; 24hr). The centre treats up to 200 people a day, and also has a dental clinic.

On the other side of immigration are more shops, restaurants and banks. A free internet lounge and a hands-on Korean traditional crafts space are near departure Gate 25. Up on the 4th floor is Incheon Airport Transit Hotel (☎ 032-743 3000; www.airgardenhotel.com; 6hr s/d from W50,000/63,000). The hotel is in two parts at both the east and west ends of the terminal. The small but smart and functional rooms are perfect for a stopover snooze. A minimum 12-hour stay is required after 6pm. Deluxe rooms are larger and have bigger beds.

KOREA CITY AIR TERMINAL

If you're booked on a Korean Air or Asiana flight, you can check-in your luggage and go through immigration at the Korea City Air Terminal (KCAT; Map p70; ☎ 551 0077; www.kcat.co.kr; 1st fl, COEX Mall, Jamsil; 5.30am-6.30pm; line 2 to Samseong, COEX Exit) and catch a nonstop limousine bus to Incheon International Airport (W14,000, every 15 minutes) or Gimpo airport (W6500).

BICYCLE

The only safe and enjoyable cycling is in Ttukseom Seoul Forest (p76) and along the excellent cycleways on both sides of the Han River (p141).

Hire

Bicycles can be hired at stalls along the Han River and at Ttukseom Seoul Forest. They cost W3000 an hour; tandems cost twice as much. Negotiate if you want a half-day or full-day hire. ID is required in lieu of a deposit, and padlocks and helmets are not supplied.

BOAT

Regular ferries connect Incheon city, west of Seoul, with a dozen port cities in China two or three times a week. Journey times vary from 12 to 24 hours. One-way fares start at W115,000 to most destinations but prices double for the more private and comfortable cabins. A through-ticket from Seoul to Beijing or Shanghai is available, which includes a ferry trip and train journeys in Korea and China – see www.korail.go.kr for details. To reach Incheon's port (ferries leave from Yeonan Pier or International Terminal 2), take subway line 1 to Incheon station and then take a taxi (around W4000).

Ferries to a number of Japanese cities leave from the southern city of Busan. See www .korail.go.kr for a Seoul–Tokyo rail-and-ferry through ticket.

BUS
Local

It is easier and usually quicker to travel around Seoul by subway, but the city has a comprehensive and reasonably priced bus system (☎ 414 5005; www.bus.go.kr), which operates from 5.30am to midnight. Some buses run on a few routes until 2am. Some bus stops have some bus route maps in English, and most buses have their major destinations written in English on the outside and a taped announcement of the names of each stop in English, but hardly any bus drivers understand English.

Long-distance express red buses run to the outer suburbs, green buses link subways within a district, blue buses run to outer suburbs and yellow short-haul buses circle small districts. The useful yellow bus 2 does a loop around Namsan from N Seoul Tower to Namsangol Hanok Village and the National Theatre. If you use a T-money prepaid card (the card costs W2500 and can be bought, charged and recharged at any subway station ticket office; p175) you save W100 less on bus fares and transfers between bus and subway are either free or discounted. Put your T-money card to the screen as you exit as well as when you get on a bus, just as you do on the subway.

Long Distance

Reasonably priced long-distance buses speed to every small town in South Korea from early in the morning until late at night. Check the terminal websites for timetables, seat availability and fares. Most major roads have a special bus lane that reduces delays. Buses are so frequent that it's not necessary to buy a ticket in advance, except perhaps on holidays and weekends. Superior-class buses have more leg room but usually cost 50% more than ordinary buses. Buses that travel after 10pm have a 10% surcharge and are generally superior class. Children go half price. Buses go to far more places than the trains, but are not as comfortable or safe (road accidents are quite common, and bus drivers have a reputation for going fast).

The **Seoul Express Bus Terminal** (Map p68; www.ko bus.co.kr, www.easyticket.co.kr; Gangnam; line 3 or 7 to Express Bus Terminal) is in two separate buildings:

Gyeongbu-Gumi-Yeongdong Terminal (535 4151; Express Bus Terminal, Exit 1) Serves mainly the eastern region and has lots of shops and restaurants. Sample express/deluxe bus fares include Busan (W19,800/29,400), Gyeongju (W17,500/26,000), Sokcho (W14,900/22,000), Gongju (W6900/7500) and Icheon (W3900/5100).

Honam Terminal (6282 0600; Express Bus Terminal, Exit 7) Serves the southwestern region. Sample express/deluxe fares include Mokpo (W17,600/26,200), Gwangju (W15,000/22,400) and Jeonju (W11,200/16,000). This terminal is linked to Central City Mall (p91).

Other bus terminals:

Dong-Seoul Bus Terminal (Map p70; 455 3161; line 2 to Gangbyeon, Exit 3) Serves the eastern part of Korea (1st floor) and major cities (2nd floor). Sample fares include Icheon (W3800), Gongju (W7700), Chuncheon (W7800), Buyeo (W12,700), Jeonju (express/deluxe W12,200/17,900) and Busan (express/deluxe W19,900/29,500).

Nambu Bus Terminal (Map p68; 521 8550; Gangnam; line 3 to Nambu Bus Terminal, Exit 5) Destinations south of Seoul such as Daecheon Beach.

Sinchon Bus Terminal (Map p64; 324 0611; Sinchon; line 2 to Sinchon, Exit 7) Has services to Ganghwado (W3400, every 15 minutes), a historical, relatively unspoiled island northwest of Seoul.

CAR & MOTORCYCLE

Due to the traffic jams, the impatience and recklessness of other drivers and the lack of street names, directional signs and parking, we recommend first-time visitors to Seoul give driving a miss. Public transport and taxis are cheap and convenient, so few tourists get behind a steering wheel.

Driving

Driving is on the right. We don't recommend getting on the road around Seoul, but for travel beyond the capital it can make sense.

Hire

To rent a car you must be over 21 (older for more powerful vehicles) and have both a driving licence from your own country and an International Driving Permit. The latter must be obtained abroad as they're not available in Korea. Incheon International Airport has a couple of car-rental agencies. Try Kumho-Hertz (www.kumhorent.com) or Avis (www.aju-avis .co.kr). Daily rates start at W60,000; hiring a chauffeur-driven car starts at W170,000 per 10 hours/125km.

TAXI

Regular taxis (*ilban*) are a good deal and are cheaper than the bus or subway for three people on a short trip. They cost W1900 for the first 2km and then W100 for every 144m or 35 seconds afterwards. A 20% surcharge is charged between midnight and 4am. Deluxe taxis (*mobeom*) and jumbos are black with a yellow stripe and cost W4500 for the first 3km and then W200 for every 164m or 39 seconds, but they don't have a late-night surcharge. You can find them lined up outside luxury hotels.

All taxis are metered, and tips are not expected. Nowadays they have GPS and some accept payment by T-money or credit card. Many run on LPG rather than petrol.

Few drivers can speak English, but some taxis have a free interpretation service (look for the sticker on the side of the taxi). In these taxis you can speak on the phone in English to an interpreter who then talks to the taxi driver in Korean. Writing your destination down on a piece of paper can help as most Koreans are better at understanding written rather than spoken English. But writing your destination in *hangeul* (Korean script) would be better, so every map key item in this guidebook has a *hangeul* translation. Otherwise ask your hotel, motel or guesthouse receptionist to write it down for you.

TRAIN
Subway

Seoul's subway system (www.smrt.co.kr) is modern, comprehensive, fast, frequent, clean, safe and cheap – but try to avoid rush hours. The system is world class, and safe even late at night. It's also a bargain. the minimum fare is W1000 (W900 with a T-money card). This takes you up to 12km. The one-hour trip to Suwon city costs only W1200 and trains run as far as Incheon city to the west, Cheonan to the south and Bukhansan National Park to the north. Trains run every few minutes from 5.30am to around midnight. Subway stations connect just about everywhere with just about everything. In central Seoul the average time between stations is just over two minutes, so it takes around 25 minutes to go 10 stops. About the only place they don't go to is N Seoul Tower on top of Namsan, which has an excellent bus service. Some top-end hotels and a few sights are a 15-minute walk from a subway station but you can hail taxis from the closest station.

A T-money card costs W2500 and can be bought and recharged at subway station ticket offices, bus kiosks and convenience stores that display the T-money logo. Each person needs their own card. Using a card saves you W100 per trip and avoids the hassle of buying a ticket for every trip. Just touch the card to the sensor when you enter and leave the subway system or bus – you don't have to take the card out of your wallet or handbag. When you leave Seoul, money on the card (up to W20,000) can be refunded at any convenience store displaying the T-money logo.

Most subway stations have lifts or stair lifts for wheelchairs. Escalators are common, but you'll do a fair amount of walking up and down stairs. Neighbourhood maps inside the stations help you decide which of the subway exits to take. North can be in any position, which makes the maps confusing, and tourist places are often omitted in favour of office or apartment blocks. This guidebook therefore gives the exit number of all listings.

The stations have clean toilets, but carry your own toilet paper just in case. Don't forget that the toilet paper is often outside the cubicle!

Every station has plenty of English signage, and the whole system is very user-friendly. Most subway stations have storage lockers, although most of them are too small to take a full-size backpack. Smoking is not permitted on trains or platforms.

At the time of writing, a new line, 9, was scheduled to open in late 2009, running from Gimpo Airport to the National Assembly on Yeouido and on to Noryangjin Fish Market and the Express Bus Station.

Rail

Seoul is the hub of an extensive domestic rail network operated by Korean National Railroad (☎ 1544 7788; www.korail.go.kr). The railway ticketing system is computerised, and tickets can be bought up to one month in advance at many travel agents as well as at train stations or online. Booking ahead is advised. Foreigners who plan to travel by train a lot over a short period should buy a 'KR pass' – see the website for details.

The fastest train is the KTX (Korea Train Express), a bullet train service that runs from Seoul to Busan, and is being extended to the southwestern route as well. It has cut the train-travel time between Seoul and Busan to just under two hours. The next-fastest and most luxurious type of train is the *saemaeul* services, which also only stop in major towns. *Mugunghwa* trains are also comfortable and fast, but stop more often, while *tongil* (commuter) trains are the cheapest and stop at every station.

BUSINESS HOURS

For most government and private offices, business hours are from 9am to 6pm Monday to Friday. Government offices usually close an hour earlier from November to February.

Banking hours run from 9.30am to 4.30pm Monday to Friday, but opening and closing may be brought forward 30 minutes. Post offices are open from 9am to 6pm Monday to Friday from March to October, and 9am to 5pm November to February.

Seoul never sleeps, and there's plenty on offer for night owls: saunas, spas, DVD rooms, internet cafés, convenience stores, fast-food and some other restaurants, and a few markets and malls. Many karaoke rooms, pool halls, bars and nightclubs stay open until dawn, particularly on Friday or Saturday night. Clubbing, gaming, watching DVDs, napping in a sauna or shopping until 5.30am means you can catch an early subway train home and save on the taxi fare.

Because business hours vary, they are listed in every review in this guide. For hours for shopping and sleeping establishments, see the corresponding chapters.

CHILDREN

See p66 for ways of keeping children entertained. If you're in Seoul with the darlings on Children's Day (5 May) take advantage of the many special events for children.

The National Museum of Korea (p73) and the National Folk Museum (p39) have fun, hands-on children's sections, and the War Memorial & Museum (p73) has outdoor warplanes and tanks that make for a popular playground.

If junior is happy to sleep on a *yo* (floor mattress), finding accommodation should be a breeze. Children are welcome in restaurants but families usually eat out in their own neighbourhood rather than in central Seoul. High chairs are not common.

For general advice about taking children abroad, check out a copy of Lonely Planet's *Travel with Children*.

Babysitting

A few top hotels and residences, such as Fraser Suites (p150) and Lotte World Hotel (p155), provide babysitting services, but that's about it. Otherwise try H & S (☎ 720 0870; www.hnskorea .com), who can supply babysitters for W10,000 an hour.

CLIMATE

Seoul has four very distinct seasons, as locals never tire of telling you. Weatherwise, the best time of year to visit is autumn (September to November) when the skies are usually blue. In October Seoul's surrounding hillsides are ablaze with autumn colours. Spring, from April to early June, is another beautiful season, with warming temperatures and cherry blossoms in late April.

Winter is dry but often bitterly cold, with average temperatures in Seoul hovering around 0°C from December to February. This is the season when you really appreciate the *ondol* (underfloor heating). But white snow on temple roofs is incredibly picturesque, and, as an added perk, the swimming pools open up as ice skating rinks. Try to avoid summer as late June to late July is the wet season, when Seoul receives 60% of its annual rainfall. Some weeks in August are unpleasantly hot and humid, although these days most places have air-con.

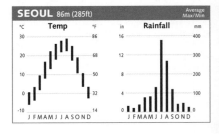

COURSES
Buddhist Temple Stays & Courses

Some Korean temples located in remote and picturesque mountain areas offer visitors the chance to participate in activities with the monks. A typical overnight temple stay includes sharing a four-bowl meal of rice, soup, vegetables and water with the monks. No talk is allowed and not even a scrap of food should be wasted – Buddhist monks and nuns still follow strict rules. A guided tour of the temple buildings is followed by half an hour of Seon (Zen) meditation. Everyone sits cross-legged and a monk tells participants to concentrate and use their minds to focus completely on their breathing.

Another experience is the tea ceremony (*dado*) when a monk prepares green tea, which must be served at exactly the right temperature and should be drunk in three sips. Tea calms the mind and body, and if Korean monks have a disagreement they settle it over a cup of green tea.

A hike in the nearby mountains and helping to clean the grounds are other likely activities. To find out more contact Templestay (www.templestay.com) or visit the KTO Tourist Information Centre (p183). In Jogyesa, visitors can also learn to make Buddhist lanterns, woodblock prints and prayer beads, as well as practice meditation.

Every Thursday at 2pm, Bongeunsa (p71) offers a temple program in English that costs W10,000. The program includes lotus lantern making, *dado*, a temple tour and Seon meditation.

Other options:

Ahnkook Zen Centre (Map p40; ☎ 3673 0772; www .ahnkookzen.org; Gwanghwamun; ◉ line 3 to Anguk, Exit 2) Buddhist teaching in English every Saturday from 2.30pm until 4pm.

Buddhist Institute English Library (Map p50; ☎ 730 0173; www.bels.kr; Jongno, Insadong; classes from W5000; ⊗ 11am–4pm Mon-Fri, 11am–2pm Sat; ◉ line 3 to Anguk, Exit 6) Besides the extensive library, the institute organises *dharma* talks, group and meditation study and lectures on Buddhist beliefs and practice. The teachers are Korean and Tibetan Buddhist monks who speak English. They offer a wonderful opportunity to study Buddhism seriously in an Asian context at beginner or advanced level. Teenagers have their own classes.

Cooking

The best way to learn Korean cooking is to do a homestay with someone willing to teach you. Failing that head to college or to Yoo's Family (right).

Korean cooking courses in English start at 10am and 2pm on weekdays at Seoul Culinary College (Map p50; ☎ 742 3567; Insadong; ⊗ office 9am–10pm Mon-Fri; ◉ line 1, 3 or 5 to Jongno 3-ga, Exit 5). Book one week ahead, no minimum number.

The one-hour kimchi course costs W60,000, while the two-hour courses cost W80,000 to W100,000. The price includes a lavishly illustrated Korean cookbook.

Korean Language

YBM Sisa (Map p50; ☎ 2278 0509; http://kli.ybmedu.com; Insadong; ⊗ office 6am-7pm Mon-Sat; ◉ line 1, 3 or 5 to Jongno 3-ga, Exit 15) Korean classes (maximum size 10) for all ability levels cover grammar, writing and conversation. Ten-day courses (W115,000) are held in the evening, 20-day courses are held during the day. Lessons last just under two hours, and courses start at the beginning of each month.

Yonsei University (Map p64; ☎ 2123 3465; www.yskli .com; Sinchon) The university runs highly recommended part- and full-time Korean language and culture classes for serious students.

Meditation

Meditation Arui Seon (Map p50; ☎ 722 1108; www.suseon jae.org; off Insadong 3-gil, Insadong; ⊗ 10am-10pm Tue-Sun; ◉ line 3 to Anguk, Exit 6), based in a *hanok* (traditional house), offers beginner and advanced meditation, breathing, stretching and other exercises designed to de-stress, relax and improve your mind and body. Students say their lives have been greatly improved. The aim is to unlock 'gi' or energy paths. Courses in English cost W20,000 for two hours and include tea. Highly recommended if you want to delve into ideas about health, and improving mind and body awareness and focus.

Traditional Culture

Housed in a *hanok*, Yoo's Family (Map p40; ☎ 3673 0323; www.yoosfamily.com; East Gwanghwamun; W40,000-60,000; ⊗ Mon-Sat; ◉ line 3 to Anguk, Exit 4) offers practical demonstrations of Korean culture in a convenient location. Lessons include the traditional tea ceremony, print-making from carved wooden blocks, Korean cooking and dressing up in *hanbok* (traditional clothing). A minimum of two persons is required. Tea was a luxury drink in the past and involved a complicated ritual – it is polite to use both hands. Young green-tea leaves, picked in April, are the best (and most expensive). There are lots of photo opportunities and the teaching style is informal and relaxed.

CUSTOMS REGULATIONS

Visitors must declare all plants, fresh fruit, vegetables and dairy products that they bring into South Korea. Meat is not allowed without a certificate. If you have more than US$10,000 in cash and travellers cheques, this should be declared and you have to fill in a form. Gifts worth more than US$400 should also be declared. Leaving the country, the duty-free allowance is 200 cigarettes, 59ml (2 ounces) of perfume and less than 1L of liquor. Log on to www.customs.go.kr for further information. Antiques of national importance are not allowed to be exported – check with the Cultural Properties Appraisal Office (☎ 662 0106).

DISCOUNT CARDS

Government-run tourist attractions generally offer discounts to senior citizens over 65, but you will need a passport or some other ID. Other organisations may restrict discounts to local residents but it's always worth asking.

See p175 for information on the T-money transport card.

ELECTRICITY

South Korea is on the 220V standard at 60Hz and uses two round pins with no earth.

EMBASSIES

Australia (Map p40; ☎ 2003 0100; www.southkorea .embassy.gov.au; 11th fl, Kyobo Bldg, Jongno 1-ga, Jongno-gu)

Canada (Map p40; ☎ 3783 6000; www.korea.gc.ca; 16-1 Jeong-dong, Jung-gu)

China (Map p40; ☎ 738 1038; 9th fl, Kyobo Bldg, Jongno 1-ga, Jongno-gu)

France (Map pp36–7; ☎ 3149 4300; ambassade.france .or.kr; 30 Hap-dong, Seodaemun-gu)

Germany (Map pp36–7; ☎ 748 4114; www.seoul.diplo .de; 308-5 Dongbinggo-dong, Yongsan-gu)

Ireland (Map p40; ☎ 774 6455; www.irelandhouse -korea.com; 13th fl, Leema Bldg, 146-1 Sosong-dong, Jongno-gu)

Japan (Map p40; ☎ 2170 5200; www.kr.emb-japan .go.jp; 18-11 Junghak-dong, Jongno-gu)

Netherlands (Map p40; ☎ 737 9514; http://southkorea .nlembassy.org; 14th fl, Kyobo Bldg, Jongno 1-ga, Jongno-gu)

New Zealand (Map p40; ☎ 3701 7700; www.nzembassy .com; 18th fl, Kyobo Bldg, Jongno 1-ga, Jongno-gu)

Philippines (Map p60; ☎ 796 7387; www.phil embassy-seoul.com; Jinsong Bldg, 34-44 Itaewon 1-dong, Yongsan-gu)

Russia (Map pp56–7; ☎ 318 2116; www.russian -embassy.org; 34-16 Jeong-dong, Jung-gu)

Singapore (Map p40; ☎ 744 2464; www.mfa.gov .sg/seoul; 28th fl, Seoul Finance Centre, 84 Taepyeongno 1-ga, Jung-gu)

Taiwan (Map p40; ☎ 399 2767; Visa Office, 6th fl, Gwanghwamun Bldg, Sejongno, Jongno-gu)

UK (Map p40; ☎ 3210 5500; http://ukinkorea.fco.gov .uk; Taepyeongno 40, 4 Jeong-dong, Jung-gu)

USA (Map p40; ☎ 397 4114; http://seoul.usembassy .gov; 32 Sejongno, Jongno-gu)

EMERGENCY

If there are no English-speaking staff available, ring ☎ 1330 (24-hour tourist information and help line).

Ambulance (☎ 119)

Fire Brigade (☎ 119)

Medical Help Line (☎ 1339; English-speaking)

Police (☎ 112)

GAY & LESBIAN TRAVELLERS

Korea has never passed any laws that mention homosexuality, but this shouldn't be taken as a sign of tolerance or acceptance. Korean law does not mention homosexuality because it is considered so bizarre and unnatural that the topic is completely taboo. Only one celebrity, TV actor Hong Seok-chun, has admitted to being gay (see boxed text, p23). Some older Koreans insist that there are no gays in Korea. Attitudes are changing, especially among young people, but virtually all Korean gays and lesbians keep their sexual orientation a secret from their family, work colleagues and friends. The few gay and lesbian clubs, bars and saunas (p131) in Seoul keep a low profile, but are more open than they used to be. Gay and lesbian travellers who publicise their sexual orientations should expect some hostile reactions.

HEALTH

South Korea is a developed country and the quality of medical care in Seoul is high. You need a doctor's prescription to buy most medications, and it may be difficult to find the exact medication you use at home, so take extra to avoid loss or theft. A letter from your physician outlining your medical condition and a list of your medications (using generic names) could be useful.

No matter how fit, careful and healthy you are, accidents can always happen and it is unwise to travel without health insurance – check www.lonelyplanet.com/bookings for more information.

There are no special vaccination requirements for visiting Korea, but you should consider vaccination against hepatitis A and B. Most people don't drink the tap water in Seoul, but those who do seem to come to no harm. Filtered or bottled water is served free in most restaurants. If you are sensitive to air pollution, particularly vehicle pollution, check for advice from your doctor before arriving. Practise safe sex in Seoul as you would anywhere else.

There is a wealth of travel health advice available on the internet. For further information, Lonely Planet (lonelyplanet.com) is a good place to start. The World Health Organization (WHO; www.who.int/ith) publishes an excellent booklet called *International Travel & Health,* which is revised annually and is available online at no cost.

HOLIDAYS

Seven Korean public holidays are set according to the solar calendar and three according to the lunar calendar, meaning that they fall on different days each year. See p12 for Seoul's festivals and annual events.

New Year's Day 1 January

Lunar New Year Three days in January or February

Independence Movement Day 1 March

Children's Day 5 May

Buddha's Birthday One day in May

Memorial Day 6 June

Liberation Day 15 August

National Foundation Day 3 October

Chuseok (Thanksgiving) Three days in September or October

Christmas Day 25 December

INTERNET ACCESS

Internet cafés can be found on every street of Seoul – just look for the 'PC 방' signs. The internet rooms charge around W1000 per hour and are usually full of teenager gamers. Addiction to these games is a major social problem. The PC rooms all have fast broadband connections, and keyboards feature English and *hangeul*. Some are open 24 hours, but they don't usually offer much refreshment beyond instant noodles, biscuits and soft drinks. Some are full of cigarette smoke, despite smoke-free zones.

The KTO Tourist Information Centre (p183), backpacker guesthouses, most post offices, some hotels and many other places offer free broadband internet access.

MAPS

The Korean Tourism Organisation (KTO) and Seoul Metropolitan Government publish numerous free brochures and maps of Seoul, which are fine for most purposes. Chungang Atlas (Map p50; ☎ 730 9191; Sambong-gil, Insadong; ☺ 9am-6.30pm Mon-Sat; subway Line 1 to Jonggak, Exit 2) has racks of maps of Seoul and Korea for W3100 each, but all are in *hangeul*. There are some hiking maps with a bit of English.

MEDICAL SERVICES

Seoul has medical-care standards equal to those of other developed countries. There are two health systems – one is Western-style and the other is based on traditional Eastern principles and makes use of herbal remedies, cupping and acupuncture. Gyeongdong Market (p91) is the place to go for traditional remedies.

It is customary for a relative or friend to stay with a patient who is in hospital (staying overnight in the case of a serious illness) to help with the nursing work. Nurses concentrate on the medicine and monitoring aspects, while relatives handle the small talk and wield the bedpans. Doctors have a heavier caseload than in the US and are not used to offering patients options or giving long explanations (even if their English is up to it). Hospitals normally require cash upfront, which you should be able to claim back from your insurance company if you have appropriate cover.

Clinics

Columbia Plus Dental Clinic (Map p68; ☎ 569 8745; www.columbiaplus.com; Gangnamdaero, Gangnam; ☺ 9.30am-6.30pm Mon-Fri, to 1.30pm Sat; ◉ line 2 to Gangnam, Exit 2) Up on the 3rd floor US-trained Kang Min-Suk has all the latest equipment and can do crowns in just one visit. An examination and X-ray costs W40,000, and fillings range from W100,000 to W350,000. Cleaning is W60,000.

Daewon Dental Clinic (Map p60; Itaewonno, Itaewon; ☎ 794 0551, fax 794 0512; ☻ 10am-1pm & 2-6.30pm Mon-Fri, 10am-2pm Sat; ☺ line 6 to Itaewon, Exit 4) Kind and gentle Dr Park can take care of your dental problems – a check-up is W20,000 to W30,000.

International Clinic (Map p64; ☎ 2228 5800, 24hr emergency only 2228 6566; www.severance.or.kr; 3rd fl, Main Bldg, Severance Hospital, Seongsanno, Sinchon; consultation W57,000; ☻ 9.30am-12.30pm & 1.30-5.30pm Mon-Fri, 9.30am-1.30pm Sat; ☺ line 2 to Sinchon, Exit 3) A 700m walk from the subway, the impressive, ultra-modern clinic has five English-speaking doctors. Ring to make an appointment – patients can usually be fitted in that day. E3 visa physical check-ups cost around W200,000.

International Clinic (Map p60; ☎ 790 0857; www.internationalclinic.co.kr; Hannam Bldg, Itaewonno, Itaewon; ☻ 9am-noon & 2-6pm Mon-Fri, 9am-noon & 2-3pm Sat; ☺ line 6 to Itaewon, Exit 2) Consultations cost W30,000 to W50,000, while a flu jab is W25,000. Appointments are a must. Natural detox is available.

Pharmacies

Almost all pharmacies stock at least some Western medicines. Pharmacists often know some English but it may help them if you write down your symptoms or the medicine you want on a piece of paper. If you have a language problem and a mobile phone, dial ☎ 1330, explain what you want in English, and ask the interpreter to explain in Korean to the pharmacist.

Pharmacists in Itaewon can communicate in English. Some brand-name medications, special sunscreens, deodorants, dental floss and specialised health products may be difficult to obtain in Seoul, so stock up on them before you arrive. Condoms can be bought from vending machines outside subway toilets.

At **Sudo Pharmacy** (Map p50; ☎ 732 3336; Insadong-gil, Insadong; ☻ 8.30am-9.20pm Mon-Sat, noon-7pm Sun; ☺ line 3 to Anguk, Exit 6) Mr Lim Jun-suk speaks English and believes Western chemical medicines are better for treating serious illnesses, while natural Eastern ones are better for minor problems. He can advise on both systems.

MONEY

The South Korean unit of currency is the won (W), with W10, W50, W100 and W500 coins.

Notes come in denominations of W1000, W5000 and W10,000. The highest value note is worth less than US$7.5 at the time of writing – you'll probably have to carry around a thick wad of notes. A W50,000 note has been promised and may be available when you travel here.

Go to www.xe.com for up-to-date exchange rates. See p14 for how far your money will stretch in Seoul.

ATMs

There are more ATMs in Seoul that accept foreign credit cards these days – look for one that has a 'Global' sign or the logo of your credit-card company. Global ATMs have instructions in English. ATM booths can be found in banks and they are also located in post offices, deluxe hotels, subway stations, airports, convenience stores and department stores.

ATMs often operate only from 9am to 11pm, but some are 24-hour. Restrictions on the amount you can withdraw vary. It can be as low as W300,000 per day, but most have a W700,000 limit. Outside banking hours you may be charged a higher commission. The exchange services listed in Changing Money all have Global ATMs. Some convenient Global ATM locations in Itaewon:

Itaewon subway station (Map p60; Itaewon; ☺ line 6 to Itaewon) 24-hour.

Korea Exchange Bank (KEB; Map p60; Itaewonno, Itaewon; ☺ line 6 to Itaewon, Exit 1)

Changing Money

Many banks in Seoul offer a foreign exchange service. There are also licensed moneychangers, particularly in Itaewon, that keep longer hours than the banks and provide a faster service, but may only exchange US dollars cash. Before exchanging money in shops or hotels, compare their rates with the banks, as banks don't usually charge any commission.

US dollars are easiest to exchange but banks accept any major currency. If you have trouble exchanging a particular currency, try the Korea Exchange Bank (KEB). Traveller's cheques usually have a slightly better exchange rate than cash. Don't forget to reconvert any surplus won into another currency before you leave the country. If you need to reconvert more than US$2000 of won at Incheon airport, you must show receipts for the money.

Exchange services:

Citibank (Map p50; ☎ 731 8100; Hwaenamu-gil, Insadong; ☷ 9.30am-4.30pm Mon-Fri; Ⓔ line 1 to Jonggak, Exit 3)

KB Star (Kookmin; Map p50; ☎ 745 1032; Donhwamunno, East Insadong; ☷ 9.30am-4.30pm Mon-Fri; Ⓔ line 3 to Anguk, Exit 4)

Korea Exchange Bank (KEB; Map p60; ☎ 792 3911; Itaewonno, Itaewon; ☷ 9.30am-4.30pm Mon-Fri; Ⓔ line 6 to Itaewon, Exit 1)

Shinhan Bank (Map p40; ☎ 774 5800; Gwanghwamun; ☷ 9.30am-4.30pm Mon-Fri; Ⓔ line 1 to Jonggak, Exit 5) Next to the KTO tourist information centre.

Credit Cards

More upmarket hotels, shops and restaurants accept foreign credit cards, but plenty of places including budget accommodation, stalls and restaurants require hard cash. Cash payment is still common in Seoul, so a stash of W10,000 notes will almost certainly be needed.

NEWSPAPERS & MAGAZINES

Korea has two English-language newspapers: the Korea Times (www.koreatimes.co.kr; W700) and Korea Herald (www.koreaherald.co.kr; W700). Both are published Monday to Saturday, and it's difficult to tell them apart. They mainly feature news agency reports and local business and political news. The websites are very useful – the *Times* has a 'jobs for foreigners' section. In the Community section there's a 'market place' for rooms and apartments for rent; in Arts & Living there's an excellent event's calendar ('Around Town'). The *Herald* website has job vacancies and accommodation classifieds.

JoongAng Daily (http://joongangdaily.joins.com) An 8-page insert in the *International Herald Tribune* (W1300) with a what's-on section on Thursdays. The website has a youthful vibe, with restaurant reviews and event listings.

Koreana (www.koreana.or.kr) Quarterly scholarly magazine on all things Korean that can be read online.

Seoul (subscription W32,000) Weighty monthly magazine that is always worth reading, with event listings, interviews, reviews and articles on cultural topics.

ORGANISED TOURS

If you join a tour, ensure it has an English-speaking guide if you want to get anything out of it. Tours usually include lunch and shopping stops. Go to www.startravel.co.kr or www.seoul

citytour.net for examples of tours and prices, and visit the KTO tourist information office (p183) for tour leaflets and advice. An Icheon Ceramics Village tour or a spin round Ganghwado costs W120,000, and a taekwondo class costs W60,000. In winter numerous package tours to nearby ski resorts (one day W75,000, overnight W300,000) are available.

Hyundai Asan (Map p40; ☎ 3669 3897; www.mtkumkang.com; 12th fl, Hyundai Bldg, Yulgongno, Insadong; Ⓔ line 3 to Anguk, Exit 3) runs tours to Kaesong (p163) and to Geumgangsan in North Korea. The North Korean government is famously unpredictable, so these tours may be altered or not running at all.

The **Royal Asiatic Society Korea Branch** (Map p40; ☎ 763 9483; www.raskb.com; Gwanghwamun; Room 611, Korean Christian Bldg; ☷ 10am-noon & 2-5pm Mon-Fri; Ⓔ line 1 Jongno 5-ga, Exit 2) organises brilliant tours to all parts of South Korea, usually at weekends. Its website has the busy schedule. Non-members are welcome to join, and all tours are led by English speakers who are experts in their field. The tours are reasonably priced, usually W30,000 to W50,000. The society also organises lectures twice a month.

Seoul City Tour Bus (☎ 777 6090; www.seoulcitybus.com; ☷ Tue-Sun) has comfortable and colourful tour buses that run between Seoul's top tourist attractions north of the Han River. You can hop on and hop off anywhere along the two routes – downtown (adult/child W10,000/8000; 9am to 9pm, half-hourly) and around the palaces (adult/child W12,000/8000, 10am to 5pm, hourly). Ticket holders receive considerable discounts on tourist attractions. Take the tour bus to see as much as possible in a short time. The routes cover the palaces, Insadong, Namdaemun and Dongdaemun markets, Itaewon and Namsan, the National Museum and the War Memorial & Museum. Buy tickets on the bus, which can be picked up outside Deoksugung. A night tour (adult/child downtown W5000/3000, palaces W10,000/6000) also operates. Check the website as tour details often change.

The **United Service Organizations** (USO; Map pp36–7; ☎ 795 3028; www.uso.org/korea; Yongsan; ☷ 8am-5pm Mon-Sat; Ⓔ line 4 & 6 to Samgakji, Exit 10), the US military's entertainment wing, organises tours for American troops, and civilians from most countries are welcome to come along. Twice a week the USO runs the best tours to the DMZ, Panmunjeom and the Third Tunnel (p160). Other all-day tours include the historical and unspoilt island of Ganghwado (US$28) and white-water rafting excursions (US$49) out in the wilds of Gangwon-do. In winter, skiing trips are organised.

POST

Korea Post (www.koreapost.go.kr) offices have a red/orange sign. Domestic postal rates start at W250 for a 25g letter, which might take three or four days, or W1840 for overnight express. A 2kg parcel costs W5000. Airmail letters (10g) cost W580 for Zone 3, which includes North America, Europe, Australia and New Zealand. A 2kg parcel costs W27,700 to the US or W22,500 to Australia.

Anguk Post Office (Map p50; ☎ 735 2005; Insadong; 🕙 9am-6pm Mon-Fri; ⊕ line 3 to Anguk, Exit 1) Free internet access.

Central Post Office (Map pp56–7; ☎ 6450 1114; Sogongno, Myeong-dong; 🕙 9am-8pm Mon-Fri, to 1pm Sat & Sun) This basement post office sells train tickets and offers free internet.

RADIO

Radio Gugak is a digital, government-funded station that broadcasts traditional Korean music on 99.1FM to the Seoul area. You can also listen online at www.gugakfm.co.kr (in Korean), although you may have to download a Gugak Player. AFN provides radio broadcasts for American troops on 1530AM (country music, news and sport) and 102.7FM (rock music and news).

SAFETY

Seoul is a safe city, except when it comes to traffic. Drivers tend to be impatient, with kimchi-hot tempers, and most of them, including bus drivers, routinely go through red lights. Don't be the first or last person to cross over any pedestrian crossing. Vehicles don't stop at pedestrian crossings not protected by traffic lights. Also keep two eyes out for cars parking on pavements and motorcyclists who routinely speed along pavements and across pedestrian crossings. A high proportion of road deaths (38%) are pedestrians, so take extra care.

Drunks in Seoul are better behaved than in the West, so walking around at 3am shouldn't pose a problem. The swaying packs of late-night revellers usually pose more of a threat to themselves than to other people. There's always an exception, of course, and as always it's best not to antagonise people who have been drinking.

Visitors are often surprised to see police in full riot gear, carrying large shields and long batons, streaming out of blue police buses that have their windows covered in protective wire. Student, trade-union, anti-American, environmental and other protests occasionally turn violent. Keep well out of the way of any confrontations that may occur.

TELEPHONE

Despite the popularity of mobile phones, there are still plenty of public telephones in Seoul, especially at subway stations. Some public phones only accept coins and can only be used for local calls. Other phones accept phonecards and can be used for local or long-distance calls. Phones that can make international calls have a sign to that effect.

Gyeonggi-do code (☎ 031) This province surrounds Seoul.

Incheon city and airport code (☎ 032)

International access codes KT (☎ 001), Dacom (☎ 002) and Onse (☎ 008)

Seoul code (☎ 02) Do not dial the zero if calling from outside Korea.

South Korea country code (☎ 82)

To send a fax, ask at your hotel or guesthouse. If they can't help, try the nearest internet room or hotel with a business centre.

Mobile Phones

The bad news is that Korea uses the CDMA network system, which few other countries use, so you will probably have to rent a mobile (cell) phone while you're in Seoul. The best place to do this is at Incheon International Airport as soon as you arrive. Mobile phone hire is available from four companies, which all have counters on the arrivals floor. Currently the rental fee is around W3000 a day, incoming calls are free and outgoing domestic calls cost around W600 a minute, while calls to the US, for example, cost around W900 a minute. Check if the price includes 10% VAT.

Korean mobile phone numbers have three-digit area codes, always beginning with 01, eg ☎ 011-0000 0000.

Phonecards

Telephone cards (W2000 to W10,000) give holders a 10% bonus and can be bought at convenience stores and many small shops. There are two types of cards, so if your card does not fit in one type of phone, try a different-looking one. For phoning abroad a much better deal is offered by the dozens of call-back cards that can be bought in Itaewon or the Filipino Sunday Market (p85).

TIME
South Korea has one time zone, Greenwich Mean Time (GMT) plus nine hours. When it's noon in Seoul it is 7pm the previous day in San Francisco, 10pm the previous day in New York, 3am in London and 1pm in Sydney (non–daylight saving hours). Korea does not have daylight saving.

TOILETS
A huge effort has gone into improving standards, so Seoul nowadays has plenty of clean, modern and well-signed public toilets. Virtually all toilets are free of charge, some are decorated with flowers and artwork, and a few even have music. Toilet paper is usually outside the cubicles, so don't forget to grab some before entering the cubicle. As always, it's wise to carry a stash of toilet tissue around with you just in case.

Restaurants, cafés and bars always have toilets, and most buildings have toilets off the stairways that are available to anyone who needs them. All major tourist attractions, parks, subway, train and bus stations have public toilet facilities. Even hikers in the mountains are well catered for, although some are rudimentary. Asian-style squat toilets are losing their battle with European-style ones, but there are still a few around. Face the hooded end when you squat.

TOURIST INFORMATION
Cheonggyecheon Tourist Information Centre (Map p40; Sejongno, Gwanghwamun; 9am-10pm; line 5 to Gwanhwamun, Exit 6)

Gyeongbokgung Tourist Information Centre (Map p40; 720 7465; Gwanghwamun; 9am-6pm; line 3 to Gyeongbokgung, Exit 5)

Hongdae Tourist Information Centre (Map p63; 1330; Seogyoro, Hongdae; noon-10pm; line 2 to Hongik University, Exit 5) Free internet.

Insadong Tourist Information Centre (Map p50; 734 0222; Insadong-gil, Insadong; 10am-10pm; line 3 to Anguk, Exit 6) Free internet. You can try on hanbok for W3000. Two more centres are at the south and north entrances to Insadong-gil.

Itaewon Subway Tourist Information Centre (Map p60; 3785 2514; Itaewon; 9am-10pm) Free internet, but may close earlier in winter.

Itaewon Tourist Information (Map p60; 1330; Itaewonno, Itaewon; 9am-6pm; line 6 to Itaewon, Exit 2)

KTO Tourist Information Centre (Map p40; 1330; www.visitkorea.or.kr; Gwanghwamun; 9am-8pm; line 1 to Jonggak, Exit 5) The best information centre; knowledgable staff, free internet and many brochures and maps.

Lotte World Tourist Information Centre (Map p70; 2143 7005; Jamsil; 9.30am-10pm; line 2 or 8 to Jamsil, Exit 3) By the Trevi fountain.

Myeong-dong Tourist Information Centre (Map pp56–7; 757 0088; Myeong-dong; 9am-6pm; line 2 to Euljiro 1-ga, Exit 6)

Namdaemun Market Tourist Information Centre (1330; Map p87; 752 1913; Namdaemun Market; 9am-6pm; line 4 to Hoehyeon, Exit 5)

Yongsan Train Station Tourist Information Centre (Map pp36–7; 1330; Yongsan; 5am-10pm; line 1 to Yongsan)

TRAVELLERS WITH DISABILITIES
In the past, Seoul has not been geared up to cater for disabled people. This is changing slowly, and the subway stations in particular have made a big effort to become more disabled-friendly. Many stations now have stair lifts and elevators, and new toilets for the disabled have been built. A few hotels, such as Ibis Myeong-dong (p153) and Metro Hotel (p153) next door, have specially adapted rooms. Tourist attractions, especially government-run ones, offer generous discounts or even free entry for disabled people and a helper.

VISAS
With a confirmed onward ticket, visitors from the USA, nearly all West European countries, New Zealand, Australia and around 30 other countries receive 90-day permits on arrival. Visitors from a handful of countries receive 30-day permits, while 60-day permits are given to citizens of Italy and Portugal. Lucky Canadians receive a six-month permit.

About 30 countries – including the Russian Federation, China, India and Nigeria – do not qualify for visa exemptions. Citizens from these countries must apply for a tourist visa, which allows a stay of 90 days.

Visitors cannot extend their stay beyond 90 days except in situations such as a medical emergency. More info is at www.mofat.go.kr or www.g4f.go.kr.

The inconveniently located Seoul Immigration Head Office (Map pp36–7; ☎ 2650 6212; http://seoul.immigration.go.kr; ⏱ 9am-6pm Mon-Fri; Ⓜ line 5 to Omokgyo, Exit 7) is in Mok-dong. This office is always busy, so take something to read. To reach it, carry straight on from the subway exit and walk along the road until it ends, where you'll see a white-tiled building on your left with a big blue sign in English. It's a 700m walk. An Immigration Office in the Seoul Global Centre (Map p40; ☎ 1688 0120; 3rd fl, Seoul Press Centre, Gwanghwamun; ⏱ 9am-6pm Mon-Fri; Ⓜ line 1 or 2 to City Hall, Exit 4) can help with re-entry permits and some visa issues.

One problem is that applicants must leave the country to pick up a work visa. Most applicants fly to Fukuoka in Japan and pick up the visa a day after it was submitted. You can apply for a one-year work visa before entering Korea but it can take a few weeks to process. Note that the visa authorities will want to see originals or notarised copies (not simply photocopies) of your educational qualifications.

It is not necessary to leave Korea to renew a work visa as long as you carry on working for the same employer, but if you change employers you must apply for a new visa and pick it up from outside Korea.

A recent change in the law requires prospective English teachers to undergo both police and health checks. This requires obtaining a police clearance certificate from your country of residence and also a medical certificate to show you don't take drugs and are not HIV-positive.

If you don't want to forfeit your work or study visa, you must apply at your local immigration office for a re-entry permit before making any trips outside South Korea. The fee is W30,000 for a single re-entry or W50,000 for a multiple re-entry permit.

If you are working or studying in Korea on a long-term visa, it is necessary to apply for an alien registration card within 90 days of arrival. This costs W10,000 and is done at your local immigration office.

For up-to-date visa information, visit lonelyplanet.com/bookings and look for the Visa Help section.

WOMEN TRAVELLERS

Seoul is a relatively safe city for women, but the usual precautions should be taken. As in any country, some men can be a bother. Many women walk alone late at night in Seoul, but it's probably not a sensible idea in any big city. The Seoul International Women's Association (www.siwapage.com) is a very active group that has been running for over 40 years and organises monthly coffee mornings, tours, classes on Korean culture and fund-raising events – its annual November bazaar raises W250 million for local charities.

WORK

Seoul is a popular place for English teachers to work, and finding a teaching job shouldn't be too difficult. A university degree in any subject is sufficient if English is your native language. However, it's a good idea to obtain some kind of English-teaching certificate before you arrive – this increases your options if not your salary. Some foreigners who go to Seoul to teach bitch about everything and would have been far better off staying at home.

Teachers can expect to teach 30 hours per week and earn over W2 million a month (income tax is around 5%), with a furnished apartment, medical insurance, return flights, paid holiday (10 days) and completion bonus all part of a one-year package. If native-speaker teachers are in short supply, as they usually are, better deals can be negotiated.

Most English teachers work in *hagwon,* small, private, neighbourhood schools that operate outside school hours. Some are part of large chains. Teaching in a *hagwon* often involves evening and Saturday classes and some split shifts. Other opportunities include working in government schools or universities. View www.epik.go.kr if you want to immerse yourself in Korean culture, teaching in a government school. Private tutoring, company classes and even teaching via the telephone are also possible.

Some *hagwon* owners don't keep the promises made in the employment contract. Sometimes this is because the *hagwon* isn't attracting enough students, other times the owner is just unscrupulous. Check out the *hagwon* before committing yourself for an entire year. Ask your prospective employer for the email addresses of some teachers who work there. Remember that if you change employers, you will need to obtain a new work visa, which means making a visa run to Fukuoka or Osaka in Japan.

The websites of the *Korea Times* (www.koreatimes.co.kr) and *Korea Herald* (www.koreaherald.co.kr) both have job vacancies, but hundreds and hundreds of English teaching jobs are on specialist websites:

Dave's ESL Cafe (www.eslcafe.com) Dozens of new English-teaching vacancies posted daily, lively discussion forums about life in Seoul and masses of help to make you a better teacher.

English Spectrum (www.englishspectrum.com) Job vacancies, classifieds, Q & A forums and more.

KoreaJoblink (www.koreajoblink.com) Jobs, jobs, jobs.

Work n Play (www.worknplay.co.kr) Jobs and more.

Doing Business

Investor Help Centre (ISC; ☎ 1600 7119; www.investkorea.org) can help with visas, legal formalities, customs and tax.

Seoul Global Centre (opposite) has brochures and advice about doing business in Seoul, including taxation. Immigration staff are on hand and can help with some issues and paperwork.

A fair number of countries have active chambers of commerce in Seoul that provide invaluable contacts and networking opportunities:

Australia & NZ (www.anzock.org) They may separate.

UK (www.bcck.or.kr)

USA (www.amchamkorea.org)

Volunteering

Willing Workers on Organic Farms (WWOOF; ☎ 723 4458; www.koreawwoof.com) is a program involving 40 farms and market gardens that lets you experience rural life outside Seoul. Volunteers work four to five hours per day in return for board and food. Most hosts speak some English. Pay W30,000 and you receive a list of participating farms.

LANGUAGE

Korean belongs to the Ural-Altaic language family and is spoken by around 80 million people throughout the world. The seven major Korean dialects, generally corresponding to the provincial boundaries, are similar enough to be mutually intelligible. The standard language of South Korea is based on the dialect of Seoul and surrounding Gyeonggi-do, while the standard for North Korea is based on the Pyongyang dialect.

Korea's neighbours have had a great impact on the nation's history, culture and language – around 70% of all Korean vocabulary is of Chinese origin, and there are strong similarities between Korean and Japanese grammar, although many scholars consider Korean to be a 'language isolate'.

You'll find that locals appreciate travellers trying their language, no matter how muddled you may think you sound. So don't just stand there, say something! If you want to learn more Korean than we've included here, get a copy of Lonely Planet's comprehensive but user-friendly *Korean Phrasebook*.

PRONUNCIATION

Writing System

Chinese characters *(hanja)* are usually restricted to use in maps and occasionally in newspapers and written names. For the most part Korean is written in *hangeul,* the alphabet developed under King Sejong's reign in the 15th century. Many users of the Korean language argue that the Korean script is one of the most scientific and consistent alphabets used today.

Hangeul consists of 24 characters and isn't that difficult to learn. However, the formation of words using *hangeul* is very different from the way Western alphabets are used to form words. The emphasis is on the formation of a syllable so that it resembles a Chinese character. Thus the first syllable of the word *hangeul* (한) is formed by an 'h' (ㅎ) in the top left corner, an 'a' (ㅏ) in the top right corner and an 'n' (ㄴ) at the bottom, with this whole syllabic grouping forming a syllabic 'box'. These syllabic boxes are strung together to form words.

Hangeul has been provided in the text for any sites that don't feature English signage.

Romanisation

In July 2000, the Korean government adopted a new method of romanising the Korean language (known as NAKL). The new system has been energetically promoted throughout the government and tourist bureaus. However, it will take a long time for everyone to fall into line, so you can expect to encounter road signs, maps and tourist literature with at least two different romanisation systems. This guidebook has adopted the new system wherever possible.

Vowels & Vowel Combinations

ㅏ	a	as in 'are'
ㅑ	ya	as in 'yard'
ㅓ	eo	as the 'o' in 'of'
ㅕ	yeo	as the 'you' in 'young'
ㅗ	o	as in 'go'
ㅛ	yo	as in 'yoke'
ㅜ	u	as in 'flute'
ㅠ	yu	as the word 'you'
─	eu	as the 'oo' in 'look'
ㅣ	i	as the 'ee' in 'beet'
ㅐ	ae	as the 'a' in 'hat'
ㅒ	yae	as the 'ya' in 'yam'
ㅔ	e	as in 'ten'
ㅖ	ye	as in 'yes'
ㅘ	wa	as in 'waffle'
ㅙ	wae	as the 'wa' in 'wax'
ㅚ	oe	as the 'wa' in 'way'
ㅝ	wo	as in 'won'
ㅞ	we	as in 'wet'
ㅟ	wi	as the word 'we'
ㅢ	ui	as 'u' plus 'i'

Consonants

Unaspirated consonants are generally difficult for English speakers to render. To those unfamiliar with Korean, an unaspirated k will sound like 'g', an unaspirated t like 'd', and an unaspirated p like 'b'.

Whether consonants in Korean are voiced or unvoiced depends on where they fall within a word. The rules governing this are too complex to cover here – the following tables show the various alternative pronunciations you may hear.

Single Consonants

The letter ㅅ is pronounced 'sh' if followed by the vowel ㅣ, even though it is transliterated as si.

In the middle of a word, ㄹ is pronounced 'n' if it follows ㅁ (m) or ㅇ (ng), but when it follows ㄴ (n) it becomes a double 'l' sound (ll); when a single ㄹ is followed by a vowel it is transliterated as r.

ㄱ	g/k
ㄴ	n
ㄷ	d/t
ㄹ	r/l/n
ㅁ	m
ㅂ	b/p
ㅅ	s/t
ㅇ	–/ng
ㅈ	j/t
ㅊ	ch/t
ㅋ	k
ㅌ	t
ㅍ	p
ㅎ	h/ng

Double Consonants

Double consonants are pronounced with more stress than their single consonant counterparts.

ㄲ	kk
ㄸ	tt
ㅃ	pp
ㅆ	ss/t
ㅉ	jj

Complex Consonants

These occur only in the middle or at the end of a word.

ㄱㅅ	–/ksk/–
ㄴㅈ	–/nj/n
ㄴㅎ	–/nh/n
ㄹㄱ	–/lg/k
ㄹㅁ	–/lm/m
ㄹㅂ	–/lb/p
ㄹㅅ	–/ls/l
ㄹㅌ	–/lt/l
ㄹㅍ	–/lp/p
ㄹㅎ	–/lh/l
ㅂㅅ	–/ps/p

SOCIAL
Polite Korean

Korea's pervasive social hierarchy means that varying degrees of politeness are codified into the grammar. Young Koreans tend to use the very polite forms a lot less than the older generation, but it's always best to use the polite form if you're unsure. The phrases included in this section employ polite forms.

Meeting People

Hello.
안녕 하십니까
annyeong hasimnikka (pol)
안녕 하세요
annyeong haseyo (inf)
Goodbye.
안녕히 계세요
annyeong·hi gyeseyo (to person staying)
안녕히 가세요
annyeong·hi gaseyo (to person leaving)
May I ask your name?
이름을 여쭤봐도 될까요?
ireumeul yeojjwo bwado doelkkayo?
My name is ...
제 이름은...입니다
je ireumeun ... imnida
Where are you from?
어디서 오셨어요?
eodiseo oseosseoyo?
I'm from ...
저는...에서 왔습니다
jeoneun ... eseo wasseumnida
I'd like to introduce you to ...
(이분은)...입니다
(ibuneun) ... imnida

Yes.	
예/네	ye/ne
No.	
아니요	aniyo
Please.	
주세요	juseyo
Thank you.	
감사 합니다	gamsa hamnida
That's fine/You're welcome.	
괜찮습니다	gwaenchan seumnida
Excuse me.	
실례 합니다	sillye hamnida
Sorry (forgive me).	
미안 합니다	mian hamnida
How are you?	
안녕 하세요?	annyeong haseyo?
I'm fine, thanks.	
네 좋아요	ne, jo·ayo

Going Out

Is anything interesting on ...?
...재미 있는 거 있어요?
... jaemi itneun·geo isseoyo?

　locally
　이 지역에　　i-jiyeoge
　this weekend
　이번 주말에　ibon jumare
　today
　오늘　　　　oneul
　tonight
　오늘 밤에　oneul bame

Where are the ...?
...어디 있어요?
... eodi isseoyo?

　clubs
　클럽　　　　keulleop
　places to eat
　음식점　　　eumsik jeom
　pubs
　호프집　　　hopeu jip

Is there a local entertainment guide in English?
영어로 된 지역 여행 가이드 있어요?
yeong·eoro doen jiyeok yeohaeng gaideu isseoyo?

PRACTICAL
Accommodation

I'm looking for a ...
...를/을 찾고 있어요
... reul/eul chatgo isseoyo

　guesthouse
　여관/민박집　yeogwan/minbak jip
　hotel
　호텔　　　　hotel
　youth hostel
　유스호스텔　yuseu hoseutel

Do you have any rooms available?
방 있어요?　　bang isseoyo?

I'd like (a) ...
...로/으로 주세요
... ro/euro juseyo

　bed
　침대　　　　chimdae
　single bed
　싱글 침대　singgeul chimdae
　double bed
　더블 침대　deobeul chimdae
　twin beds
　침대 두개　chimdae dugae

to share a room
같이 쓰는 방　gachi sseuneun bang
Western-style room
침대 방　　　chimdae bang
room with sleeping mats
온돌 방 주세요　ondol bang juseyo
room with a bathroom
욕실있는 방　yoksil itneun bang
　주세요　　　juseyo

How much is it ...?
...에 얼마에요?
... e eolma eyo?

　per night
　하룻밤　　　harutbam
　per person
　한사람　　　han saram

Directions

Where is ...?
...이/가 어디 있어요?
... i/ga eodi isseoyo?
Go straight ahead.
똑바로 가세요
ttokbaro gaseyo
Turn left.
왼쪽으로 가세요
oen·jjogeuro gaseyo
Turn right.
오른쪽으로 가세요
oreun·jjogeuro gaseyo
at the next corner
다음 모퉁이에서
da·eum motung·i e-seo
at the traffic lights
신호등에서
sinhodeung eseo

Language Difficulties

Do you speak English?
영어 하세요?
yeong·eo haseyo?
What does ... mean?
...가/이무슨뜻 이에요?
... ga/i museun tteusieyo?
I don't understand.
잘 모르겠는데요
jal moreuget·neun deyo
Please write it down.
적어 주실래요
jeogeo jusillaeyo
Can you show me (on the map)?
보여 주실래요?
boyeo jusillaeyo?

Numbers

Korean has two counting systems. One is of Chinese origin, with Korean pronunciation, and the other is a native Korean system – the latter only goes up to 99 and is used for counting objects, expressing your age and for the hours when telling the time. They're always written in *hangeul* or digits (never in Chinese characters). Sino-Korean numbers are used to express minutes when telling the time, as well as dates, months, kilometres, money and floors of buildings. Numbers above 99 may be written in *hangeul*, in digits or in Chinese characters. Either Chinese or Korean numbers can be used to count days.

	Sino-Korean		Korean	
1	일	il	하나	hana
2	이	i	둘	dul
3	삼	sam	셋	set
4	사	sa	넷	net
5	오	o	다섯	daseot
6	육	yuk	여섯	yeoseot
7	칠	chil	일곱	ilgop
8	팔	pal	여덟	yeodeol
9	구	gu	아홉	ahop
10	십	sip	열	yeol
11		십일		sibil
12		십이		sibi
13		십삼		sipsam
14		십사		sipsa
15		십오		sibo
16		십육		simnyuk
17		십칠		sipchil
18		십팔		sippal
19		십구		sipgu
20		이십		isip
21		이십일		isibil
22		이십이		isibi
30		삼십		samsip
40		사십		sasip
50		오십		osip
60		육십		yuksip
70		칠십		chilsip
80		팔십		palsip
90		구십		gusip
100		백		baek
1000		천		cheon

Question Words

Who? (as subject)
누구?   nugu?
What? (as subject)
무엇?   mu·eot?

When?
언제?   eonje?
Where?
어디?   eodi?
How?
어떻게?   eotteoke?

Banking

I want to change ...
....를/을 바꾸려고 하는데요
.. reul/eul bakku ryeogo haneun deyo
  money
  돈   don
  travellers cheques
  여행자 수표   yeohaengja supyo

Where's the nearest ...?
제일 가까운...이/가 어디있어요
jeil gakkaun ... i/ga eodi isseoyo?
  automatic teller machine/ATM
  현급지급기
  hyeon·geup jigeupgi
  foreign exchange office
  외한 거래소
  oe·hwan georaeso

Post

I'm looking for the post office.
우체국을 찾고 있어요
uchegug·eul chatgo isseoyo

I want to send a ...
...보내고 싶은데요
... bonaego sipeundeyo
  fax
  팩스   paekseu
  parcel
  소포   sopo
  postcard
  엽서   yeopseo

I want to buy ...
...사고 싶은데요
... sago sipeundeyo
  an aerogram
  항공우편   hanggongupeon
  an envelope
  편지 봉투   peonji bongtu
  a stamp
  우표   upyo

Phones & Mobiles

I want to buy a phonecard.
전화 카드를 사고 싶어요
jeonhwa kadeu·reul sago sipeoyo

I want to make ...
…하고 싶어요
... hago sipeoyo ...
  a call (to ...)
  전화를…
  jeonhwareul ...
  a reverse-charge/collect call
  수신자 부담으로/콜렉트 콜을
  sushinja budameuro/collectcall eul

Where can I find a/an ...?
… 어디서 살 수 있어요?
... eodiseo salsu isseoyo
I'd like a/an ...
…주세요
…juseyo
  adaptor plug
  어댑터
  eodaepteo
  charger for my phone
  핸드폰 충전기
  haendupon chungjeon·gi
  mobile/cell phone for hire
  임대핸드폰
  imdae haendupon
  prepaid mobile/cell phone
  선불 요금 핸드폰
  seonbul yogeum haendupon

Internet
Where's the local internet café?
제일 가까운 PC방 어디에요?
cheil gakka·un pissi bang eodi·eyo?

I'd like to ...
…하려고 하는데요
... haryeogo haneun deyo
  check my email
  이 메일 확인   imeil hwagin
  get online
  인터넷을   inteo·neseul

Days
Monday	월요일	woryoil
Tuesday	화요일	hwayoil
Wednesday	수요일	suyoil
Thursday	목요일	mogyoil
Friday	금요일	geumyoil
Saturday	토요일	toyoil
Sunday	일요일	iryoil

Transport
What time does the ... leave/arrive?
…이/가 언제 떠나요/언제 도착해요?
... i/ga (eonje tteonayo/eonje dochak-haeyo)?

airport bus
공항버스   gonghang beoseu
boat (ferry)
여객선   yeogaek seon
bus
버스   beoseu
(city) bus
(시내)버스   (sinae) beoseu
train
기차   gicha

the first
첫   cheot
the last
마지막   maji mak
bus station
버스정류장   beoseu jeongnyu jang
subway station
지하철역   jihacheol yeok
ticket vending machine
표 자판기   pyo japan·gi
timetable
시간표   sigan pyo
train station
기차역   gicha yeok
I want to go to ...
…에 가고 싶습니다
... e gago sipseumnida

HEALTH
Where's the nearest ...?
가장 가까운…어디있어요?
gajang gakka·un ... eodi isseoyo?
  chemist
  약국   yakguk
  dentist
  치과   chikwa
  doctor
  의사님   uisanim
  hospital
  병원   byeong·won

I'm ill.
저 아파요
jeon apayo
I need a doctor (who speaks English).
(영어하는) 의사가 필요해요
(yeong·eo haneun) uisaga piryo haeyo

I'm allergic to ...
…알레르기가있어요
... allereugiga isseoyo
  antibiotics
  항생제   hangsaengje
  nuts
  땅꽁   ttang kkong

Symptoms

I have (a) ...
전...
jeon ...

diarrhoea
설사를 해요   seolsa-reul haeyo
fever
열이 나요   yeori nayo
headache
두통이 있어요   dutong-i isseoyo
pain
통증이 있어요   tongjeung-i isseoyo

EMERGENCIES

Call ...!
...불러 주세요!
... bulleo juseyo!

a doctor
의사   uisa
the police
경찰   gyeongcha
an ambulance
구급차   gugeupcha
Help!
사람살려!   saram sallyeo!
I'm lost.
길을 잃었어요   gireul ireosseoyo
Go away!
저리가!   jeori ga!

FOOD & DRINK

breakfast
아침   achim
lunch
점심   jeomsim
dinner
저녁   jeonyeok
snack
스낵   seunaek
eat
먹어요   meogeoyo
drink
마셔요   masheoyo

Can you recommend a ...?
...추천 해주실래요?
... chucheon hae jusillaeyo?

bar/pub
호프 집   hopeu jip
café
까페/커피숍   kkape/keopi-shop
restaurant
식당   sikdang

We'd like the nonsmoking/smoking section, please.
금연석으로/흡연석으로 주세요
geumyeon seogeuro/heupyeon seogeuro juseyo
Do you have seating with tables and chairs?
테이블 있어요?
teibeul isseoyo?
Do you have an English menu?
영어로 된 메뉴 있어요?
yeong-eoro doen menyu isseoyo?
Could you recommend something?
뭐 추천해 주실래요?
mwo chucheonhae jusillaeyo?
Will a service charge be added to the bill?
서비스료도 포함이 되나요?
seobiseu ryodo pohami doenayo?
Excuse me! (please come here)
여기요!
yeogiyo!
Is this dish spicy?
이 음식 매워요?
i eumsik maewoyo?
Bon apetit.
맛있게 드세요
masitge deuseyo
Water, please.
물 주세요
mul juseyo
It was delicious.
맛있었어요
masisseosseoyo
The bill/check, please.
계산서 주세요
gyesanseo juseyo
Do you have any vegetarian dishes?
고기 안 들어간 음식 있어요?
gogi andeureogan eumsik isseoyo?
I don't eat meat.
전 고기를 안 먹어요
jeon gogireul anmeogeoyo
I can't eat dairy products.
전 유제품을 안 먹어요
jeon yujepumeul anmeogeoyo
Does it contain eggs?
계란이 들어가요?
gyerani deureogayo?
I'm allergic to (peanuts).
전 (땅콩)에 알레르기가 있어요
jeon (ttangkong)e allereugiga isseoyo

Food Glossary
CHINESE DISHES
bokkeumbap   볶음밥
fried rice

jajangmyeon 자장면/짜장면
noodles in black bean sauce
tangsuyuk 탕수육
sweet and sour pork

FISH & SEAFOOD

chobap 초밥
raw fish on rice
daege 대게
spider crab
galchi 갈치
silver-skinned fish
gwang-eohoe 광어회
raw halibut
hoe 회
raw fish
jang-eogui 장어구이
grilled eel
jeonbok-juk 전복죽
rice porridge with abalone
kijogae 키조개
razor clam
kkotge-jjim 꽃게찜
steamed blue crab
modeumhoe 모듬회
mixed raw fish platter
nakji 낙지
octopus
odeng 오뎅
processed seafood cakes in broth
ojing-eo sundae 오징어순대
stuffed squid
saengseon-gui 생선구이
grilled fish
saeugui 새우구이
grilled prawns
samchigui 삼치구이
grilled mackerel
sannakji 산낙지
baby octopus
ureok 우럭
raw fish

GIMBAP (KOREAN SUSHI)

chamchi gimbap 참치김밥
tuna *gimbap*
modeum gimbap 모듬김밥
assorted *gimbap*
samgak gimbap 삼각김밤
triangular *gimbap*

KIMCHI

baechu kimchi 배추김치
cabbage *kimchi*; the spicy classic version
kkakdugi 깍두기
cubed radish *kimchi*

mulkimchi 물김치
cold *kimchi* soup

MEAT DISHES

bulgogi 불고기
barbecued beef slices and lettuce wrap
bulgogi jeongsik 불고기정식
bulgogi with side dishes
dakgalbi 닭갈비
pan-fried chicken
dakkochi 닭꼬치
spicy grilled chicken on skewers
dwaeji galbi 돼지갈비
barbecued pork ribs
galbi 갈비
beef ribs
jjimdak 찜닭
spicy chicken pieces with noodles
jokbal 족발
steamed pork hocks
moksal sogeumgui 목살 소금구이
barbecued pork
neobiani/tteokgalbi 너비아니/떡갈비
large minced patty
samgyeopsal 삼겹살
barbecued bacon-type pork
tongdakgui 통닭구이
roasted chicken

NOODLES

bibim naengmyeon 비빔냉면
cold buckwheat noodles with vegetables, meat and sauce
bibimguksu 비빔국수
noodles with vegetables, meat and sauce
japchae 잡채
stir-fried noodles and vegetables
kalguksu 칼국수
thick handmade noodles in broth
kongguksu 콩국수
noodles in cold soy milk soup
makguksu 막국수
buckwheat noodles with vegetables
mul naengmyeon 물냉면
buckwheat noodles in cold broth
ramyeon 라면
instant noodle soup
udong 우동
thick white noodle broth

RICE DISHES

bap 밥
boiled rice
bibimbap 비빔밥
rice topped with egg, meat, vegetables and sauce
boribap 보리밥
boiled rice with steamed barley

dolsot bibimbap 돌솥비빔밥
bibimbap in stone hotpot
dolsotbap 돌솥밥
hotpot rice
dolssambap 돌쌈밥
hotpot rice and lettuce wraps
sanchae bibimbap 산채비빔밥
bibimbap made with mountain vegetables
sinseollo 신선로
meat, fish and vegetables in broth cooked at your table
ssambap 쌈밥
assorted ingredients with rice and wraps

SNACKS
bung-eoppang 붕어빵
fish-shaped cake with red-bean filling
hotteok 호떡
pitta bread with sweet filling
tteok 떡
rice cake
tteokbokki 떡볶이
pressed rice cakes and vegetables in a spicy sauce

SOUPS
chueotang 추어탕
minced fish soup
galbitang 갈비탕
beef-rib soup
gamjatang 감자탕
meaty bones and potato soup
haemultang 해물탕
spicy assorted seafood soup
kkorigomtang 꼬리곰탕
ox tail soup
manduguk 만두국
soup with meat-filled dumplings
oritang 오리탕
duck soup
samgyetang 삼계탕
ginseng chicken soup
seolleongtang 설렁탕
beef and rice soup

STEWS
budae jjigae 부대찌개
ham-and-scraps stew
doenjang jjigae 된장찌개
soybean paste stew
dubu jjigae 두부찌개
tofu stew
nakji jeon-gol 낙지전골
octopus hotpot
sundubu jjigae 순두부찌개
spicy uncurdled tofu stew

OTHER
bindaetteok 빈대떡
mung bean pancake
donkkaseu 돈까스
pork cutlet with rice and salad (Japanese *tonkatsu*)
dotorimuk 도토리묵
acorn jelly
gujeolpan 구절판
eight snacks and wraps
hanjeongsik 한정식
Korean-style banquet
jeongsik 정식
smaller banquet meal
juk 죽
rice porridge
mandu 만두
filled dumplings
manduguk jeongsik 만두국정식
dumpling soup with side dishes
omeuraiseu 오므라이스
omelette with rice
pajeon 파전
green onion pancake
patbingsu 팥빙수
shaved ice, fruit and red bean dessert
sangcharim 산차림
banquet of meat, seafood and vegetables
shabu shabu 샤브샤브
DIY beef and vegetable casserole
sigol bapsang 시골밥상
countryside-style meal
siksa 식사
budget-priced banquet
sujebi 수제비
dough flakes in shellfish broth
sundae 순대
noodle and vegetable sausage
sundubu 순두부
uncurdled tofu
twigim 튀김
seafood and vegetables fried in batter
wangmandu 왕만두
large steamed dumplings

Drinks
NONALCOHOLIC DRINKS
boricha 보리차
barley tea
cha 차
tea
daechucha 대추차
jujube (red date) tea
hongcha 홍차
black tea
juseu 주스
juice

keopi	커피
coffee	
kolla	콜라
cola	
mukapein keopi	무카페인 커피
decaffeinated coffee	
mul	물
water	
nokcha	녹차
green tea	
omijacha	오미자차
berry tea	
saenggang cha	생강차
ginger tea	
saengsu	생수
mineral spring water	
seoltang neo-eoseo/	설탕 넣어서/
ppaego	빼고
with/without sugar	
sikhye	식혜
rice punch	
ssanghwacha	쌍화차
herb tonic tea	
sujeonggwa	수정과
cinnamon/ginger punch	

sungnyung	숭늉
burnt-rice tea	
uyu	우유
milk	
uyu neo-eoseo/	우유 넣어서/
ppaego	빼고
with/without milk	
yujacha	유자차
citron tea	

ALCOHOLIC DRINKS

dongdongju	동동주
fermented rice wine	
insamju	인삼주
ginseng liqueur	
maekju	맥주
beer	
makgeolli	막걸리
unstrained rice wine	
sansachun	산사춘
rice wine	
soju	소주
vodkalike drink	

GLOSSARY

ajumma – a married or older woman
-am – monastery
anju – bar snacks
banchon – side dishes
bang – room
bong – peak
buk – north
buncheong – Joseon-era pottery decorated with simple folk designs
cheon – stream
Chuseok – Thanksgiving holiday
DMZ – the Demilitarized Zone that separates North and South Korea
-do – province
do – island
-dong – ward, subdivision of a *gu*
dong – east
DVD bang – minicinemas that show DVDs
-eup – town
-ga – section of a long street
gang – river
geobukseon – 'turtle ships'; iron-clad warships
gibun – harmonious feelings; face
-gil – small street
-gu – urban district
-gun – county
gung – palace
gugak – traditional Korean music
gut – shamanist ceremony
gwageo – Joseon-era civil-service examination
hae – sea
hagwon – private schools where students study after school or work
hanbok – traditional Korean clothing
hangeul – Korean phonetic alphabet
hanja – Chinese-style writing system
hanji – traditional Korean handmade paper
hanok – traditional Korean one-storey wooden house with a tiled roof
ho – lake
hof – bar or pub
insam – ginseng
ipgu – entrance
jaebeol – huge conglomerate business, often family-run
jeon – hall of a temple
jeong – pavilion
jjimjilbang – luxury sauna and spa

KTO – Korea Tourism Organisation
KTX – Korean bullet train
minbak – a private home in the countryside with rooms for rent
mobeom – deluxe taxi
mudang – shaman, usually female
mugunghwa – limited-stop express train
mun – gate
-myeon – township
nam – south
neung – tomb
no – large street, boulevard
noraebang – karaoke room
oncheon – hot-spring bath
ondol – underfloor heating
ondol room – traditional, sleep-on-a-floor-mattress hotel room
pansori – traditional Korean opera with a soloist and a drummer
PC bang – internet café
pojagi – traditional wrapping cloth
pungsu – Korean geomancy or feng shui
pyeong – a unit of measurement equal to 3.3 sq m
ramie – see-through cloth made from pounded bark
-ri – village
ro – large street, boulevard
ROK – Republic of Korea (South Korea)
ru – pavilion
-sa – temple
saemaeul – luxury express train
samullori – farmer's percussion music and dance
-san – mountain
sanseong – mountain fortress
seo – west
Seon – Korean version of Zen Buddhism
si – city
sijo – short, Chinese-style nature poetry
ssireum – Korean-style wrestling
taekwondo – Korean martial arts
tap – pagoda
tongil – slow local train
trot – foot-tapping country music
USO – United Service Organizations; it provides leisure activities for US troops and civilians
yangban – aristocrat
yeogwan – small, family-run hotel, usually older than a motel
yo – padded quilt or futon mattress for sleeping on the floor

BEHIND THE SCENES

THIS BOOK

Regular Korea traveller Martin Robinson has written the last three editions of Lonely Planet's *Seoul* guide, including this, the sixth edition. Seoul-resident Jason Zahorchak wrote Introducing Seoul and the Background chapter. Dr Trish Batchelor wrote the Health section. Seoul was commissioned in Lonely Planet's Melbourne office and produced by:

Commissioning Editor Errol Hunt

Coordinating Editor Daniel Corbett

Coordinating Cartographer Barbara Benson

Coordinating Layout Designer Jacqui Saunders

Managing Editor Bruce Evans

Managing Cartographer David Connolly

Managing Layout Designer Sally Darmody

Assisting Editor Charlotte Harrison

Assisting Cartographer Andrew Smith

Assisting Layout Designer Indra Kilfoyle

Cover Designer Pepi Bluck

Language Content Coordinators Quentin Frayne, Branislava Vladisavljevic

Project Manager Chris Love

Thanks to Lucy Birchley, Melanie Dankel, Stefanie Di Trocchio, Nicole Hansen, Craig Kilburn, Yvonne Kirk, Kim Kyung-Hee

Cover photographs by Lonely Planet Images: Colourful patterns on the wall of Changgyeonggung, Juliet Coombe

(top); Tourists and ceremonial guards outside the entrance to Gyeongbokgung, Neil Setchfield (bottom).

Internal photographs the Seoul city government p7 (#1), p121, p123 (top), p128; Penelope Brook p126 (bottom). All other photographs by Lonely Planet Images, and by Anthony Plummer except Manfred Gottschalk p4 (#3); Martin Robinson p6, (#2) p7(#3), p8 (#1), p123 (bottom), p125, p126 (top); Neil Setchfield p8 (#3); Juliet Coombe p124 (top); John Elk III p127 (right).

All images are copyright of the photographer unless otherwise indicated. Many of the images in this guide are available for licensing from Lonely Planet Images: www .lonelyplanetimages.com.

THANKS
MARTIN ROBINSON

Thanks to Oh Jee-chul, Han Young-hee, Koo Bon-sik, Sung Lee, Kim Seok-jin, Kang Soon-deog, Robert Koehler, Tania Campbell, Jenny Flinn, Seo Bong-sik, Joe McPherson, James Hendicott and Eddie Hwang. Special thanks to Kim Kyunghee, Park Min-jung and to interviewees chef Gwak Joongseob, artist Min Jung-soo and bass guitarist Park Ji-won — you were all great. Special special thanks as always to Marie.

This book is dedicated to my dad, Eric Robinson, who passed away while I was working on it.

JASON ZAHORCHAK

Thanks to Bak Mi-kyung, Chun Su-jin, Kang Yunjung, Lee Ho-jeong, Lee Sin-ae, Park Jihoon, Park Soomee and Yoo

THE LONELY PLANET STORY

Fresh from an epic journey across Europe, Asia and Australia in 1972, Tony and Maureen Wheeler sat at their kitchen table stapling together notes. The first Lonely Planet guidebook, *Across Asia on the Cheap*, was born.

Travellers snapped up the guides. Inspired by their success, the Wheelers began publishing books to Southeast Asia, India and beyond. Demand was prodigious, and the Wheelers expanded the business rapidly to keep up. Over the years, Lonely Planet extended its coverage to every country and into the virtual world via lonelyplanet.com and the Thorn Tree message board.

As Lonely Planet became a globally loved brand, Tony and Maureen received several offers for the company. But it wasn't until 2007 that they found a partner whom they trusted to remain true to the company's principles of travelling widely, treading lightly and giving sustainably. In October of that year, BBC Worldwide acquired a 75% share in the company, pledging to uphold Lonely Planet's commitment to independent travel, trustworthy advice and editorial independence.

Today, Lonely Planet has offices in Melbourne, London and Oakland, with over 500 staff members and 300 authors. Tony and Maureen are still actively involved with Lonely Planet. They're travelling more often than ever, and they're devoting their spare time to charitable projects. And the company is still driven by the philosophy of *Across Asia on the Cheap*: 'All you've got to do is decide to go and the hardest part is over. So go!'

Hyun-sook for all their guidance on things Korean and otherwise – and for their friendship through the years; Park Byong-su and Seo Sumin for delving deep into the issues; Hal Piper, Hal Lipper, Toby Smith and David Moll for their mentorship; Kim Kyung-hee and the Seoul City Government; my co-author and editors at Lonely Planet for making this experience so rewarding; and, of course, Sam, my fellow traveller.

OUR READERS

Many thanks to the travellers who used the last edition and wrote to us with helpful hints, useful advice and interesting anecdotes:

Ann Ang, Hannah Bae, Paulo Cheong, Young Geun Choi, Mary Donnellan, David Fletcher, Jamison Folland, Mike Forster, Vickie Frater, Jooseok Han, Robert Kienzle, Walter King, Sr, Marisa Lavoratore, Triona McHugh, Peter Messingfeld, Jordan Orscheln, Clifton Phua, Sheena Pia, Katherine Pinckney, Brent Robson, Matteo Romitelli, Mary Roohan, Richard Royston, Lindsey Simon, Patricia Skully, Alissa Smith, Peter Song, Nicole Speedy, David Tan, Linda Tisue, Michael Verga, Jin Whittington

SEND US YOUR FEEDBACK

We love to hear from travellers – your comments keep us on our toes and help make our books better. Our well-travelled team reads every word on what you loved or loathed about this book. Although we cannot reply individually to postal submissions, we always guarantee that your feedback goes straight to the appropriate authors, in time for the next edition. Each person who sends us information is thanked in the next edition – and the most useful submissions are rewarded with a free book.

To send us your updates – and find out about Lonely Planet events, newsletters and travel news – visit our award-winning website: lonelyplanet.com/contact.

Note: We may edit, reproduce and incorporate your comments in Lonely Planet products such as guidebooks, websites and digital products, so let us know if you don't want your comments reproduced or your name acknowledged. For a copy of our privacy policy visit lonelyplanet.com/privacy.

Notes

Notes

Notes

INDEX

63 Building 62

A

accommodation 146-58, *see also* Sleeping index
 booking 148
 costs 147
 renting 147
activities 140-3, *see also* Sports & Activities index
air quality 30
air travel 171-3
ambulances 178
amusement parks, *see* Sights index
April Revolution 18-19
aquariums, *see* Sights index
area codes, *see inside front cover*
architecture 27-9
 books 30
art galleries, *see* Arts index
arts 23-7, 85, 136-8, *see also* Arts index
 dance 136-8
 festivals 14, 136
 theatre 136-8
ATMs 180

B

babysitters 176
backpacker guesthouses 146
bargaining 82
bars, *see* Drinking index
baseball 141, 143
basketball 143
bathrooms 183

beaches 168-9
beondegi 92
bicycle travel, *see* cycling
Blue House, *see* Cheongwadae
boat travel, *see* ferry travel
Bongeunsa 71-2
books, *see also* literature
 architecture 30
 history 17
bowling 71, 142
Buddha's Birthday 13
Buddhism 20
 courses 176-7
Bukhansan National Park 164-5
bus travel 173-4
business hours 45, 176, *see also inside front cover*
 restuarants 98
 shops 82

C

cafés, *see* Drinking index
calligraphy 24-5
car travel 174
 hire 174
cathedrals, *see* Sights index
cell phones 182
ceramics 25
Changdeokgung 39-42
Changgyeonggung 42-3
chemists 180
Cheondogyo 20-1
Cheondogyo Temple 52
Cheonggye Stream 30, **8**
Cheongwadae 44
Cherry Blossom Festival 12
children, travel with 66, 176
Children's Grand Park 76
chopsticks 96
Christianity 20
churches, *see* Sights index
Chuseok 14
cinema 26-7, 138, *see also* Arts index, films
 festivals 12, 13
climate 12, 176
clothing sizes 92
clubs 130-2, *se1e also* Nightlife index

COEX Mall 68-9
Confucianism 22
consulates 178
costs 14-15, 83
 accommodation 147
 discount cards 175, 178
 drinking 115
 food 98
courses 176-7
credit cards 181
culture 3, 21, 22-3
 bargaining 82
 courses 177
currency exchange 180-1, *see also inside front cover*
customs regulations 177-8
cycling 15, 141, 173, **8**
 bicycle hire 76, 173

D

Daehangno 49-54, **52**
 accommodation 150-1
 drinking 115-16
 food 101-4
 shopping 83-5
 transport 51
dance 27, 136-8
Dano Festival 13
Demilitarized Zone 160-2
disabilities, travellers with 183
Dobongsan 164-5, **165**
drinking 114-19, *see also* Drinking index
DVD *bang*, *see* Arts index

E

economy 3, 18
education 22-3
 history 48
electricity 178
embassies 178
emergencies 178, *see also inside front cover*
 language 191
environmental issues 29-30, *see also* sustainable travel
Everland 167-8
exchange rates, *see inside front cover*

F

ferry travel 173
 Han River ferries 65
festivals & events 12-14
 Bucheon International Fantastic Film Festival 13
 Buddha's Birthday 13
 Cherry Blossom Festival 12
 Chuseok 14
 Dano Festival 13
 Gugak Festival 14
 Hangeul Day 14
 Hi Seoul 13
 Jonhmyo Daeje 13
 Kimchi Expo 14
 Korea International Art Fair 14
 Korean Queer Cultural Festival 13
 Lunar New Year 12
 Seoul Drum Festival 14
 Seoul Fringe Festival 14
 Seoul International Cartoon & Animation Festival 13
 Seoul Medicinal Herb Market Festival 14
 Seoul World DJ Festival 13
 Women's Film Festival in Seoul 12
films 27, *see also* cinema
fire services 178
food 94-111, *see also* Eating index
 booking 98
 customs 95, 96
 history 94-5
 Jongno 100
 kimchi 14, 69, 97
 language 191-4
 royal cuisine 95, 105, **7**
 sampling 111
 self-catering 98-9
 tipping 98
football, *see* soccer
four ball 142

G

Gangnam 67-72, **68**
 accommodation 154-7
 drinking 119

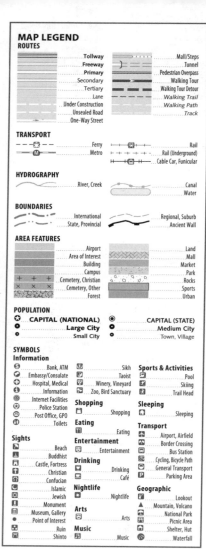

MAP LEGEND
ROUTES

Tollway	Mall/Steps
Freeway	Tunnel
Primary	Pedestrian Overpass
Secondary	Walking Tour
Tertiary	Walking Tour Detour
Lane	Walking Trail
Under Construction	Walking Path
Unsealed Road	Track
One-Way Street	

TRANSPORT

Ferry	Rail
Metro	Rail (Underground)
	Cable Car, Funicular

HYDROGRAPHY

River, Creek	Canal
	Water

BOUNDARIES

International	Regional, Suburb
State, Provincial	Ancient Wall

AREA FEATURES

Airport	Land
Area of Interest	Mall
Building	Market
Campus	Park
Cemetery, Christian	Rocks
Cemetery, Other	Sports
Forest	Urban

POPULATION

CAPITAL (NATIONAL)	CAPITAL (STATE)
Large City	Medium City
Small City	Town, Village

SYMBOLS
Information

Bank, ATM		Sikh	**Sports & Activities**
Embassy/Consulate		Taoist	Pool
Hospital, Medical		Winery, Vineyard	Skiing
Information		Zoo, Bird Sanctuary	Trail Head
Internet Facilities	**Shopping**		
Police Station	Shopping		**Sleeping**
Post Office, GPO			Sleeping
Toilets	**Eating**		
	Eating		**Transport**
Sights	**Entertainment**		Airport, Airfield
Beach	Entertainment		Border Crossing
Buddhist			Bus Station
Castle, Fortress	**Drinking**		Cycling, Bicycle Path
Christian	Drinking		General Transport
Confucian	Café		Parking Area
Islamic	**Nightlife**		**Geographic**
Jewish	Nightlife		Lookout
Monument	**Arts**		Mountain, Volcano
Museum, Gallery	Arts		National Park
Point of Interest			Picnic Area
Ruin	**Music**		Shelter, Hut
Shinto	Music		Waterfall

Published by Lonely Planet Publications Pty Ltd
ABN 36 005 607 983

Australia Head Office, Locked Bag 1, Footscray, Victoria 3011,
☎03 8379 8000, fax 03 8379 8111, talk2us@lonelyplanet.com.au

USA 150 Linden St, Oakland, CA 94607,
☎510 250 6400, toll free 800 275 8555, fax 510 893 8572, info@lonelyplanet.com

UK 2nd fl, 186 City Rd, London, EC1V 2NT,
☎020 7106 2100, fax 020 7106 2101, go@lonelyplanet.co.uk

Printed by SNP Security Printing Pte Ltd, Singapore.